PLANTING AN EMPIRE

p. 60 – servitude –
① women seem to have come unmarried.
② seemingly, no interest in
planting families
④ difference between gov't's
policy and colonists
needs/interests ?

Regional Perspectives on Early America

JACK P. GREENE AND J. R. POLE, ADVISORS

Planting an Empire

THE EARLY CHESAPEAKE IN
BRITISH NORTH AMERICA

Jean B. Russo and J. Elliott Russo

THE JOHNS HOPKINS UNIVERSITY PRESS
BALTIMORE

Printed in the United States of America on acid-free paper
9 8 7 6 5 4 3 2 1

The Johns Hopkins University Press
2715 North Charles Street
Baltimore, Maryland 21218-4363
www.press.jhu.edu

LIBRARY OF CONGRESS CATALOGING-IN-PUBLICATION DATA
Russo, Jean Burrell
Planting an empire : the early Chesapeake in British North America / Jean B. Russo, J. Elliott Russo.
p. cm. — (Regional perspectives on early America)
Includes bibliographical references and index.
ISBN-13: 978-1-4214-0555-1 (hardback)
ISBN-13: 978-1-4214-0556-8 (pbk.)
ISBN-13: 978-1-4214-0694-7 (electronic)
ISBN-10: 1-4214-0555-5 (hardback)
ISBN-10: 1-4214-0556-3 (pbk.)
ISBN-10: 1-4214-0694-2 (electronic)
1. Chesapeake Bay Region (Md. and Va.)—Economic conditions.
2. Chesapeake Bay Region (Md. and Va.)—Social conditions.
3. Chesapeake Bay Region (Md. and Va.)—Religious life and customs.
4. Tobacco industry—Chesapeake Bay Region (Md. and Va.)—History.
5. Slavery—Chesapeake Bay Region (Md. and Va.)—History. 6. United States—History—Colonial period, ca. 1600–1775. 7. Great Britain—Colonies—America—History. I. Russo, J. Elliott. II. Title.
HC104.R87 2012
975.2′02—dc23 2011047300

A catalog record for this book is available from the British Library.

For Lois Green Carr

Contents

Acknowledgments

OUR INVOLVEMENT WITH the Chesapeake volume of this series began, much longer ago than we care to remember, with an invitation from Robert J. Brugger of the Johns Hopkins University Press. Bob has waited very patiently ever since for the results and we thank him both for the opportunity and for the patience. We are also indebted to a number of colleagues for their direct assistance. The late Emory G. Evans never asked us to return his copy of *Colonial Virginia* and graciously answered many questions about the minutiae of Virginia history. Lorena S. Walsh not only answered all our questions but also read the manuscript and offered valuable guidance and corrections. We also thank the two anonymous readers for the Johns Hopkins University Press, especially Reader A, for their perceptive critiques and helpful suggestions.

We are grateful to Douglas Bradburn and John C. Coombs for inviting us to attend the symposium "Early Modern Virginia: New Thoughts on the Old Dominion" (Monticello, VA, 2007), thus enabling our work to benefit from the path-breaking research presented during its sessions. At the JHU Press, we express our gratitude to Deborah Bors, Juliana McCarthy, and Kara Reiter for guiding us and the manuscript through the editorial process with efficiency and thoughtfulness. We thank Dennis Marshall for his careful, insightful copyediting and humorous exchanges and Robert Cronan for his skillful work in preparing the maps that enhance our volume. We also wish to acknowledge our considerable debt to the scholarship of the Chesapeake School (sometimes known as the Maryland Mafia).

Finally, but never least, we thank our extended family and friends for living with TDB—our unusual version of a mother-daughter book club—for far too long.

We dedicate this book to Lois Green Carr: friend, colleague, inspiration, as she has been to so many of the people engaged in Chesapeake scholarship for the last forty years.

Material quoted from primary sources is cited in notes at the back of the book. The original spelling and punctuation of this material have been retained. The essay on sources expresses our debts to the work of others and provides suggestions for additional reading.

PLANTING AN EMPIRE

PROLOGUE

Leah and Rachel

For three months in the summer of 1608, about a dozen Englishmen led by Captain John Smith explored the body of water that Algonquian-speaking Native Americans called Chesepiooc, or great water. Smith and his companions covered more than seventeen hundred miles traveling in an open shallop, a thirty-foot-long boat equipped with oars and sail and well-suited to the Chesapeake Bay's shallow waters. After the men left their new settlement called Jamestown on June 2, they began their voyage by traveling up two rivers on the bay's eastern shore, identified by Smith as the Wighcocomoco and Cuskarawaok, but known today as the Pocomoke and Nanticoke Rivers. Crossing back to the western shore, they stopped along the Patapsco and Potomac Rivers before turning south to Jamestown. Three days later the shallop set sail again, heading for the upper bay to explore the Susquehanna River, whose estuary (or drowned river bed) forms the bay. On the return voyage the expedition surveyed the Patuxent and Rappahannock Rivers, two major waterways of the western shore, and several smaller tributaries before arriving back at Jamestown on the 7th of September.

From these two brief voyages, Smith and his men brought back to the English their first detailed information about the bay, its surrounding territory, and its inhabitants. Their explorations mapped the setting for the colonial drama enacted in Virginia, England's first permanent North American settlement, and her sister colony, Maryland.

THE CHESAPEAKE—"A FAIRE BAY"

In describing the territory that he explored, Smith wrote that "heaven and earth never agreed better to frame a place for mans habitation."[1] The "frame" provided by the Chesapeake Bay has shaped the region from the earliest days of human settlement. The bay begins at the northern edge of territory that England's king granted to Lord Baltimore for the Maryland colony; nearly two hundred miles to the south, its waters empty into the Atlantic Ocean near Virginia's present-day southern border. This vast body of water divides the Chesapeake region into two very unequal parts. On the eastern shore, a narrow peninsula runs south toward the mouth of the bay, bounded by the Delaware River to the north and the Atlantic Ocean to the east.

The western shore comprised the bulk of the two colonies' territory, with a broad swath of coastal plain giving way to the plateau known as the Piedmont region and then to the Blue Ridge and Allegheny Mountains. Forty-eight major tributaries reach far into the interior on both shores. During the colonial period, ocean-going vessels could navigate many of the rivers for considerable distances—more than one hundred miles upriver for the James, Rappahannock, and Potomac Rivers, for example. For English colonists seeking to settle in the region, the many rivers and creeks offered access to the tidewater (the area where waterways rise and fall with the bay's tides) and its hinterland. Or, in Smith's words, "here are mountaines, hils, plaines, valleyes, rivers and brookes, all running most pleasantly into a faire Bay compassed . . . with fruitfull and delightsome land."[2]

As Smith's account of his explorations makes abundantly clear, the English sought to settle in Indian country. The narrative describes at length the Native Americans whom Smith and his men either encountered or learned about during their voyages. Traveling along the western shore, for example, Smith reported that "The fifth river is called Pawtuxunt. . . . Upon this river dwell the people called Acquintanacksuak, Pawtuxunt and Mattapanient. . . . These of al other were found the most civill to give intertainement." When the shallop reached the head of the bay, its crew encountered the Susquehannock, who "came to the discoverers [Smith's party] with Skins, Bowes, Arrowes, Targets, Beads, Swords, and Tobacco pipes for presents." Five of the

Susquehannock leaders crossed the bay in the English shallop; "the greatest of them is signified in the Mappe"—the map Smith drew to accompany his narrative. Smith noted that the Susquehannock lived "pallisadoed in their Townes to defend them from the Massawomekes their mortall enimies."[3] He also observed that these northern Indians were "scarse knowne" to Powhatan, the paramount chief of the Indians who inhabited the territory surrounding Jamestown.*

Well before European explorers reached the Chesapeake region in the sixteenth century, its Native American inhabitants comprised three distinct populations, each sharing broadly similar linguistic and cultural characteristics. The English settlers who arrived in 1607 most frequently came into contact with Indians led by Powhatan, but soon learned that the region encompassed numerous other Native American groups. Archaeological evidence indicates that the Algonquian-speaking peoples who predominated in the coastal plain had migrated into the area as early as A.D. 200, perhaps displacing Siouan-speaking tribes whose territory then occupied the Piedmont area to the west. A buffer zone between these two cultural groups developed at least as early as A.D. 1000 along the fall line, the juncture between the coastal plain and the adjoining Piedmont plateau, and was used by both for hunting. Iroquoian-speaking tribes were concentrated well to the north, but the territory of several groups, including the Susquehannock warriors whom Smith met, stretched south along the Delaware and Susquehanna Rivers to the Chesapeake region's perimeter.

The label *European* identifies the English, Spanish, and others, as populations with similar economic, political, and social institutions, but glosses over significant differences and points of conflict. So too are the labels *Algonquian, Siouan*, and *Iroquoian* useful—but imperfect—collective terms. Common linguistic heritages did not preclude territorial competition, as Smith frequently noted, and cultural borders existed within, as well as among, these Native American populations. For example, both oral histories and archaeological evidence suggest that the Algonquian-

*Although sometimes referred to by his informal name, Wahunsunacock, as paramount chief Powhatan used the name of his people and their principal town.

The Sasques= ahanougs
are a Gyant like peo= ple &
Utchowig
thus a= tyred

Susquehannock Warrior. This warrior appears as an inset image on John Smith's map of Virginia published in 1612. Smith identified the Susquehannock as a "Gyant like people . . . thus attyred." Courtesy of the Geography and Map Division of the Library of Congress speaking Piscataway migrated into the Chesapeake region several centuries after the ancestors of the Powhatan, likely in response to Iroquoian expansion farther north. Occupying lands surrounding the Potomac River, the Piscataway not only resisted encroachments from Siouan groups to the west and Iroquoian populations to the north but also from other Algonquian tribes to the south. In the early seventeenth century, Powhatan sought to exert influence over villages on the south side of the Potomac River that were previously part of a broad Piscataway confederacy, creating a conflict that the English tried to exploit to their advantage.

The English who migrated to Virginia and Maryland settled in a world described by the language of its Indian inhabitants, but over time, English and anglicized names usurped many of those used by Native Americans, just as the English and other Europeans usurped the sovereignty of many Indian peoples. For Europeans, the process of renaming was a fundamental part of colonization: to commemorate their arrival and extend their claim to the Chesapeake region, for example, Virginia's English explorers quickly named the bay's southernmost river and its capes after King James and his sons, Prince Henry and Prince Charles. Renaming took place in advance of attempts to establish sovereignty or dominion—efforts that proved considerably more challenging than many settlers anticipated. Native Americans persisted in both Chesapeake colonies throughout the colonial period with a complex history of strategies for survival.

VIRGINIA AND MARYLAND—"TWO FRUITFULL SISTERS"

In a 1656 pamphlet about "the two fruitfull Sisters of Virginia and Mary-land," an English colonist named John Hammond told his readers that "these two Sister Countries (though distinct Governments) are much of one nature, both for produce and manner of living." In writing about the two colonies, Hammond used the names Leah and Rachel, referring to the biblical story of two sisters married to Jacob. (Hammond also decided to "Treat of the elder Sister Virginia, and in speaking of that [thereby] include both," thus setting the pattern for many future accounts of the region.)[4] Hammond regarded Virginia and Maryland as two parts of a whole; to understand one was to appreciate the essence of both. But the context in which he wrote—a time when many Virginians contested Lord Baltimore's right to his colony—belies any assumption that these two sisters lived in harmony. Tensions existed between the two settlements, and their arenas of conflict, as well as their points of agreement, helped shape the course of Chesapeake development.

As a basic point of similarity, both colonies emerged from English participation in Europe's age of exploration. The English government supported these colonial endeavors to further national interests, hoping that colonies would produce raw materials and foodstuffs to replace costly imports from Asia and that gold and silver mines would increase the country's wealth. Encouraging English settlement in the Chesapeake region was also a strategic move to counter England's European rivals. Virginia served as a barrier to Spanish settlement on the North American mainland, while Maryland, carved out of territory originally included in the Virginia grant but not yet occupied, bolstered English claims in the northern Chesapeake region when the Dutch and Swedes showed interest in establishing colonies along the Delaware River.

In pursuit of these goals, England's government relied upon private investors who financed the two settlements and expected personal profit from the ventures, a circumstance that resulted in similar patterns of migration. In both colonies the first waves of European migrants were young, unmarried, and mostly male workers who labored as servants, in contrast to the New England colonies, where most early migrants settled as part of family groups. Family formation in the two Chesapeake colonies, which brought greater social cohesion and stability to the region, occurred only gradually. Native-born families did not become the dominant social group in either colony until the end of the seventeenth century.

With their common origin as early English colonizing ventures, the two Chesapeake colonies shared a political and civic culture that more closely resembled public life in the mother country than was true of the later-settled colonies to the north. By the middle of the seventeenth century, each had an assembly (similar to the English Parliament), composed of representatives elected by male property owners and empowered to pass laws, as well as a council (a variant of the Privy Council of England) appointed by the governor to advise him on provincial affairs. Although legal structures and practices were modified in the colonial setting, English settlers throughout the region retained fundamental features of England's legal system, including jury trials and the role of precedent, known as common law. In both colonies, the county was the foundation of the court system as well as the unit of local administration, in contrast to the town-based government of New England settlements.

English and other European settlers in the Chesapeake colonies found themselves, by chance rather than design, in a region geographically suited to tobacco cultivation, complete with an extensive network of waterways that facilitated export of their crop. The Virginia Company's initial plans for its colony did not include cultivation of any crop, much less an economy dominated by tobacco's production and export. Investors expected to profit by mining precious metals and iron, exchanging goods with the native population, and producing exotic commodities like wine and silk. But a dozen years of failure to establish a successful colony along those lines gave way to a scramble to plant tobacco once colonists perceived the crop's potential for profit. Maryland's settlers, arriving after the initial boom period for tobacco, wasted no time in following the Virginians' example. In the Chesapeake, the *planting* of a colony, a term used for all English efforts to establish overseas settlements, took the form of cultivating tobacco as the staple, or main export, crop. Men who cultivated land were known as *planters* and their landholdings, whether large or small, were called *plantations*.

The consequences of relying on tobacco as the primary export crop shaped settlement patterns in similar ways in both colonies. Because planters learned from experience that the quality and quantity of their tobacco declined after the first few years of cultivation on the same plot of land, they tried to maintain productivity by acquiring enough acreage to rotate the crop periodically to new fields. This practice resulted in dispersed settlement along the region's many waterways, where the best soils could be found, and landholdings much larger than was common in either England or the New England colonies. The perceived need to cultivate fresh land together with significant population growth repeatedly pushed English settlement outward in both Chesapeake

Virginia, 1612. John Smith's map of Virginia (including territory that later became the colony of Maryland) is the first detailed rendering of the Chesapeake Bay region. Smith marked with crosses the limits of the territory he personally explored and placed on his map symbols for Native American villages and the names of native peoples who lived in the area claimed by England's new colony. Courtesy of the Geography and Map Division of the Library of Congress colonies. Although the English held only precarious dominion over small stretches of the tidewater region in the first decades of settlement, each colony's eventual prosperity displaced thousands of Native Americans.

In Virginia and Maryland, the common goal of establishing tobacco plantations created another point of similarity, an early and persistent reliance on exploitative labor practices. Influenced by the Spanish model of conquest, the men who established the Virginia colony initially expected to commandeer Native American labor. When that plan proved untenable, settlers adapted two systems of bound labor: indentured servitude and chattel slavery. The lure of tobacco profits provided motivation for individual planters to buy laborers to work their fields if they could save or borrow capital to invest in bound workers. In the early years, most workers, male and female, were immigrants from the British Isles who agreed to labor as servants to repay the costs of their passage. A shift from indentured servants to enslaved Africans (and then African Americans) began early in the colonial period. Well before the middle of the seventeenth century, wealthier planters started acquiring enslaved workers, first from slave traders in the West Indies, somewhat later from occasional ships bringing cargoes from Africa. By the end of the seventeenth century, when access to enslaved Africans substantially increased, Chesapeake colonists shared a deepening commitment to enslaved labor to increase their economic well-being, enhance their claims to political power, and secure their social position.

Virginia and Maryland differed in several significant respects despite their broad similarities. Virginia enjoyed advantages of greater size, with far more territory available as English population growth exceeded the tidewater area's capacity to provide land for all. For Virginia's earliest settlers and their descendants, proximity to the mouth of the bay, through which all shipping entered and exited, conferred better access to inbound cargoes of merchandise and laborers and to outbound convoys of tobacco ships, particularly during times of international conflict in the late seventeenth and early eighteenth centuries. Geography also favored Virginia with a longer growing season, and her territory included all of the tidewater soil suitable for the sweet-scented variety of tobacco that commanded the highest prices in

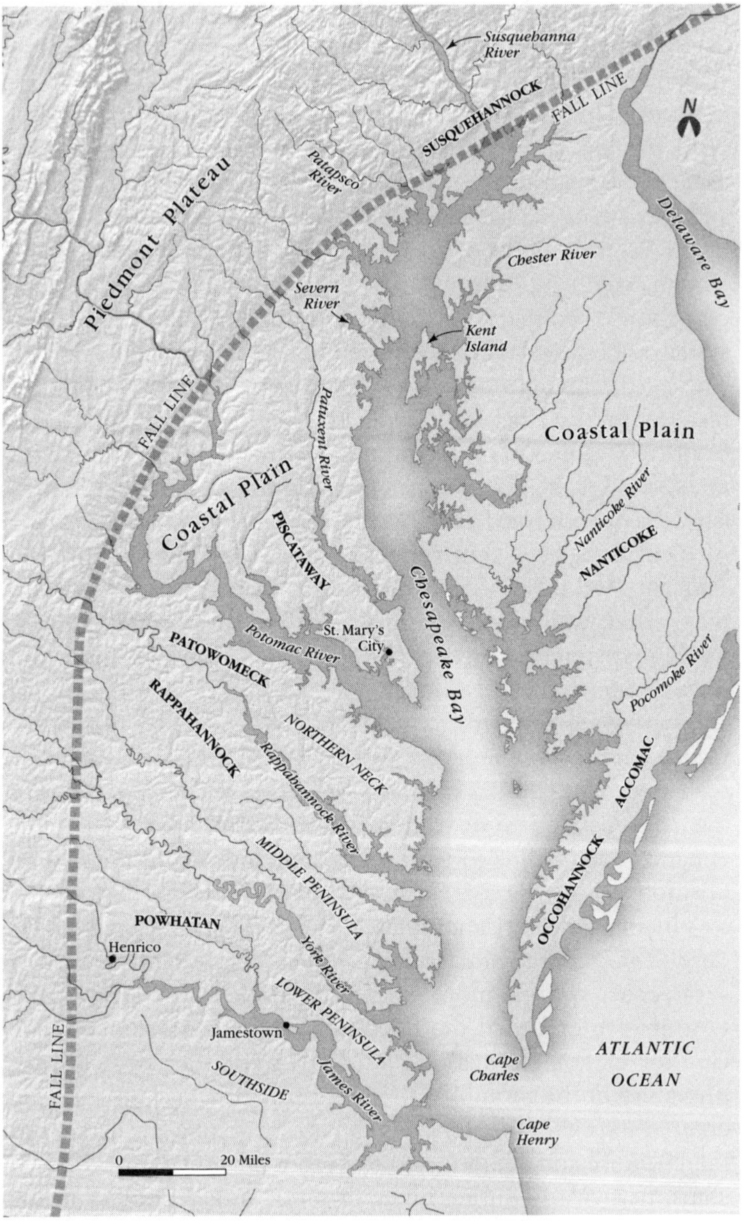

The Chesapeake region, c.1635, with early English settlements and approximate locations of principal Native American groups. Map by Robert Cronan, Lucidity Information Design, LLC

England. Such advantages enabled a small subset of Virginia planters to achieve levels of wealth and power that placed them at the top of the region's economic and social structure.

As the second English colony in the region, Maryland replicated some, but not all, aspects of the Virginia model. Early Marylanders, for example, never experienced the level of starvation that characterized Virginia's first decade because they could draw upon the older colony for food and livestock supplies. Maryland planters also benefited from Virginia's development of tobacco as a marketable commodity, but grew only oronoco tobacco, a strain that sold at a lower price than sweet-scented. In comparison with Virginia, moreover, much more of the younger colony's territory lay on the bay's eastern shore or in the northern Piedmont, regions with land unsuited to either variety of tobacco. Consequently, Maryland's economy diversified earlier and more fully than was the case for its older sibling. With its less robust tobacco economy, Maryland experienced neither Virginia's extremes of wealth nor the expensive, large-scale investment in land and enslaved labor that left many of Virginia's great planters seriously indebted in the middle of the eighteenth century.

English settlers in the two colonies also differed in their relations with the region's Native Americans, despite sharing cultural understandings of ecology (the relationship between man and the natural environment) and diplomacy (the use of trade, alliances, and warfare to negotiate relationships among people) that were largely incompatible with those of Indians. In contrast to the Virginians at Jamestown, Maryland colonists purchased land for their first settlement, and the government generally continued the practice of acquiring land through treaties and purchases before allowing settlement in new territory. In addition, Maryland's English population grew more slowly than Virginia's throughout the first century of colonization and was always much smaller in absolute numbers during the colonial period. Thus the spread of settlement on Maryland's western shore stayed largely east of the fall line until well into the eighteenth century. Within its smaller territory, the provincial government exercised jurisdiction over interactions between settlers and Native Americans in ways that diffused large-scale conflict. Perhaps most important, Maryland's first colonists arrived at a time when Native Americans in the northern Chesapeake region faced significant threats from the Susquehannock, leading the Piscataway and others to view the new English arrivals as potential allies. Although Maryland did occasionally participate as an ally in intra-Indian warfare and experienced intermittent hostility among individuals, settlers in Lord Baltimore's colony avoided the protracted military conflict with Native Americans that characterized Virginia's early years.

Another major distinction arose from the colonies' different political structures. Virginia, although initially settled by the private, joint-stock Virginia Company, became a royal colony in 1624, while Maryland was the personal undertaking of George Calvert and his son Cecilius, the second Lord Baltimore, to whom Charles I granted the colony as private property. Although the Maryland charter provided for an assembly of freemen, the proprietor could disallow legislation it passed and could use the powers of his prerogative, or exclusive right, to establish policies without legislative consent.

The political distinction between royal and proprietary colonies was further complicated by religious differences, particularly because religion and politics were inextricably linked during the seventeenth century. The contemporary practice of expressing political identities and allegiances in religious terms contributed to instability within each colony and to conflict between the two. Promoters of each shared an imperative to bring Christianity to people they perceived as pagan and uncivilized, but differed not only over specific tenets of faith but also over the colonial government's role in promoting religious belief. Virginia was founded explicitly as a Protestant colony to counter Catholic Spain's ambition to dominate North America's southern coast, and from its beginnings the government maintained an established, state-sponsored, and Protestant church. The Calverts, on the other hand, who were themselves Roman Catholic, envisioned in Maryland a civil society where religion was a private affair, clearly separated from government activities. The intertwined differences of polity and religious belief created tensions between the two sisters relating to issues of legitimacy and authority.

In the seventeenth century, with the Maryland colony settled on land that Virginians considered an integral part of *their* colony, both sides tended to emphasize the two colonies' distinctiveness. Colonists generally understood themselves to be English, but also separately Virginians and Marylanders, loosely united by common origin but never unified. Yet the frame provided by the bay that washed the tidewater shores of both Leah and Rachel, Hammond's colonial sisters, ensured that they would continue to resemble one another, linked by bonds of kinship that grew and strengthened over nearly two centuries.

Despite the occasional quarrels and periods of intense competition that occur naturally among siblings, the two fruitful sisters prospered as colonies of England (and, after the union of England and Scotland in 1707, of Great Britain). They enriched the mother country more than any of her other mainland offspring, conforming well to the mercantile ideal: they produced valuable raw materials for export and consumed an abundance of manufactures as well as exotic imports from around the world profitably channeled through British ports. As they matured and began to resemble more closely the metropolis to which they owed political and cultural allegiance, the two colonies drew closer together, and together became a trifle rebellious, as children often do. In time, Virginia and Maryland, finding that they had more in common with their younger siblings along the seaboard than with their distant parent, declared their independence.

ONE

Great Expectations

IN APRIL 1635, William Claiborne, an Englishman in his mid-thirties who had lived in the nascent Virginia colony for more than two decades, faced a decision. Over the past several years he had created a viable trading community in the upper Chesapeake Bay, using his skill at negotiating with Native Americans, his authority as a colonial official, and his contacts with influential London merchants and politicians. Claiborne had a royal license granting exclusive rights to trade with the Susquehannock people, whose territory encompassed the southern stretches of the river now bearing their name. He exchanged English tools, cloth, ribbon, and beads for thick beaver pelts highly prized in Europe for making fine hats. Claiborne had recently established a fort on an island he named Kent, located roughly 150 miles north of Jamestown. By 1634, nearly one hundred men and women worked there as traders, farmers, cooks, shipwrights, washerwomen, hog keepers, coopers, and millers. Yet despite this success, Claiborne's position was vulnerable.

England's king, Charles I, had in 1632 granted a charter for a new colony to Cecilius Calvert, the second Lord Baltimore. Named Maryland in honor of the king's wife, Lord Baltimore's colony encompassed unsettled territory between Delaware Bay and the Potomac River, including nearly two-thirds of Chesapeake Bay. Claiborne's protests that his trading license predated Maryland's charter and that the Kent Island settlement should be exempt from a grant of land "not yet cultivated and planted" had failed to prevent establishment of the new colony.[1] The first Maryland colonists arrived in March 1634 and quickly negotiated trading alliances and land for their settlement with Indians who lived along the Potomac River. The colony's governor, Lord Baltimore's brother Leonard Calvert, not only demanded that Claiborne yield his Kent Island proprietorship but also prohibited Virginia vessels from trading in the northern bay. Now in 1635, Henry Fleet, a former associate of Claiborne who had allied with Maryland, seized a Kent Island ship for trading without Lord Baltimore's license; both ship and cargo were condemned and sold. Claiborne had to choose: should he submit to Lord Baltimore's authority or should he continue to fight for his monopoly and land rights?

On 23 April 1635, Claiborne's choice became dramatically clear. In retaliation for seizure of his property, Claiborne ordered one of his armed sloops to intercept Maryland vessels to stop their trade with northern Indians. Governor Calvert responded by dispatching ships to counter Claiborne. When the two forces engaged in the Pocomoke River, Maryland's vessels captured Claiborne's sloop in a battle that left three of Claiborne's men dead. Two weeks later, the two sides shed blood again. Although the Kent Islanders were victorious in this second battle, and although Claiborne continued to lobby for his license and his settlement, Lord Baltimore ultimately won the day. The Privy Council of England (the executive body made up of the king's closest advisors) upheld Maryland's charter, Governor Calvert seized the Kent Island trading fort, and Claiborne's London partners withdrew financial and political support.

The struggle for Kent Island brings into focus significant themes in the history of the Chesapeake region. The immediate objective to monopolize access to furs highlights the critical importance of trade, while the refusal of the Kent Islanders to operate under the Maryland government raises issues of sovereignty and authority. Above all, the clash between William Claiborne and the Calverts—including the skirmish some regard as North America's first naval battle—illustrates that the early years of English settlement involved competing interests and violent conflicts that did not always break down along ethnic or racial lines.

Men and women living in the bay's tidewater area before about 1640 separate into clusters that can be characterized as Native American, European, and—to a limited extent—African, but such labels mask internal variations and divisions that were often more significant than the broad categories. The dispute over Kent Island, for example, involved not only economic competition but also religious conflict. The Calverts founded Maryland in part as a refuge for Roman Catholics, who could not worship openly in England, while Claiborne's supporters in Virginia and London were predominantly Puritans, hostile to Roman Catholicism and favoring simplicity in doctrine and worship. Because differences of religion affected many aspects of seventeenth-century life, the Catholic Calverts and Claiborne's Puritan allies were natural adversaries. Territorial disputes among Native Americans played a similarly significant role. The relatively warm welcome the Marylanders received from the Piscataway and Yaocomico who lived in territory where they wished to settle owed much to the Indians' expectation that this English group would offer them military support against Claiborne's Susquehannock allies. When Lord Baltimore's prohibitions disrupted Claiborne's trade in the northern Chesapeake, the Susquehannock elected to carry their pelts overland to Dutch and Swedish settlements along the Delaware River, where they could obtain European goods without violating their alliance with Claiborne. A simple story of Maryland versus Virginia (or European versus Native American) thus quickly becomes one of Calvert-Maryland-Piscataway-English Catholic versus Claiborne-Virginia-Susquehannock-London Puritan, with a smattering of English versus Dutch and Swede thrown into the mix.[2]

The history of the Chesapeake colonies requires a wide lens to encompass shifting alliances and developments throughout both Europe and the North American coast. Conflicts with roots in European issues are critical to understanding the region's early history, but so too are conflicts among Native American groups that only tangentially involved Europeans. This is a drama with many actors whose histories predated particular moments of contact and shaped subsequent developments. Key events occurred along the shores of the Chesapeake Bay, but the drama and its participants, with all of their motivations, expectations, and misconceptions, reflected broader trends in the economies and societies of both Europe and North America.

EUROPE BEFORE JAMESTOWN

For centuries before the eras of exploration and colonization, Europe's orientation toward the Mediterranean basin played a critical role in its economic and social development. The Atlantic and Arctic Oceans presented formidable barriers to the west and north because navigation tools and ship design were inadequate for long-distance voyages across open waters. Instead, trade flowed naturally overland south and east to the Mediterranean Sea, which could be safely traversed by medieval mariners, facilitating exchanges with Islamic realms along its eastern and southern perimeter. Muslims dominated the trade routes that stretched south into Africa and east to India and thus monopolized access to precious metals, spices, silks, perfumes, and drugs, sources of wealth and luxury coveted by Europeans. In addition to their geographic disadvantage, Europeans suffered epidemics of bubonic plague and waves of famine that decimated populations, while successive wars over territory and religion disrupted economic development. Rather than expanding outward, to spread Christianity and acquire valuable lands and resources, Europe was shrinking, losing influence and territory to Muslims. The ascendancy of non-Christians became all too evident by the mid-fifteenth century, when Ottoman Turks captured Constantinople and invaded southeastern Europe.

Attempting to circumvent Muslim trading monopolies, European merchants and sailors first navigated around the African continent during the fifteenth century. In the process they discovered and conquered three island groups in the eastern Atlantic: the Canaries, Madeira, and the Azores. With technological improvements in shipbuilding and navigation making longer voyages possible, ambitious merchants contemplated sailing still farther west to find a new route to India and China. In addition, northern Europeans, seeking a competitive edge in fishing and whaling, used the new technologies to explore farther in the North Atlantic and began establishing seasonal camps along the coasts of Greenland, Labrador, and Newfoundland. The development of the printing press and rising literacy in Europe helped disseminate new information about these distant lands and peoples. An era of discovery was well under way by 1492 when Christopher Columbus set off for the Pacific but made landfall first in the Bahamas and then in the Greater Antilles.

Subsequent Spanish conquest of large regions in Central and South America had significant consequences for Europe as well as the Americas. By the late sixteenth century, the Spanish used the extensive wealth of their colonial silver mines to import luxury items from the Far East. Spain's king, Philip II, also employed this wealth to expand his army and influence throughout Europe. A fervent and militant Roman Catholic, Philip sought to eradicate Protestantism on the European continent. The dramatic rise in Spanish fortunes sparked both envy and fear among northern, mostly Protestant, Europeans. Envy motivated rulers and merchants of other European nations to seek wealth through exploration and colonization. Fear operated on two levels, as political motivation for countering Spain's expanding influence and as religious motivation for Protestant nations to counter Spain's efforts to convert natives to Roman Catholicism.

The opportunities of overseas expansion inspired a cluster of merchants and politicians to promote England's earliest colonization efforts. This group, known as the West Country men because of their concentration in England's southwestern counties, included Sir Francis Drake, Sir Humphrey Gilbert, Gilbert's half brother Sir Walter Ralegh, Richard Hakluyt the elder, and his cousin, Richard Hakluyt the younger. Together, these men developed a rational for establishing overseas colonies that blended economic, political, and religious objectives. Promotional literature emphasized the benefits of English migration to and trade with overseas settlements. Established colonies would supply raw materials and luxury goods otherwise imported from southern Europe, North Africa, or Asia. As Hakluyt the younger argued, no longer would England have to "depende upon Spaine for oyles, . . . orenges, lemons, Spanish skinnes, etc. Nor uppon Fraunce for . . . baysalt, and Gascoyne wines, nor on Estlande for flaxe, pitch, tarre, mastes, etc.," and thus, "we shoulde not so exhaust our treasure, and so exceedingly inriche our doubtfull friendes."[3]

Colonies would also create consumer demand. Explorers and traders would sell commodities produced in England to the indigenous population, particularly cloth, glass and pewter wares, knives, and tools. As the English established permanent North American settlements, colonists would be useful consumers of the mother country's exports. For England, the need to manufacture more goods for sale overseas would ease unemployment. Moreover, colonies would relieve England of her surplus population by encouraging the able-bodied poor to migrate. Promoters argued that relocation would be of greater benefit to the poor than the assistance being provided by churches, prisons, and hospitals. In addition, settlement in North America would enable Protestants to proselytize among Native Americans to counter the spread of Roman Catholicism in Spanish America. Strategic placement of colonies on the seaboard would also provide secure harbors for privateering, or government licensing of privately owned vessels to attack an enemy nation's commercial shipping. English promoters hoped that successful privateering would disrupt the flow of Spanish silver from the Americas and divert a significant share of that wealth into their hands.

Reliance on privateers to further national objectives illustrates the contrast between England's approach to exploration and settlement and the activities of Spain and Portugal. England's rulers did not have sufficient resources to finance exploration as a government enterprise, but instead issued royal grants of authority to individual initiatives or multiparty ventures organized as joint-stock companies. London-based investors and merchants had successfully used the joint-stock method to fund the East India and Russia companies that traded with Asia and eastern Europe. Such companies raised capital to finance trading voyages by selling "stocks," or shares, in the enterprise to a pool of investors, who then divided any profits.

Despite their enthusiasm for overseas exploration and settlement, the West Country men's first ventures were largely unsuccessful. Martin Frobisher explored the North American coast between 1576 and 1578 but located neither gold nor the coveted northern sea route to the Pacific Ocean known as the Northwest Passage. Shortly thereafter, Sir Humphrey Gilbert claimed the Newfoundland fisheries for England and explored the coast of Maine, but his death at sea ended his plans to establish a colony. Although these efforts failed, they kept alive the possibility of English control in the North Atlantic. In 1584, after Gilbert's death, the task of realizing that goal fell to Sir Walter Ralegh, his half brother. Queen Elizabeth I granted Ralegh authority to explore the area north of Spanish Florida in search of suitable land for settlements.

Elizabeth promised Ralegh dominion over any colony he founded, but neither the queen nor her courtier had a clear idea of what that territory might offer. Ralegh therefore sent two small vessels commanded by Philip Amadas and Arthur Barlowe to explore the area. The ships sailed up the east coast of Spanish Florida and in July passed through barrier islands off present-day North Carolina. In mid-September, after their return to England, Barlowe wrote an account of the venture's experiences in the territory Ralegh had named Virginia in honor of Elizabeth I, England's "virgin queen." In keeping with the tradition of promotional literature, Barlowe emphasized the region's most positive features and glossed over potential difficulties. He described a fertile land inhabited by a docile and friendly people: "We found the people most gentle, loving and faithfull, void of all guile, and treason." Barlowe made no mention of the Indians' desire to trade for hatchets, axes, knives, and swords or of the wars fought between native groups. He asserted that the land itself promised riches for those who settled there, having "the most plentifull, sweete, fruitfull, and wholsome [soil] of all the world." Game abounded, grapevines flourished, and a half hour of fishing could "laden [a] boate as deepe as it could swimme."[4] But Barlowe seriously misjudged the area's suitability for oceangoing vessels, ignoring both the shallow depths of the coastal sounds and the dangerous waters off Cape Hatteras. Nor would the region's Indians prove to be easily conscripted to labor on behalf of settlers.

Barlowe's account nonetheless fulfilled its goal of gathering support for the ill-fated effort that began in 1585, an enterprise that takes its name of Roanoke from one of the islands Barlowe and Amadas visited. Seven ships left England in April, but a slow passage delayed their arrival until too late in the year to plant crops. Many supplies were lost immediately when one ship went aground in a shallow inlet, and the men lacked skills needed to gather food from the wild. These circumstances, combined with inadequate leadership and unrealistic expectations of Native American assistance, made for a difficult winter, yet the settlers showed little inclination to toil in the "fruitfull and wholsome" soil once a new growing season began. In June 1586, Sir Francis Drake arrived with supplies and equipment, but a hurricane damaged both the cargo and Drake's fleet. Richard Lane, the expedition's leader, decided to use the one remaining large vessel to carry everyone back to England. The following year, Ralegh sent another three ships under the leadership of John White. In August 1587, White sailed back to London to procure additional supplies, but the threat of a Spanish invasion of England delayed his return trip. By the time White finally returned to Roanoke in August 1590, virtually all traces of the settlers had vanished.

Well before the colony's disappearance, Lane recognized that lack of a sheltered deep-water harbor made the Carolina coast an unsuitable place for settlement. In the fall of 1585 he had sent a small party to explore farther along the Atlantic coast for the protected harbor any colonizing effort required. Over the winter, this group ventured up several rivers on the Chesapeake Bay's western shore, where they found more favorable conditions. As Lane reported, "the Territorie and soyle of the Chesepians . . . was for pleasantnes of seate, for temperature of Climate, for fertilitie of soyle, and for the commoditie of the Sea . . . not to be excelled by any other whatsoever."[5] Once again, the account of a cursory visit painted a glowing picture of a land ideally suited to English ambitions. Relying on Lane's account, the next organized effort to plant an English colony in the Virginia territory selected the region of the Chesepian.

THE TIDEWATER BEFORE JAMESTOWN

Just as Europeans had gathered information about foreign lands from explorers and merchants, so too did Native Americans throughout North America use networks of trade and diplomacy to learn about distant places and people. Well before the first English settlement efforts, some of the news that arrived with people and goods included tales of Europeans. Not infrequently, Spanish, French, Dutch, and English mariners exploring the coast of North America interacted with Indians they encountered. Such meetings could be relatively peaceful. In 1524, for example, Giovanni da Verrazano reported to his employer, the king of France, that during his first encounter with Native Americans, they "showed the greatest delight on beholding us. . . . and offered us some of their provisions." Other interactions were decidedly less benign, including a subsequent meeting when Verrazano had no hesitation about taking a "little boy eight years of age. . . . to carry with us to France."[6] Verrazano's early voyage established enduring parameters for sixteenth-century encounters between European mariners and Native Americans: enthusiastic trade and callous kidnapping.

More sustained contact occurred in the late sixteenth century, with encounters that foreshadowed the early Jamestown settlers' experiences. A decade before the Roanoke settlers appeared, a Spanish Jesuit priest, Father Juan de Segura, offered to lead a mission to the Chesapeake Bay. Father Segura's desire to convert Native Americans meshed with the Spanish government's desire to extend control farther up the North American seaboard. The Jesuits anticipated a fruitful mission in part because of encouragement from an Indian they knew as Don Luís de Velasco, who offered to lead them to his homeland. Don Luís, who had been taken from the Chesapeake Bay nine years earlier, had traveled, not entirely by choice, widely since that time: to Portugal and Spain, then Mexico (where he was baptized), and Florida. Arriving in Havana in 1570, he joined the small Jesuit group sailing from Cuba that summer.

After anchoring in the Chesapeake Bay in September, the missionaries and Don Luís left their ship and trekked overland to a Kiskiack village, where they set about building a chapel. In a letter sent back to Cuba, the missionaries reported a warm welcome, both for Don Luís, whose relatives felt he had "risen from the dead and come down from heaven," and for the missionaries, whom the Indians "begg[ed] . . . to remain in this land with them."[7] Yet the Spanish quickly discovered that local populations were suffering extreme hunger because of a severe drought. Far from being able to supply the Jesuits with material goods while the priests went about their spiritual work, Native Americans looked to the Spanish for both material and spiritual relief.

Although mindful of the risk of starvation, the missionaries chose to stay and proselytize, but their letter to supporters in Cuba underscored the necessity of receiving "a generous quantity of corn . . . with all speed possible."[8] The situation deteriorated rapidly after the Spaniards' ship set sail for Cuba, according to later testimony of the only European survivor, a young boy named Alonso de Olmos. Don Luís returned to his village some weeks after their arrival at the Kiskiack village, leaving the Jesuits without an interpreter. The fathers bartered with neighboring Indians for food as best they could and tried repeatedly to compel Don Luís to return and to stop behaving "more like a pagan than a Christian in his manners, dress, and habits." After struggling through the winter months, Father Segura sent several men to find Don Luís, believing that "the devil held him in great deception."[9] Don Luís killed Segura's envoys, then went to the missionary settlement and killed the remaining Spaniards except the boy, Olmos. A Spanish supply ship arrived in the spring of 1571, observed Indians on shore clothed in Jesuit vestments, captured two, and learned of Olmos's survival but not the fate of the priests. Pedro Menéndez de Aviles, the Spanish governor, personally led a second expedition in 1572 seeking more information. After recovering Olmos and learning of the attacks on the Jesuits, Menéndez demanded that the Indians deliver Don Luís. When Don Luís failed to appear, the Spaniards hanged a number of captured Native Americans from the flagship's rigging and indiscriminately killed additional Indians gathered on shore before returning to Cuba.

The actions of both parties—the Jesuit fathers' persistent efforts to correct Don Luís's behavior and his violent response—suggest the intensity of cultural misunderstandings that fueled conflicts between Native Americans and Europeans in the period of exploration and settlement. Misunderstanding flowed from fundamental differences in the two groups' cosmologies, or ideas about the universe's origin and structure. Although Native Americans and Europeans recognized each other as similarly human (that is, distinct from animals), they held radically different conceptions about man's place within a framework that incorporated the natural world and spiritual phenomena.

As prescientific people, both Europeans and Indians explained the phenomena they observed in the world around them as the work of superhuman forces, but held different ideas about the relationship between humans and those forces. Native Americans understood the universe as a unified whole, with the supernatural and natural intertwined. Human beings were one element within a complicated universe that existed in a precarious state of equilibrium. This perception contrasted with that of most Europeans, whose religious teachings—whether Catholic or Protestant—included the concept of human dominion over a world created specifically for man's benefit and distinct from the celestial home of man's creator. For Europeans, an external and omnipotent God or his spiritual assistants could intercede to help humans, or the machinations of external demons could undermine the well-being of humans, but these powerful spirits stood at a remove from worldly affairs. The distinction between earthly and heavenly was central to European ideas about human origins and purpose, but absent from Native American cosmologies. Indians saw themselves instead as coexisting with animals and spirits, neither entirely dominant over the former nor fully subservient to the latter. The natural and spiritual worlds, fully interconnected, required careful stewardship to maintain the balance essential for all to survive.

The need to maintain an appropriate balance of power to hold the universe in equilibrium shaped Indian conceptions of governance, warfare, trade, and religion in ways that Europeans rarely understood. For example, European explorers and traders identified Native American men and women who exerted authority over others with titles such as emperor or queen, attempting thereby to reconcile their observations with European assumptions about hierarchical power and social organization. Thus the English, who occasionally witnessed Powhatan ordering the death of one or more of his people, believed this indicated Powhatan's status as a "great king" with absolute power over his subjects. Ethnographic evidence, however, indicates that the nature of Powhatan's authority was more complicated. Tribal structures generally featured a chief who exercised power with the consent and support of a council composed of elders, priests, and warriors. Chiefs derived a measure of their individual power from the extent to which they exemplified moral and proper behavior; chiefs who failed to lead with circumspection and reason could be deposed.

A similar emphasis on appropriate behavior and leadership shaped relationships among Native American groups, whose diplomatic alliances were continually in flux. When the English established their Jamestown settlement, many Indians in the lower Chesapeake region recognized Powhatan as a *mamanatowick* (a paramount chief), but the strength of their allegiance varied. Similar alliances or confederacies occurred elsewhere in tidewater and Piedmont areas, such as the Piscataway confederacy, whose paramount chief assumed the title of *tayac*. Although there is evidence that tributary offerings flowed upward from households to the *werowance* (or lesser chief) of each village or town and then to a confederacy's paramount chief, the extent of tribute and precise nature of gifting rituals are unclear. The English overestimated the degree of commitment and authority these relationships represented, expecting them to entail more subservience than was the case and to persist unless explicitly broken. Native Americans, by contrast, viewed alliances as ongoing processes of gifting and renegotiation to maintain balanced relationships among neighboring groups.

Indian and European approaches to armed conflict similarly reflected their distinct cosmologies. In addition to differences in the mechanics and weapons of war (raids and ambushes versus sieges and frontal attacks; arrows versus firearms), broader conceptions of warfare contrasted in two significant respects. First, Native Americans did not generally recognize "at war" as a distinctly separate state from "at peace." War and peace coexisted and required the same careful attention to balance as did all other aspects of life. Raids, taking captives, and similar tactics could be used at any time by one group as corrective measures to counter another group's actions. Indian warfare thus included a moral component, as punishment for improper behavior, and success in war could be understood as evidence of moral, as well as military, superiority. But such superiority was transitory, with the balance of power—and the balance between war and peace—always in flux. Second, in contrast to European concepts of territorial conquest, for Native Americans legitimate motivations for warfare did not explicitly include an objective of acquiring land or other resources. Native American groups used war to restructure relationships, by incorporating defeated villages as subordinate polities. This distinction reflected an Indian emphasis on individual behavior and a proper relationship with the natural world—through stewardship and occupation rather than mastery and possession.

Native American trade practices similarly differed from European methods in ways that emphasized equal exchange rather than maximized profit. Europeans perceived the goal of trading as obtaining the greatest possible benefit at the least possible cost and they thus marveled at the willingness of Indian hunters to exchange beaver pelts or deerskins for such items as glass beads and copperware. But for Native Americans the goal of trading was not to acquire more for less; rather, exchanging goods was part of the continual process of obtaining and redistributing power to maintain the Earth's equilibrium. In assessing the value of trade goods, Native Americans considered not only the utility of items for specific tasks but also objects' inherent spiritual power that connected people to spirits. Objects with certain characteristics, such as reflectivity or uncommon colors, were understood as particularly potent, able to confer status and authority to those who possessed them.

Rarity as well as physical characteristics enhanced the power of objects that came to Chesapeake Indians from great distances. For example, the Powhatan, Piscataway, and other groups placed a high value on items made from or decorated with copper, which they obtained from Indians who mined the ore in mountains to the west. When Europeans began to trade in the region, Native Americans valued the items they offered, including objects made from copper and glass as well as iron tools and woven cloth, not only because such goods fit into preexisting patterns of exchange but also because they were brought over a great distance by an unfamiliar people.

Native Americans similarly expressed interest in the religious objects and teachings that European explorers and missionaries brought from their distant lands, but again fundamental differences in cosmology contributed to misunderstandings and conflict. When the Spanish tried to establish their mission, for example, Indians who demonstrated curiosity about Jesuit teachings may have hoped to draw into their lives the spiritual power they perceived in the missionaries, but they were not amenable to the radical changes Jesuits tried to impose on their way of life. The distinction between an Indian practice of "incorporation" versus a European preoccupation with "conversion" lies beneath the quarrel with Don Luís and other early conflicts between Native Americans and proselytizing Europeans.

For many tidewater Indians, power and authority originated in the spiritual world. Ahone, who created the Earth, represented the source of all spiritual power. Another spirit, Okeus, taught humans how to live in the earthly world. A variety of lesser spirits, including werowances and priests, provided guidance in behaviors that maintained the universe's delicate balance between good and evil forces. Native Americans cultivated their connection to these spirits through such means as rituals, gifts, sacrifices, and possession of powerful objects. When they encountered Europeans, and the spiritual and material possessions that connected these newcomers to unfamiliar sources of power, Indians were often amenable to incorporating these people, objects, and spirits into their pantheistic world.

Missionaries and other Europeans, by contrast, insisted upon a complete conversion from "primitive" and "uncivilized" ways to their ideal of Christian behavior. Europeans expected Indians to abandon their gendered division of labor, customs of polygamy, and spiritual practices. Europeans pressured Indian men to become sedentary agricultural workers, despite the dependence of Native American economies upon a system of labor in which men engaged in hunting and warfare while women cultivated crops and foraged for additional foodstuffs. Similarly indifferent to the ways in which multiple marriages were an essential strategy that linked different families and groups into broader social organizations, Europeans regarded polygamy as sinful. Upholding a belief in one true God, Europeans commanded Indians to destroy representations of their gods and cease honoring ancestral spirits. Native Americans found these expectations not only deeply offensive but also dangerous, because European practices threatened to upset the delicate balance of natural and supernatural forces coexistent in the universe.

At the beginning of the seventeenth century, when the English came to the Chesapeake region intent upon establishing a permanent colony, Native Americans already had reason to believe that the precarious equilibrium of their universe was in jeopardy. Analysis of tree-ring data indicates that settlers arrived as Native Americans struggled with recurring periods of drought. From about 1570 until about 1610, a series of multiyear periods when rainfall was below average meant that Indian populations were experiencing the driest decades in seven centuries. Because Native American economies depended upon a complex balance of cultivated crops and hunted game, supplemented by a wide variety of foraged fruits, vegetables, and nuts, such climatic changes had significant consequences. Unusually severe weather conditions could increase competition for scarce resources, with possible outcomes including migration, warfare, and population loss due to famine. Archaeological evidence from Native American skeletons, such as early ages at death and loss of teeth or bone, reveals significant malnourishment among groups inhabiting the region at the beginning of the seventeenth century. Extended periods of drought appear to have adversely affected Native American economies and health, destabilizing patterns of land use and precipitating a reconfiguration of alliances. In the midst of this period of instability, the region's Indians faced new challenges from European explorers and settlers who once more arrived in their territory seeking food, labor, and land.

JAMESTOWN

There is no evidence that English participants in Virginia's settlement knew about the earlier Jesuit attempt to establish a mission in the region. There is little doubt, however, that Indians inhabiting the tidewater area in 1607 not only remembered Spanish actions in the 1570s but were also familiar with English behavior at Roanoke in the 1580s. In both instances, Europeans expected that Native Americans would willingly share scarce food resources and labor on their behalf. Initial interactions that were relatively peaceful quickly gave way to violence when Europeans demanded assistance. These successive appearances of aggressive newcomers likely contributed to the region's principal development during the late sixteenth century: the rapid expansion of the Powhatan chiefdom.

Sometime after 1570, Powhatan inherited the core of his chiefdom, comprised of six small tribes near the falls on the James River. By 1607, his authority extended over roughly thirty groups across the coastal plain, from south of the Potomac River to the James River basin. During this time, Powhatan moved his principal town eastward to a new site on the York River, closer to the center of his expanding chiefdom. Over the three decades preceding English settlement, Powhatan achieved this remarkable expansion of authority through a combination of marital and diplomatic alliances, military actions, and threats. Military action subdued some groups, such as the Kecoughtan near the mouth of the James River whom the Powhatan defeated in 1596–97, and later the Chesepian, whose settlement the Roanoke party had visited in 1585 but who had been decimated by 1607. Other groups, like the Accomac and Occohannock on the bay's eastern shore, joined Powhatan's tributary network when faced with threat of attack but otherwise maintained independent sovereignty. Kinship ties played a pivotal role, as Powhatan could draw upon support from brothers and sons who held authority as werowances and warriors in allied groups. Most importantly, three of Powhatan's brothers were werowances among the Pamunkey, whose territory stretched along the upper York River and two of its tributaries. One brother, Opechancanough, not only commanded Pamunkey warriors, reputed to be exceptionally skilled and fierce, but also served as Powhatan's war chief, or leader in external affairs (in contrast to Powhatan's more powerful position as peace chief, or ruler within the chiefdom).

Powhatan's success in expanding his chiefdom so dramatically may also have resulted from a distinctive combination of political status (inherited through his mother) and spiritual authority (acquired through religious rituals and moral conduct). The etymology of Powhatan's name and his status as mamanatowick suggest as much—that he commanded particular respect because he held an unusually high degree of priestly power as well as his inherited position of political power. In addition, it is possible that the violence that followed the two earlier settlement attempts, first at the Spanish mission and then farther south at Roanoke, induced smaller groups to ally with the Powhatan as protection against this new, albeit intermittent, threat. At the very least, the increasing frequency of European ships sailing into Chesapeake Bay added an element of instability that Powhatan could use to his advantage.

Loss of the Roanoke settlers in the 1580s and preoccupation with European wars set back English efforts to establish a North American colony, yet interest in colonization persisted. A formal peace treaty with Spain, negotiated shortly after James I succeeded Elizabeth I as England's monarch in 1603, reduced the risk that the Spanish would move quickly against any new colonizing effort and at the same time ended privateering as an investment opportunity for wealthy merchants and aristocrats. Circumstances thus favored a renewed commitment to establishing North American colonies. Warships still protected Spain's claim to the eastern seaboard as far north as the Savannah River, while the French had established themselves along the St. Lawrence River and asserted control over the North Atlantic fisheries. English entrepreneurs therefore focused their efforts between the Bay of Fundy and Carolina's Outer Banks.

A royal charter issued on 10 April 1606 satisfied the interests of both West Country merchants and rival London investors by dividing North America's coast into two overlapping grants. The charter gave the northern half to the West Country group, organized as the Plymouth Company, including merchants and investors from Bristol, Exeter, and smaller ports. It granted the southern half, from Long Island Sound to present-day North Carolina, to the London group, organized as the Virginia Company of London. As neither group was expected to inhabit its entire region, a precise boundary between the grants was unnecessary. Instead, the grants authorized each cluster of investors to establish a settlement, with jurisdiction over territory one hundred miles inland and fifty miles north and south. Although each company was to be privately financed and managed, the charter also established a royal council to oversee their operations and to resolve any conflicts between company policies and national interests.

The Virginia Company's first expedition left England late in 1606. Three ships carrying 144 sailors and colonists set out for Chesapeake Bay, commanded by Christopher Newport, an experienced mariner. Apart from the sailors, nearly one-half of the men who set sail were members of the gentry and/or former soldiers or privateers, including three of the colony's chief promoters: Edward Maria Wingfield, Bartholomew Gosnold, and John Smith. Wingfield and Gosnold were well-born cousins with experience in, respectively, privateering and European wars. Smith, a farmer's son, was decidedly less well-born, but he had parlayed a successful military career into status as a gentleman-knight. The group also included about a dozen skilled artisans, but somewhat more than one-half consisted of unskilled laborers and young boys.

Early colonization efforts did not envision settlements with permanent residents. The Virginia Company's mix of goals included identifying resources such as precious metals or timber that could be exploited, searching for the elusive Northwest Passage to the Pacific, converting Native Americans to Protestant Christianity, and establishing a presence to solidify England's territorial claim. Most of the men who arrived in Jamestown did so in hope of quickly making a fortune and returning to England in far better circumstances. Because the Virginia Company did not envision an agricultural community, few expedition members had skills necessary for self-sufficiency. The colony's sponsors and leaders expected to emulate the Spanish model of colonization. The conquistadors successfully placed themselves at the top of an existing tributary ladder, supported by Indians who labored as miners and farmers. Promotional tracts encouraged the idea that Native Americans would willingly supply food and trade goods, leaving the adventurers free to take possession of the land and begin extracting the region's resources. When this expectation proved to be as illusory as it had been for the Roanoke expedition, this new group of English men was similarly unprepared for the hardships that beset them almost as soon as they disembarked.

Entering the capes of the bay on 26 April 1607, Captain Newport and his men anchored near the mouth of a wide river they named after their monarch, James I. The English spent several weeks exploring the lower bay, during which time they named the capes after the king's sons, Henry and Charles, and ceremoniously claimed possession of the region by erecting a cross at Cape Henry. Their first days in Virginia included numerous interactions with the region's Native Americans, some violent and others peaceful. On the first night, a small group exploring the lower James River was attacked while preparing to return to the ships. Several days later, as the vessels moved up the river to Cape Comfort, another scouting party was welcomed at a Kecoughtan village. Following this promising encounter, the colonists explored farther up the James to find a site for their initial settlement.

After some debate, the expedition's leaders chose a neck of land extending into the river, connected to its northern shore only by an isthmus, which they named Jamestown Island. Several practical considerations led to this decision. With a water barrier on three sides and a narrow land connection, the site was easy to defend. The location, well upriver, meant there would be ample warning if the Spanish entered the bay and the deep channel enabled sailors to anchor large vessels close to shore to transfer cargo, with the added benefit that the ships' cannon could be used for defense. In addition, the peninsula was large enough to provide timber and game but not overgrown with trees, which permitted rapid construction of a fort without first creating a clearing in dense forest.

Despite these advantages, the location had numerous flaws that became all too evident over time. Although the English perceived the site as vacant and unoccupied, it was part of the hunting territory of the neighboring Paspahegh, who had previously extended hospitality but did not welcome this permanent intrusion. Simmering Indian hostility compounded the misery that soon resulted from the dubious decision to settle in the middle of a swamp. The terrain's relative openness was due to the preponderance of low-lying marshland, which aided hunting and defense but was terribly unhealthy. As spring turned to summer, stagnant marsh water bred mosquitoes, which tormented settlers and infected them with malaria, as well as bacteria that caused typhoid and dysentery. The site lacked any springs for fresh water; when supplies of ale ran out, colonists drank from the river, despite its high salt content and contamination with sediment and organic waste during summer months. The combination of heat, humidity, disease, and salt poisoning proved lethal for many, while those who lived were often too debilitated for agricultural labor, which led to starvation come winter.

As the Jamestown settlers began to build their fort, however, these latent dangers remained unrecognized. Captain Newport set sail late in June to collect more supplies and settlers from England, leaving a few more than one hundred men to improve the site and explore the region. By the end of September, fully one-half had died. As George Percy later recalled, "Our men were destroyed with cruell diseases, as Swellings, Flixes, Burning Fevers, and by warres, . . . but for the most part they died of meere famine."[10] Those who lived owed their survival to Native Americans, who intermittently supplied Jamestown with food as the harvest season progressed. Although grateful for the sustenance, the English largely attributed Indian generosity to divine intervention, believing that it had "pleased God . . . to send those people which were our mortall enemies to releeve us with victuals."[11] Because they ascribed hostile actions to an innate Native American savagery but peaceful actions to intervention by a

Christian God, English acceptance of support did not greatly lessen their perception of Indians as likely enemies.

Leadership problems compounded the suffering experienced during the first fall and winter. The Virginia Company had named a council of seven men to govern the colony, led by a president elected by the council from among its members. Conflict beset this small, ill-assorted group who found themselves in an unexpectedly harsh environment and weakened by disease and hunger. The council was chronically divided, fracturing into subgroups that bickered about how to deal with their adversity, and caught between the Company's instructions and the realities of their situation. The council deposed Wingfield, its first president, in a flurry of accusations and counteraccusations in early September; his successor proved equally ineffectual; and other likely leaders died during the first waves of sickness and famine. Eventually, Captain John Smith, an enduringly controversial figure, emerged to fill the leadership void.

Although the Company had named Smith as a councilor, Wingfield denied him his seat, believing Smith guilty of encouraging mutiny during the Atlantic voyage. Opinionated, vocal, and lacking in deference, or the expected respect for authority, Smith was also unpopular with some of the other leaders. But he was undeniably intelligent, energetic, and successful in obtaining food from the Indians, which won him critical support, and he proved to be an effective leader. Serving first as supply master, Smith explored the region surrounding Jamestown and made contact with a number of nearby Indian groups, trading with some but using force to seize supplies of food from others.

Late in 1607, as he traveled up the James River to explore its tributaries and search for food, Smith was captured by Powhatan's brother and war chief, Opechancanough. According to Smith's later accounts, he was twice spared death, first when he "amazed" Opechancanough with the wonder of his compass, and second after Pocahontas, "Powhatan's dearest daughter, when no intreaty could prevail, . . . laid her own head on his" to prevent her father's men from beating "out his braines."[12] In all likelihood, Smith misinterpreted the meaning Native Americans attached to both events, particularly the second, which Powhatan may have intended as a ritual adoption to destroy Smith's English identity so that he could be reborn as Powhatan. Smith's earliest account of the event, written in 1612, makes no mention of Pocahontas; she enters only in later versions and likely played a minor part in the ceremony. Under the layers of literary embellishments and cultural misunderstandings that cloud Smith's narrative, there is evidence that Powhatan wished to draw the English into his tributary system to supply European copper for redistribution to allies and European weapons for use against enemies. Smith was accordingly dispatched back to Jamestown with guides who were to return with a grindstone and two "great gunnes" (medium-sized cannons) that, weighing more than one ton each, proved to be "somewhat too heavie."[13]

Smith's return to Jamestown in early January 1608 after weeks of captivity coincided with the arrival of Captain Newport with the influx of settlers and goods known as the "first supply." Coming from opposite directions, the two men found the same desperate situation, with fewer than forty settlers still alive. Smith's news of an accord with Powhatan, and Newport's supply of healthy men and food, provided ample cause for celebration. Yet the supply proved to be of little use. Within a few days, a fire consumed the fort and most provisions, leaving nearly three times as many men to face the remaining winter months with even less food than before Newport's return. There was little love lost between Smith and Newport, but the two men worked in tandem to alleviate the situation. Smith took Newport upriver to meet Powhatan, with whom they traded for provisions to tide the settlers over until spring. When Newport returned to England in April, he once again left behind a colony that appeared to be on a reasonably secure footing.

Smith left shortly thereafter to continue exploration of Chesapeake Bay, its resources, and its people. Although the expedition discovered neither precious metals nor a route to the Pacific, Smith and his men traveled nearly two thousand miles, identified more than two hundred Indian towns and villages, and made contact with numerous groups of Native Americans, including the Susquehannock and Massawomeck to the north and the Mannahoac to the west. Smith's *A Map of Virginia*[,] *With a Description of the Countrey,* published in 1612, provided Europeans with their first detailed portrait of the Chesapeake region. The comprehensive and visually dramatic map, illustrated by scenes of native life, showed the bay's immensity, the many rivers that fed into it and provided interior access, and the numbers and varieties of people who already inhabited its territory.

Extensive as Smith's explorations had been, however, the English occupied only Jamestown Island, where Smith returned in September 1608 to find the hot, humid Virginia summer taking its toll once again. Mismanagement, corruption, and spoilage had depleted the food supply and little had been done toward growing or gathering winter provisions. Smith, who understood that survival required hard work, agreed to serve as council president and did what he could to impose order and discipline. Captain Newport arrived soon after on the *Mary and Margaret* with the second supply, which also carried the small settlement's first English women: Margaret Forrest, probably joining her husband, and Anne Burras, her fourteen-year-old servant. Newport's arrival also added about seventy more men with inadequate skills and unrealistic expectations. The survivors of the first disastrous year knew that it was not possible to ship back precious metals or to send news of a passage to Asia, yet the Virginia Company had ordered Newport to continue the search for both. In addition, he was commanded to subjugate Powhatan in a ceremony crowning the Indian leader as the English king's vassal, a task that proved less than satisfying for all concerned. Powhatan clearly recognized the negative significance of kneeling before the English and flatly refused to relinquish sovereign authority over his people and their land, ultimately exchanging only "his old shooes and his mantell" for the coronet and scarlet mantle Newport offered.[14]

Regrouping after this setback, Jamestown's settlers faced another Virginia winter, while Newport left for England to deliver a disappointing cargo of lumber products and small quantities of naval stores and glass. The uneasy peace with the Powhatan and more distant Indians deteriorated during the winter, particularly when Smith went searching for food. Finding few native groups willing to trade, he resorted to subterfuge and force. Smith also found himself repeatedly in danger of capture and again escaped through self-reported acts of bravado, such as seizing Opechancanough by his hair to use him as a shield, and through the timely intervention of Pocahontas, who supposedly defied her father to warn Smith of an imminent attack. Using a combination of

Powhatan's Mantle. This deerskin mantle, with figures worked in shells, may have been given to Christopher Newport in 1608 as part of the ceremony by which Virginians attempted to make Powhatan a vassal of the English king. Denver Public Library, Western History Collection, X-31119; original at the Ashmolean Museum, Oxford, England shrewd calculation and brutal force, Smith was able to keep most settlers alive through the winter, and in the spring he began preparations for the expected arrival of a third supply.

WAR, PEACE, AND TOBACCO

The nine ships that sailed from England in May 1609 not only included roughly five hundred men, with additional women and the first children to emigrate, but also brought notice of new leadership and reorganization of the settlement. Under a new royal charter, granted in 1609, the Virginia Company began selling stock publicly and received direction from a treasurer and council elected by stockholders, rather than from a royally appointed council. These changes prompted the wave of investment that financed the third supply. The colony's revival was delayed, however, by a hurricane that scattered the fleet. One ship was lost with no survivors, while the flagship *Sea Venture*, bearing Sir Thomas Gates, one of the new leaders, was shipwrecked at the Bermuda Islands off the North American coast. Crew and passengers made it safely to shore but were stranded until they could build a seaworthy vessel. The remaining ships limped up the James River in August, bringing several hundred hungry and ill settlers. The arrival of new Company orders—but not the leaders authorized to carry them out—touched off another wave of discord among the councilors, resulting in Smith's loss of the presidency. Nursing a debilitating wound, Smith departed with the ships that sailed for England in October, knowing that he left behind a colony without adequate winter provisions but unable to correct the problem.

As cold set in, so did death; the winter's misery surpassed even that of previous years. Efforts in the fall to extract food from the Powhatan and Patawomeck proved disastrous. Because of drought conditions Native Americans had no surpluses to trade, and violent attempts to seize food by force destroyed any pretense of Anglo-Indian friendship. Frustrated by the settlers' unreasonable demands, Powhatan ordered his warriors and allied Indians to keep the English hemmed in on Jamestown Island. This strategy turned the defensible fort into a besieged prison, with deadly arrows and hatchets on the outside, ready to kill anyone trying to escape, and deadly plague, typhoid, dysentery, and famine on the inside, ready to kill the rest. Of nearly three hundred colonists alive in the fall, barely one hundred lived until the spring of 1610.

The English inside Jamestown's fort might have suffered less from disease and hunger had the Virginia Company planned its project as a permanent, agriculture-based colony. Women who arrived with the ships of the second and third supplies, for example, brought skills the colony sorely needed, but the Jamestown settlement offered little scope for their employment. Tending kitchen gardens that could improve the diet; looking after dairy herds and processing surplus milk into cheese and butter; making cider and other beverages from orchard fruit; spinning, knitting, and sewing to provide clothing; and nursing the sick and wounded—all essential activities that English women customarily performed—could have made important contributions to the colony's well-being. Instead, intent upon exploiting tidewater resources rather than cultivating a self-sustaining village, Jamestown's settlers had not planted orchards or gardens and had slaughtered their livestock (even the horses) for meat, while the colony's leaders (according to Smith) hoarded medical supplies for their own use. When Sir Thomas Gates and the colonists shipwrecked on Bermuda arrived in May 1610, Gates quickly determined that the settlement was so wasted by disease, neglect, and Native American hostility as to be unsalvageable. On his orders, the English prepared to abandon Jamestown and were sailing down the river just as an advance party brought word that Thomas West, Lord De La Warr, had arrived in the bay with three ships, supplies, and 150 new colonists.

As part of this dramatic turnaround, De La Warr brought explicit authorization to reform the colony's day-to-day management. The Virginia Company had appointed him to the new post of governor, with power to choose his own council, thus placing him above the factional discord that undermined the authority of previous presidents. De La Warr imposed military-style discipline, with work schedules and assigned tasks; when illness persuaded De La Warr to return to England in 1611, Gates served as deputy governor and continued the military model. The colony now had a series of regulations, published in 1612 as the *Lawes Divine, Morall and Martiall*, that established punishments for a variety of moral and civil offenses, including blasphemy, treason, murder, adultery, and unauthorized Indian trade. More important to the community's immediate survival, article 1.28 ordered that every "souldier or tradesman" be "readie, both in the morning, & the afternoone, upon the beating of the Drum, to goe out unto his worke, nor shall hee return . . . before the Drum beate againe."[15] The authority given to the governor ensured, at last, that settlers planted crops, built shelters, dug wells, and maintained order.

A codification of rules could not ensure, however, that Native Americans would tolerate English settlers' continued presence. Lord De La Warr initially renewed efforts to negotiate with Powhatan as a fellow subject of the English king, but Powhatan firmly rebuffed his overtures. In response, De La Warr and his successors extended the new military approach to the colony's interactions with Native Americans. Taking the offensive, the English organized militias and conducted a series of brutal raids on Native American towns, using as their model practices employed in Ireland in the 1590s, campaigns in which many leading colonizers had participated. Militias burned native villages, carried away ripening corn, and killed not only warriors but women, children, and elderly men as well. These aggressive military actions brought a measure of security, but at the cost of any semblance of peaceful coexistence.

A new policy of English expansion lay behind the military effort. To secure more territory and establish healthier settlements, the Company instructed the colony's leaders to disperse the inhabitants of Jamestown fort. Between 1611 and 1614, Sir Thomas Dale, the colony's military leader, used the militias to secure English occupation of much of the James River valley, from the river's mouth upstream as far as the falls. Amending the earlier policy that required settlers to work exclusively for the Company and be supplied from common stores, Gates and Dale introduced a limited amount of private enterprise. For the first time, individual men, receiving grants of time and land for personal use, established private holdings along the James River. Creation of a settlement at Henrico (near modern-day Richmond) and successful campaigns against the Paspahegh, Kecoughtan, Arrohateck, and Appamattuck forcefully demonstrated that colonists were gaining the upper hand against the Powhatan.

In addition to securing territory in the heart of Powhatan's inherited domain, the English negotiated alliances with groups that had maintained some independence, including the Chickahominy, the Patawomeck, and the Accomac and Occohannock on the east side of the bay. In the course of trade and diplomatic meetings with the Patawomeck, moreover, the English envoy, Captain Samuel Argall, abducted Powhatan's daughter Pocahontas in the spring of 1613. Offers to return the girl in exchange for English captives and weapons held by Powhatan became imbedded in broader negotiations for a general truce, which finally took hold in April 1614. By that time, Pocahontas had absorbed much of the language and culture of her English captors, converted to Christianity, and expressed a desire to marry a colonist, John Rolfe. Although their union may have symbolized to Dale and others that the English and Native Americans could be "united together, and made one people" through conversion and intermarriage, there is no evidence that Powhatan saw Pocahontas's marriage as more than confirmation of the truce and a means to gather information about the English and their plans.[16]

The truce endured somewhat longer than the marriage of Pocahontas, who created a sensation when she traveled to England in 1616 but became ill, died, and was buried in London in 1617. The interruption of hostilities enabled each side to tend its fields and settlements, while the English still had the task of finding an exportable commodity to satisfy the Virginia Company's investors. John Rolfe provided a possible answer, one that had far more lasting impact than the model of Anglo-Indian intermarriage. As early as 1612, Rolfe began trying to cultivate tobacco, a plant known to Europeans since explorations in the sixteenth century. Smoking tobacco had become fashionable throughout England, first among the aristocracy and gentry but gradually gaining popularity with artisans and laborers, once expanding production increased supplies and lowered prices. Rolfe worked to cross the oronoco variety of tobacco grown in the Spanish Caribbean colonies with the indigenous plant grown by the Powhatan and other Native Americans for use in religious rites. The oronoco strain grew wild on Bermuda (most likely introduced by Spanish castaways); Rolfe, who spent ten months on the island after the *Sea Venture* shipwreck in 1609, probably carried seeds with him to Virginia. After sending small amounts to England in 1613 and 1614, colonists shipped twelve hundred pounds of tobacco in 1615. The next year, Rolfe and others grew, harvested, and cured a crop of nine thousand pounds, which Rolfe marketed while in London with Pocahontas. When Samuel Argall became Virginia's governor in May 1617, he reportedly found tobacco planted in "the Store-house they used for the Church, the market-place, and streets, and all other spare places" in Jamestown.[17]

In addition to his bride and his tobacco, John Rolfe carried to England an assessment of the colony's population and resources as of the spring of 1616. He documented six settlements inhabited by a little more than 350 people. About 200 officers and laborers worked by contract for the Virginia Company, while 80 farmers supported themselves and their families on lands granted in exchange for annual deliveries of corn, a month's service to the Company, and military duties. The 65 women and children who rounded out the colony's numbers included many servants, but they also represented the first English families to make Virginia their home. Despite these signs of progress, however, the Company's shareholders had poured more than £50,000 into the colony and transported more than 1,700 settlers over ten years with virtually no return on their investment.

Recognizing the reality that Virginia would thrive only as an agricultural colony, the Company sought to attract new investment and settlers through a significant shift in land policy. In 1616, the Virginia Company began offering stockholder dividends in land rather than cash and in 1617 introduced the headright system of land distribution. The Company promised individuals paying passage costs the right to fifty acres of land for every person (or head) transported to the colony. Yet English investors continued to advocate projects to supply agricultural products presently being imported from tropical regions, rather than encourage tobacco, the one crop with a demonstrated prospect of success. Suggestions ran the gamut of crops and raw materials produced in Mediterranean lands that shared the same latitude as Virginia. These included wine, olives, ginger, dyewoods and dye-producing plants, citrus and other tropical fruits, silk, flax, hemp, cotton, naval stores (pitch, tar, and potash), medicines, and oil-producing plants like rape that were used in the textile industry. Although every enterprise to produce these commodities failed, largely due to the colder winter climate and the labor shortage, support for diversified, import-replacing economic activities continued to be part of government policy through the seventeenth and early eighteenth centuries.

The Virginia Company also sent a new treasurer, Sir Edwin Sandys, and a new governor, Sir George Yeardley, who relaxed the military-style government imposed by Dale in the *Lawes Divine*. Through a series of instructions and policy statements known collectively as the "Great Charter," Sandys and Yeardley instituted more liberal land policies (including grants of land to colonists who arrived before the headright system took effect) and introduced systems of local government that resembled administration of law in England. Capping these reforms, in 1619 Yeardley called for an assembly of elected representatives, chosen from the colony's free male property holders, to meet with him and the council in Jamestown. Although illness and bad weather cut short this first meeting of burgesses, their convocation established the precedent of representative government in English America.

Giving colonists a share in the governance of their new home served several purposes. Establishing a local assembly modeled after a familiar political institution, England's Parliament, protected settlers' rights as English subjects and helped make their new home seem less alien. Although the early assembly had only limited power to initiate legislation, even a minor voice in local affairs meant that colonists no longer merely took orders from company officials. Through their representatives, settlers could express grievances and negotiate reforms. Over the course of the seventeenth century, the challenges of creating a successful colony provided opportunities for Virginia's legislators to assert broad control over local affairs.

For a time, this assortment of new policies and enthusiasm for tobacco succeeded in stimulating interest in Virginia. The Company sent several thousand additional settlers between 1619 and 1621, luring male migrants and investors with the promise of land and the possibility of making a fortune. The Virginia Company also made a concerted effort to send more women, transporting ninety in 1620 and an additional fifty-seven in 1621. By sending these "*young, handsome, and honestlie educated Maides* to Virginia: Ther *to be disposed in Marriage to the most honest and industrious Planters*," the Company hoped to "make the men there more setled & lesse moveable."[18] Some women, the daughters of craftsmen, had knowledge of their families' trades. Others, noted for their needlework, could turn imported cloth into clothing and household linens. Two were singled out as able to brew, bake, and make butter and cheese. By this time, the latter skills could be fruitfully put to use because settlers had successfully imported cattle, which adapted well to the colonies' forests and marshes.

The thousands of men, women, and children sent to Virginia produced only a modest increase in population. The continuing ravages of infectious disease and contaminated water kept mortality rates at appallingly high levels. From roughly 350 survivors reported in 1616, the number of settlers early in 1622 barely exceeded 1,200, despite the arrival of almost three times that number of immigrants during the intervening five years. And worse was to come. Seemingly without warning, the fragile, uneasy truce between the English and the Powhatan shattered on 22 March 1622.

The English were caught entirely by surprise, thanks to careful preparations by Opechancanough, who led the attack, and wishful thinking by the colony's leaders, who interpreted the relative peace of recent years as evidence that Native Americans accepted a subjugated and tributary status. A transfer of power in the Powhatan chiefdom from Powhatan, who died in 1618, to his brothers, Opitchapam and Opechancanough, had not appeared to destabilize Anglo-Indian relations. Indeed, Opechancanough showed friendliness toward the English and invited settlers to disperse themselves across his territory. In hindsight, it is evident that Opechancanough encouraged the English to regard him as an ally, patiently building a sense of trust to relax settlers' defenses. By promoting peaceful interactions, Opechancanough gained essential information about daily routines and points of vulnerability. Using this knowledge, he directed warriors under his command to fan out among outlying settlements early in the morning. Moving quickly from farm to farm, and frequently taking up tools and weapons readily at hand in colonists' homes and fields along a one-hundred-mile stretch of the James River, warriors killed the English regardless of age or gender, burned fields and buildings, and slaughtered livestock. Employing many of the tactics that Dale and his militias had used before the 1614 truce, Indians killed 347 colonists, nearly one-third of the English population, and forced survivors to seek refuge in a handful of fortified settlements.

Yet even this brutal assault and the months of warfare that followed failed to dislodge the English. In fact, Opechancanough's attack, which the English perceived as unprovoked, strengthened their resolve to occupy tidewater lands and establish themselves as overlords of the Chesapeake region. Ironically, the "great Massacre" removed the one constraint that had kept the English from pressing the advantage provided by their supply of weapons and growing numbers. Up until 1622, a persistent imperative to cast the Virginia enterprise as a godly mission to Christianize and civilize Native Americans dictated at least a veneer of humane treatment and moral behavior. Now the Company's leaders abandoned all efforts to proselytize and ceased any negotiation for permission to settle in Indian territory. Instead, the colonists' "first worke" henceforth would be "expulsion of the Salvages to gaine the free range of the countrey," and they quickly reverted to Dale's methods for subjugating the countryside through raids that destroyed villages and crops as well as people.[19]

As the settlers regrouped, Virginia Company leaders struggled to retain their hold over colonial affairs. But years of mismanagement, internal disputes, and failure to secure profits, capped by the tremendous loss of life, proved too damaging. In May 1624, the Crown officially revoked the Company's charter and assumed control, making Virginia the first English royal colony. (The Bermuda colony, established in 1612, and the Plymouth colony, established in 1620, were each controlled by investors until much later in the seventeenth century.) Settlers in Virginia worked to ensure that the Crown actually had a colony to administer. First securing their hold on the peninsula between the lower James and York Rivers, colonists used their military assets to extend the territory under their control, particularly in a decisive battle against the Pamunkey in the summer of 1624. Although hostilities continued for several more years, the Powhatan were never able to amass enough weapons or warriors to reassert their sovereignty in the lower Chesapeake tidewater.

MARYLAND, "THE YOUNGER SISTER"

The next challenge to Virginia's hold over the Chesapeake region came from neither Native Americans nor such European rivals as the Spanish, French, or Dutch, but rather from fellow Englishmen. As William Claiborne discovered in 1635, competing colonial interests could also deprive Anglo-Virginians of territory and trade.

In contrast with Virginia, Maryland was the property and creation of a single family, the Calverts. George Calvert had served as secretary of state and member of James I's Privy Council and had been rewarded for his service first with land in Ireland (the manor of Baltimore in County Longford) and later with the title Baron of Baltimore. Building on his participation in the East India and Virginia Companies, Lord Baltimore sought to plant a North American colony. He first established a successful settlement in Newfoundland, but in the face of harsh northern winters and conflict with Native Americans sought a more congenial location for a new colony. He attempted to secure a grant for land south of the James River, but was opposed by powerful investors alarmed at any encroachment on territory within the bounds of the Virginia Company grant. Lord Baltimore's interest in a colony, however, coincided with an English desire to counter Dutch claims to territory surrounding the Delaware River, creating royal support for his project. Consequently, the king granted Calvert a charter for land in the northern Chesapeake region.

Because George Calvert died two months before the charter became final on 20 June 1632, the document that received royal assent named Cecilius Calvert, second Lord Baltimore, as Lord Proprietor of Maryland. In addition to giving Calvert the northern portion of the Virginia Company's Chesapeake land (roughly seven million acres), the charter also gave him extensive powers over his territory. As proprietor, Lord Baltimore could grant land to encourage settlement. He could regulate trade, including setting taxes and customs duties, to promote economic well-being. He could establish local and provincial courts and appoint government officials. He could defend his colony by declaring war or imposing martial law in times of crisis. In exchange, the proprietor owed to the Crown an annual tribute of two Indian arrows and one-fifth of any gold and silver found within the colony. The only check on Lord Baltimore's extensive powers was the requirement that he convene periodic assemblies of Maryland's freemen (or their deputies) to give their "advise assent and approbation" for any legislation he proposed.[20]

As Roman Catholics, both George and Cecilius Calvert needed considerable adroitness to guide their colonization project through

Cecilius Calvert (1606–1675). Calvert, the second Lord Baltimore, and his grandson are depicted holding Augustine Herrman's map of Maryland that Calvert commissioned, c. 1660. Note the presence of an African page dressed in fine livery. By Gerard Soest, c. 1670. Courtesy of Enoch Pratt Free Library, Maryland's State Library Resource Center, Baltimore, Maryland the political and religious shoal waters of the mid-seventeenth century. The Calverts demonstrated that national and spiritual loyalties were intertwined and could work together to promote their objective. The Maryland colony would further the national goal of expanding and protecting English imperial interests, while also providing an opportunity to send missionaries intent on converting Native Americans to Christianity. Thus the project could appeal to general English patriotic and religious impulses while also garnering financial support from the Jesuit order, which sent priests and indentured servants at its own expense. The Calverts also hoped that the Jesuits' activities among the region's Indians would lead to profitable trade in furs and pelts.

Learning from Virginia's experience, George Calvert had set out conditions of plantation offering land as an incentive for prospective settlers. To encourage men of substance to sponsor investment and rapid immigration, the Calverts awarded larger grants to investors paying the passage of five or more able men and offered the privilege of erecting these large tracts into manors. Manor lords enjoyed considerable powers over their domains, including rights to collect rents from tenants and to hold manorial courts to settle local disputes. Although the concept harkened back to English feudal relationships, the Calverts likely placed a different value on the manorial system, envisioning it as creating an enclosed community to shelter residents from interference with their religious practices. Catholicism survived in England in part because Catholic manor lords protected their tenants and laborers from English legal penalties for practicing their faith. Perhaps a similar arrangement in Maryland could keep religion private, enabling colonists of different faiths to enjoy liberty of conscience. At the same time, wealthy immigrants enticed from England could provide the seasoned leadership the fledgling colony needed to survive. The Calverts also expected recipients of large land grants to be loyal supporters of proprietary government. In practice, few men of substance took Lord Baltimore's manorial bait, and retaining control of a colony founded on principles of religious neutrality required all the diplomatic skills Cecilius Calvert possessed to keep the project afloat in the coming years.

Two ships, the *Ark* and the *Dove*, carried about 130 settlers to Maryland, arriving in the Potomac River in March 1634. They anchored off St. Clement's Island, where most of the passengers remained to build a defensive palisade and guard the ships. Leonard Calvert, Lord Baltimore's brother and the colony's governor, traveled upriver with a few advisors to the Piscataway's principal town, where, aided by trader Henry Fleet as interpreter, he entered into a "parley" with the tayac. The tayac may well have been wary of the English in light of the contested encounters at Roanoke and Jamestown, but he also had to consider pressures from hostile Native American groups: William Claiborne's bellicose allies, the Susquehannock at the head of the bay; the Massawomeck, who inhabited territory to the northwest in the Potomac valley; and more distant Indians such the Seneca (part of the Five Nations in eastern New York), whose warriors had massacred residents of a Piscataway village about 1630. The English, therefore, offered the prospect of a useful alliance. When asked by Calvert if "hee would be content that [Calvert] and his people should set downe in his Countrey," the tayac answered " 'that he would not bid [Calvert] goe, neither would hee bid him stay, but that he might use his owne discretion.' "[21]

The new arrivals established their permanent settlement a few miles up the east bank of the St. Mary's River. This choice may well have been guided as much by the tayac and Fleet as by Calvert's own preference. By positioning the English on the coastal plain, near the Potomac's mouth, the tayac established a buffer between his people and the Susquehannock. By moving the English away from the upper Potomac, Fleet protected his trading interests with Potomac basin Indians. Calvert negotiated settlement with the Yaocomico and "thought fit to present the Werowance . . . with some English Cloth, (such as is used in trade with the Indians) Axes, Howes, and Knives."[22] In return, the Indians gave the English one-half of their village immediately and agreed to cede the remainder in a year's time. Father Andrew White attributed the Yaocomico's willingness to trade so much land for "a trifle" to divine intervention, but the Yaocomico viewed the exchange differently.[23] They expected, in return for selling a village that they had already decided to abandon, not only the "trifle" but also assistance in fighting their enemies. The English planted corn and gardens in the already cleared fields, while the Yaocomico provided supplies of corn and fish. They placed the English further in their debt by sharing useful advice about hunting, fishing, building canoes, planting crops, and harvesting wild herbs and roots for dyes and medicinal use. Lord Baltimore's instructions included directions for laying out a town, and Leonard Calvert accordingly named the settlement St. Mary's City in anticipation of its growth. Work began on a fort and a storehouse for trade goods brought from England, as well as laying out streets and marking off town allotments for large investors.

Lord Baltimore and the adventurers who invested with him expected profits from beaver pelts and animal skins, not hogsheads of tobacco, despite Virginia's success with the crop. The colony's prominent settlers and merchants only shifted attention to tobacco when conflict with William Claiborne, his fellow Virginia merchants, and his Susquehannock allies made the prospect of wealth from fur unlikely. But the majority of Maryland's colonists, no less ambitious but with fewer resources at hand, wasted little time in following Virginia's lead. As settlers turned their headrights for land into title to tracts along the waterways, they cleared fields using techniques learned from Native Americans, planted enough corn to feed their households, and devoted the rest of their energies to cultivating the sotweed (a derisive term for tobacco). Once in possession of land, a planter needed only a hoe to cultivate tobacco. The crop could be as successfully grown on a small plantation with one or two laborers as on a larger one with a dozen or more workers. With demand continuing to increase in Europe in the 1620s and 1630s, English merchant ships visited the Chesapeake region annually in pursuit of tobacco. Of all the options available to Chesapeake planters, tobacco production promised the greatest financial return for the labor invested.

Successful planting and marketing of tobacco fueled Maryland's growth but undermined the Calverts' plan for a peaceful settlement organized into manors. As servants transported to clear land and grow crops completed their terms of servitude, individual enterprise engulfed the handful of manors that had been established. With their freedom, men gained the opportunity to set up their own plantations once they had sufficient capital or credit to pay the costs of securing a patent, or legal title, for the land. Few wished to enter into long-term contractual obligations as manorial tenants when outright ownership was within reach. Their domestic skills and the headright received after completing their service made freed women attractive marriage partners for freed men; they, too, had better prospects than life on a manor. Abundant land together with relatively low entry costs thus offered independence and land ownership to freed men and women. For men, this change in status also carried the right to participate in civic government as independent heads of household. Former servants might benefit from credit or ad hoc assistance from members of the gentry, but the manorial ties that Lord Baltimore had envisioned as the glue holding his colony together faded away within two generations. Freeholders, not tenants, working their own land with the help of family members and perhaps a servant or two, emerged as the backbone of the planter class by the 1640s.

Lord Baltimore's vision of a manorial society did not survive the realities of life in the Chesapeake tidewater, just as the Virginia Company's dreams of precious metals and a docile Indian labor force ran afoul of geographic and cultural reality. Powhatan's aspiration to annex and control the new arrivals as a tributary people similarly failed in the face of fundamental conflicts between the role he tried to assign the English and the settlers' own aspirations for wealth and dominion. For all participants in this drama, unfounded expectations and imperfect knowledge created situations rife with misunderstandings and deadly consequences.

By the early 1630s, English settlers were establishing themselves more firmly in the tidewater landscape. Tobacco had emerged as a marketable crop with enough potential for gain to entice thousands of migrants. From their precarious and vulnerable position at Jamestown in 1607, the English had conjured two expanding colonies that exported a profitable crop to the mother country while importing sizeable quantities of manufactured goods and servants. In hindsight, this colonial success can be understood as disastrous for the Chesapeake region's Native Americans. But for numerous Indian groups who inhabited the region and charted their own course through these unfamiliar waters, the arrival of the English and their successful establishment of settlements were not immediately negative developments. As the actions and choices of the Powhatan and Piscataway illustrate, Native American populations assessed the situation with regard to their own needs; in light of their long histories of intragroup conflict, many

Indians perceived the English more as an opportunity than as a threat. In this respect, the complexity of the world the English invaded in some measure secured their eventual success: Native American groups had little motivation to set aside their particular interests in favor of a common response to European arrivals. Once established, however, the English proved impossible to expel. For better or worse, Virginia and Maryland would henceforth be England's "tobacco coast."

TWO

Troubled Times

In November 1638, new arrivals in the Maryland colony included an unusual family group. Two brothers, Fulke and Giles Brent, and two of their sisters, Margaret and Mary, migrated to Maryland together, leaving behind their parents and nine siblings in England. Claiming headrights in exchange for transporting themselves and at least fourteen servants, the Brents received allotments in St. Mary's City and warrants for outlying tracts. Giles's land included one thousand acres he acquired on Kent Island just a few years after Maryland gained control of Kent from William Claiborne. The Brent siblings were members of a prominent Roman Catholic family and distant cousins of the governing Calverts, circumstances that likely account for the unusually elevated status they enjoyed upon arrival. Fulke and Giles Brent, for example, served together with a handful of other well-connected men as members of the governor's council. Although Fulke's political career was brief, Giles held numerous provincial and military offices, including treasurer of the colony and commander of Kent Island's militia. When Leonard Calvert traveled to England in the spring of 1643, he appointed Giles Brent as acting governor during his absence.

Ineligible for similar roles by virtue of her sex, Giles Brent's sister Margaret nevertheless appears frequently in early records, engaged in activities reflecting her position as a wealthy and influential proprietary relative. As a *feme sole*, the legal term for an unmarried adult woman, Margaret held land and conducted business in her own name, independent of any male relative. In addition, Margaret periodically appeared in court as an attorney-in-fact, someone with authority to act for another individual in business or legal matters (distinct from an attorney-at-law, a licensed lawyer). Margaret Brent's numerous court appearances demonstrate her active engagement in the colony's economic life. In 1647, when Leonard Calvert became ill and anticipated death, he named Margaret as his executor, instructing her to "Take all [of his property], & pay all [of his debts]."[1] At the time, Leonard Calvert held power of attorney to supervise Lord Baltimore's Maryland plantations and property. The governor's council therefore recognized Margaret's authority, as Calvert's executor, to act as the proprietor's attorney-in-fact. Thus both Giles and Margaret Brent wielded significant power in Maryland, and each served for a time as direct representative of Lord Baltimore.

Despite their early prominence and connections, the Brents' Maryland experience proved contentious and ultimately unsuccessful, with Fulke soon returning to England and Giles and Margaret moving to Virginia in 1649. Giles, rather than fulfilling the proprietor's expectation of support from a loyal councilor, was among the colonists who insisted that provincial laws include an expiration clause to specify the number of years each law would remain in effect. These clauses, by compelling the governor to convene assemblies to renew expiring laws, countered Lord Baltimore's loose interpretation of his charter obligation to solicit approval of the colony's freemen before enacting legislation. The proprietor was also dissatisfied with Brent's failure as a military official to lead a 1642 expedition against Susquehannock warriors in retaliation for raids on outlying settlements. Two years later, Lord Baltimore viewed with disfavor Brent's marriage to the young daughter of the Piscataway tayac, who had been sent in 1640 "to be educated among the English at St. Mary's," where she was baptized and became "proficient in the English language." When the tayac died in 1641, Margaret Brent and Leonard Calvert served as guardians of "the young Empress."[2] The marriage in 1644 took place during Calvert's absence, timing that suggests Brent knew the Calverts would not have permitted the union. Lord Baltimore suspected that Brent planned to claim, through his wife, ownership of Piscataway territory within Maryland's boundaries. Because Margaret Brent must have agreed to the marriage, Giles's action also compromised the proprietor's faith in her loyalty.

The developing rift between the Calvert and Brent families widened considerably during the period known as the "plundering time," an episode of violence that nearly destroyed Maryland in the mid-1640s. Disagreements in England over religious practices and royal authority during the 1620s and 1630s had escalated into civil war by the early 1640s, forcing colonial governments to tread warily between the opposing sides. Giles Brent precipitated the local crisis in the winter of 1643/44 when he leveled charges of treason against Richard Ingle, a ship captain trading in Maryland. Ingle's subsequent armed attack on the colony disrupted Lord Baltimore's government for the better part of two years. While Ingle and his supporters, all Protestants, looted the property of Maryland's wealthy, mostly Catholic planters, Leonard Calvert fled across the Potomac River, regaining control of Maryland only late in 1646 with help from armed men hired in Virginia. Calvert's inability to pay wages promised to these men, however, raised the danger of a mutiny. After Calvert's death in the summer of 1647, Margaret Brent, as Calvert's executor, not only disbursed Calvert's estate but also sold off proprietary livestock to pacify the soldiers. Brent's sale of Lord Baltimore's cattle may have averted further violence, but her authority to act was questionable, and Lord Baltimore was outraged. In the wake of these controversies, Giles left Maryland for Virginia's Northern Neck. Margaret Brent soon joined her brother, and in July of 1650 informed Maryland's governor that she would no longer "intangle" herself in Maryland affairs "because of the Ld Baltemore's disaffections."[3]

During three decades of settlement before the arrival of the Brents, English men and women planted literal and metaphorical roots along the Chesapeake Bay's shores. The literal roots included the corn plants that yielded essential food, the meadow plants and woodland trees that augmented diets and sustained livestock, and above all the tobacco plants, whose central place in the region's economy made the two colonies a "tobacco coast." Tobacco fueled migration from the British Isles and brought profits not only to planters but also to the Crown, the proprietor, and the English mercantile community. The metaphorical roots comprised the families that formed and reproduced, some to establish lineages that extend down to the present day, others to wither away in a generation or two. As the Brents anticipated, opportunity existed for social and economic advancement, but as they also discovered, circumstances in both colonies were unstable, with unclear lines of authority and competing claims to power. The region's nascent economy relied heavily on one crop, whose high price could plummet drastically with overproduction. As settlement expanded into new territory, colonists' land-use practices repeatedly created conflict with Native Americans whose homelands were invaded. When political and religious disputes in England were added to the mix, the resulting turmoil threatened the fortunes of all the region's inhabitants.

SOTWEED

Once colonists abandoned attempts to discover gold or produce exotic commodities and turned instead to growing tobacco, expanding demand in Europe enabled planters to earn a tidy profit in most years until the mid-seventeenth century. The spectacular fortunes earned during the earliest boom phase were short-lived because production increased rapidly in the 1630s and 1640s, but settlers still considered tobacco their most promising export commodity throughout the century. Tobacco was literally the cash crop: both the largest source of income and the most common currency. George Alsop, a Maryland indentured servant in the early 1660s, noted that tobacco was "the currant Coyn," universally used in lieu of money not only to "purchase Commodities from the Merchant" but also to settle local accounts and pay public taxes.[4] Tobacco's continued dominance prompted the Reverend Hugh Jones's similar comments in 1699 that "tobacco is our meat, drinke, cloathing and monies" and that "we have no trade att home or abroad but that of tobacco."[5]

Cultivation, processing, and marketing of tobacco set the parameters for much of daily life. After an initial period of experimentation, the method of producing a crop for sale overseas varied little during the colonial period. The tasks involved little skill, but timing each step necessitated experienced judgment, and many phases required specific weather conditions, making planters' fortunes vulnerable to climatic vagaries. Furthermore, unlike wheat and other grains that were the mainstay of English agriculture, and unlike Indian corn, grown as a substitute for those grains, tobacco's cultivation demanded year-round attention. A Chesapeake worker needed fewer than 10 days to plant enough corn to feed one adult for a year, perhaps 20 days to tend the plants over a five-month growing season, and another 4 or so autumn days to gather and store the crop. One worker cultivating tobacco, on the other hand, annually labored roughly 125 days.

Planters began with clearing fields by girdling trees, burning brush, and digging in the ashes for fertilizer. Following Native American practice, girdling was a quick means of killing trees by cutting the bark; once foliage died, planters could grow tobacco on fields no longer shaded by leaves. Workers also prepared seed beds, a task that had to be well under way by late January and completed by early spring, when seeds were sown. While seedlings developed, workers finished preparing fields for transplanting in late spring. Adopting another Indian technique, workers built up about twenty-five hundred hills per acre to create loose earth needed for root development. Using a hoe, a laborer gathered soil into a mound around one of his legs, then withdrew the leg to leave a hole for a seedling. Once leaves were well-established, planters needed to complete the transfer from seedbed to tobacco field by mid-June; otherwise, an early autumn frost could destroy the crop before it fully ripened. As plants grew they were checked daily for pests or signs of disease to avoid contamination of an entire crop. An infestation of hornworms, for example, could destroy a crop in less than a week. Constant pruning promoted growth of leaves, the only marketable part of the plant. "Priming" took off bottom leaves to encourage fullness; "topping" eliminated flowers and seeds; and "suckering" pinched off weaker shoots between stem and leaves. No one task was particularly difficult or time consuming per plant, but by the mid-seventeenth century planters expected each worker to cultivate roughly six thousand plants annually.

Successful planters needed to exercise good judgment in order to time transplanting and pruning. They also needed favorable weather, especially damp spring days for transplanting, and consistent moisture thereafter. The critical test of experience, skill, and meteorological good fortune came in the fall as plants neared maturity. Planters tried to extend the growing season to maximize leaf size and weight, but generally they had to cut the crop by late September to avoid a killing frost. Workers left cut plants to wilt for a few hours before hanging the stalks upside down to begin curing. As early as the 1620s, Virginians developed "tobacco houses" that featured tiers of rails to maximize storage while still permitting air to circulate to dry the leaves. Later improvements included moveable siding on the walls to increase circulation during favorable weather. During the curing period, planters monitored leaf condition so as to end the process just when leaves were moist enough to transport without becoming brittle but not so damp that the crop would become moldy or rot. Weather again was an uncontrollable variable; an unusually wet, dry, or brief autumn could ruin the crop.

When a planter judged his crop adequately cured, workers prepared the leaves for shipment. The first crops were shipped in bulk, generally gathered into loose rolls, but it quickly became the usual practice to pack leaves into large wooden barrels called hogsheads. By mid-seventeenth century, the two legislatures set a maximum height and diameter for hogshead size. Standard cask sizes simplified loading cargo and calculating freight charges. Because rates were determined by space rather than weight, planters had an incentive to pack each cask tightly to save costs. Typical weights rose from an early average of about 150 pounds per hogshead to around 400 by midcentury with more efficient packing. Hogsheads were rolled to the nearest navigable waterway and loaded onto merchant ships, which generally left Chesapeake waters as spring arrived. Planters had to be prepared for loading when merchants came calling, as tobacco that missed the shipping would not keep long enough to be marketed the following year. The entire cycle thus took more than a year from first preparing seedbeds to loading hogsheads aboard a ship.

For much of the century, planters and merchants utilized a variety of trading arrangements to market tobacco. Many early traders were English merchants acting alone or as part of a small group, who "adventured," or sent, a shipment of merchandise in hope of exchanging the cargo for tobacco. Numerous ships sent by adventurers arrived during the winter months to sail along the bay's wide rivers, gradually emptying their holds of goods from England and refilling them with tobacco before recrossing the Atlantic. As George Alsop described the process: "Between November and January there arrives . . . Shipping to the number of twenty sail and upwards, all Merchant-men loaden with Com-

Processing Tobacco for Market. Tatham's "The Tobacco House and its Variety" depicts various steps in the processing of tobacco, including curing leaves in tobacco houses, packing tobacco into casks, and rolling hogsheads for storage. From William Tatham, *Historical and Practical Essay on the Culture and Commerce of Tobacco* (London, 1800)

modities to Trafique and dispose of, . . . Silks, Hollands, Serges, and Broad-clothes, with other necessary Goods."[6] A planter who bargained directly with a ship captain or merchant traded his cured tobacco for the cloth, tools, or servants he needed.

Two other trading methods involved credit exchanges that enabled planters to buy goods in advance of their harvest or in excess of their crop's value. In the first, planters with sufficient resources acted as resident merchants. These merchant-planters served as middlemen, setting aside space on their plantations to store surplus imported merchandise for sale to neighboring planters, who could buy either directly with tobacco or on account for payment at a future date. Merchant-planters profited by selling the goods they kept on hand at higher prices than they paid to import them. In addition, by consolidating their neighbors' smaller crops into one larger shipment, merchant-planters could negotiate better terms when they sold the sotweed. In the second, known as the consignment system, a planter sent tobacco directly to England "on consignment" to a firm that earned a commission for arranging its sale and applying proceeds as the planter directed. Planters profited because they retained ownership until the crop sold in England, where prices were higher. In doing so, however, they assumed considerable risk, as potential profits vanished if the tobacco suffered damage en route or was lost at sea. Generally, only wealthier planters, particularly those who grew the more-valued sweet-scented variety, could afford the risks of marketing tobacco in this fashion.

Tobacco cultivation in the early seventeenth century yielded a marketable crop whose proceeds could support a family working a small plantation. To move beyond a subsistence livelihood, however, planters needed to maximize the use of their land. One worker could tend about three acres of tobacco plants, but plantations also needed land for corn and woodland to provide forage for cattle and hogs, as well as sufficient acreage to let old tobacco fields lie fallow during a twenty-year cycle. In all, planters considered fifty acres for each hand to be a ratio that maximized production while protecting soil quality. Thus even a planter with a small holding of 200 to 250 acres needed four or five hands to make the best use of his acreage. For most of the seventeenth century, family labor was not a likely option. Cultural norms considered intensive agricultural work unsuitable for women. As John Hammond noted, a wife's labor within the Chesapeake household economy involved "such domestique imployments and houswifery as in England."[7] Wives, therefore, did not count as potential tobacco hands, and few men had grown sons to assist them. Tobacco's demand for year-long attention made hired labor a prohibitively expensive way to acquire more workers. Planters turned instead to two types of bound laborers: servants and slaves.

SERVITUDE

Permanent English settlements in the Chesapeake region rested upon three key ingredients. Colonists assumed the first to be theirs for the taking—abundant, fertile land along rivers and creeks feeding into the bay. They added the second by developing tobacco as a profitable export crop. They then sought the third element: labor to clear land, cultivate tobacco, and harvest it for shipment to England. Although planters occasionally hired workers to satisfy short-term labor needs and made use of family members when they could, in both colonies the labor system that evolved rested upon bound labor. In both servitude and slavery, an individual was legally required to work for another individual's exclusive benefit. Under servitude, the term of service was fixed to a period of years, while enslavement subjected men, women, and children to lifetime bondage. Of the two, servitude was the more fully established by the mid-seventeenth century, but Chesapeake planters utilized both types of bound labor throughout the colonial period. Responding in part to land policies that linked importing workers to claiming acreage, planters invested tobacco profits in successive waves of land and labor.

Under the headright system instituted in 1617, every Virginia immigrant paying his or her own passage received the right to fifty acres of land; those who paid the passage for others, such as family members or servants, received an additional fifty acres for each person. When the first Lord Baltimore in 1632 laid out Maryland's conditions of plantation, he set the headright allotment at one hundred acres for each person entering the colony, with the expectation that transported servants would receive rights to one-half of the acreage. In time, it became the practice to grant fifty acres to the master, with men and women who migrated as servants entitled to claim fifty acres from the land office at the end of their servitude.

In both colonies, the headright was only the *right* to acquire land. Actual possession required securing a warrant from the land office for a survey, having the surveyor lay out the tract and issue a certificate of survey, and finally registering the survey as a patent granting title. Each step required payment of fees to clerks and officials who drew up papers, surveyed land, and recorded documents. Landholders also owed annual payments, known as quitrents, set at two shillings per hundred acres and paid to the titular owner—the king, for Virginia, and Lord Baltimore, for Maryland. Although such fees meant that land could not be claimed without some capital to secure title and pay quitrents, costs were surmountable and the prize was outright ownership. In England, by contrast, most men and women could not expect to acquire more than a leasehold (long-term possession as tenants). Less than 10 percent of English heads of household held freehold title to land, with ownership highly concentrated in the aristocracy. The lure of land ownership stimulated Chesapeake immigration for most of the seventeenth century.

In England, farmers seeking extra workers made use of "servants in husbandry," young men and women who signed yearly contracts to work as farmhands and dairy maids. Similarly, English craftsmen took on apprentices for whom they provided training in return for increasingly skilled assistance. Chesapeake colonists developed their own variation called indentured servitude, a contractual arrangement blending and adapting elements of both English models to meet the steadily growing need for agricultural workers. In exchange for passage costs of between £5 and £7, an individual signed a contract, or "indenture," to work for someone else's benefit for a term ranging from about four years to seven. If a migrant made the agreement with a ship captain in England, the captain then sold the contract to a Chesapeake planter to recoup the transportation expenses. Prospective servants who left England without written indentures were sold on arrival to serve by "custom of the country." Legislation to protect servants' rights required the new master to bring any such servant before the county court for an age judgment that set the term of service. Mariners' potential profit from transporting servants led to less-than-honest recruitment practices; false promises and outright kidnappings were not uncommon. But many men and women, facing high unemployment and rising prices for food and other necessities in England, chose to gamble on the chance of a better life through emigration and indenture. As a result, more than 70 percent of Europeans who arrived in the Chesapeake region during the seventeenth century spent their first years there as indentured servants.

Headrights and indentured servitude laid the groundwork for population expansion in a region that did not attract much family migration. Initial recruitment efforts by the Virginia Company focused on men who would labor for shareholders in exchange for sustenance and the possibility of a better future than they could expect in England. When the Company instituted headrights, and when Lord Baltimore adapted the system in Maryland, men of means could transport their families in exchange for land, but few took advantage of the opportunity. The region's reputation for conferring ill health and an early death was well known. After the 1620s, as settlement moved away from Jamestown, mortality rates improved, but dysentery, typhoid, and a new, more virulent strain of malaria (introduced from Africa) continued to take a high toll. Not many families reckoned the potential reward outweighed the probable risk. The absence of families contrasted with New England colonies, which before 1640 were settled largely by family groups. Although a smattering of the Chesapeake region's early colonists, like the Brent siblings, did arrive with kin, men and women traveling independently dominated the stream of English migrants.

Both the supply of available labor and the requirements of planters looking for workers fostered emigration through servitude primarily of young, single, and largely unskilled males. The first ships arriving in Virginia carried only men, and the Virginia Company transported only about 140 women before 1624, not all of whom were servants. In Maryland, Father Andrew White's account of the 1634 voyage documents the presence of a few women among the first settlers. He noted that after the *Ark* dropped anchor at St. Clement's Island, the settlers "allmost lost our mades [maids] which wee brought along" when a shallop taking the women ashore to do laundry overturned.[8] Immigrants to Maryland continued to include some female servants, but as in Virginia men outnumbered women among servants by about three or four to one for several decades. Men engaged in promoting initial settlement perceived little immediate need for female skills. Only a small number of free women migrated to either colony, usually with or to join spouses.

Driven by servant migration, the region's English population increased dramatically during the century. In 1660, for example, Maryland's non-Indian population stood at about eight thousand souls spread over six counties. Five years later, the colony's population had nearly doubled to fifteen thousand. In Virginia, a census of 1625 counted about twelve hundred settlers; fifty years later Governor William Berkeley estimated that the population numbered more than forty thousand. The appearance of new counties, created by provincial assemblies to make local government accessible in frontier areas, reflected the spread of settlement. Maryland began with one county, St. Mary's, but expanded to ten by 1675. Virginia experienced even more dramatic growth. The assembly created the colony's first eight counties in 1634, added two before 1638, and established another nine along the midcentury frontier by 1670. The county lines imprinted on maps of the colony testify to expansion sparked by tobacco and fueled by servitude.

Labor indentures, being legal agreements between masters and servants, spelled out obligations each owed the other and could be enforced in a court of law by either party. Typical indentures required servants to "doe and performe true and faithfull service" and to "be tractable and obedient," while masters and mistresses were obligated to provide "sufficient meate drink apparrell and other necessaryes for [a servant's] livelihood and maynetenance."[9] Servants frequently petitioned for release from bondage by claiming they had served the full contractual term. Courts often granted such petitions, although masters could be awarded extra service if the justices imposed penalties for running away, theft, or other illicit activities. Servants could also petition for aid if subjected to excessive physical abuse, including lack of adequate food or shelter. Thus in 1664 John Helmes pleaded to a Maryland court that he had only "one shirt which is at Presant on his back Besids the Rest of his apparrell very baer and thin for the time of year." He requested either proper clothing or freedom from his master, John Meekes, "befor[e] hee is quit[e] naked," upon which the justices ordered Meekes to clothe Helmes "from top to toe."[10]

Most migrants experienced a period of illness, referred to as seasoning, while adjusting to the Chesapeake climate and disease environment. Servants who survived seasoning and completed their term had several options to bridge the gap between achieving freedom and becoming a landowner. For their immediate needs, servants were entitled to freedom dues, which were spelled out in law. These generally consisted of a set of clothing, basic tools, and enough seed to grow a year's supply of corn. Freedmen could rent a small tract of land, either independently or in partnership with another recently freed servant. Men and women could hire themselves out to a planter, either for wages or for a share of the year's crop. More rarely, a freed servant could marry someone who already possessed land or other property. Because men dramatically outnumbered women in both colonies, newly freed women were more likely than freed men to marry quickly, but the fortunate man who married a propertied widow advanced himself significantly.

If all went well for a few years—no illness or injury, no extremes of weather to destroy the crop, and no slump in tobacco prices—a former servant might save enough to acquire land and establish a household. In both colonies, freed servants (with property requirements after 1670) could participate in civic life, with the significant qualification that only men could hold office or vote for provincial delegates. When Margaret Brent addressed the Maryland assembly in 1648 and "requested to have vote in the howse for her selfe," on the strength of her status as a landowner, and "voyce allso" as Lord Baltimore's attorney, Governor Thomas Greene denied her request without any recorded debate or discussion.[11] English common law allowed widows and never-married women like Brent to own property, but social practice in England and in both Chesapeake colonies prevented women from exercising the political rights of an independent freeholder.

Indentured servitude was primarily a system that transported English people, but the broader category of servants working for a term of years embraced both non-English Europeans and non-Europeans. Most European migrants who were not English came from elsewhere in the British Isles, particularly Scotland and Ireland, but small numbers of Dutch and German colonists settled in both colonies. The servant population at midcentury also included an uncertain number of Native Americans and

Africans. Surviving records for each colony's first few decades contain references to non-Europeans living in planter households, but they rarely specify the person's precise status—that is, servant or enslaved. At least some of these Indians and Africans labored under terms of servitude, with a finite period of service. Passengers on the same *Ark* that carried the "mades" in 1634, for example, included two indentured servants described in headright claims as mulattoes, probably men of mixed Portuguese and African parentage. Scattered evidence similarly indicates the presence of Native Americans in Chesapeake households, such as that of Simon Overzee, a tobacco merchant with land and business connections in both colonies. The inventory of his Virginia estate, compiled when Overzee died in 1662, included two "Indians," a boy and a girl, explicitly identified as servants.

In each colony, moreover, freed servants included both Native Americans and Africans, and some of these former servants became householders and landowners. In addition to his Native American servants in Virginia, Overzee's Maryland household included John Baptista, "a moore of Barbary."[12] Overzee acquired Baptista's labor in 1650 and released him from service in 1655. Baptista remained in Charles County, working with John Cain for crop shares in 1659 and appearing in court several times between 1660 and 1663 as both plaintiff and defendant. The free-householder status of former African or Native American servants complicated the frequent assumption within colonial law that *free* was synonymous with *European* or *Christian*. But even in the years before 1662, when slavery had not yet been legally established as a system of hereditary lifetime bondage largely defined by race, individuals like Baptista, who were neither white nor held in long-term service, were by far the exception. The few non-Europeans who completed terms of servitude and established independent households found their situations increasingly precarious as more and more Africans were forcibly brought to the Chesapeake colonies for sale as slaves.

SLAVERY

Slavery presented an alternative form of bound labor. The use of slaves—workers forced to toil without wages for life—was widespread throughout the Spanish and Portuguese colonies that English colonizers hoped to emulate. The Virginia Company had expected to coerce Native Americans but failed to do so because the region lacked sedentary, hierarchical Indian populations. The infrequent presence of enslaved workers in the early period of settlement thus reflects the planters' inability to acquire slaves rather than any ideological or cultural reluctance to use forced labor. Although there are scattered early examples of Indians held to cultivate tobacco, widespread enslavement of native people did not occur until late in the seventeenth century when conflicts in other colonies created an opportunity for trade in captives. But in 1619, only two years after development of the headright system that drove investment in indentured English servants, the first trickle began of a second stream of migration that ultimately delivered tens of thousands of workers. In that year, the captain of "a Dutch man of Warr" sold to Virginia planters a cargo of "20. and odd Negroes."[13] These individuals are generally acknowledged as the first enslaved Africans sold in England's North American colonies.

There is little evidence that African slaves were seen at the time as the key to solving the labor shortage. But the merchants and military leaders who guided Virginia's settlement in its earliest decades knew that Africans were treated as trade goods within the Atlantic basin. As privateers, some had captured ships carrying slaves and profitably sold the cargoes. By the mid-1600s, colonists in various early English settlements—from the mouth of the Amazon to Caribbean islands to Bermuda—were buying slaves as workers for agricultural plantations. Although indentured servants dominated the Chesapeake region's bound labor for many decades, individual planters with access to Caribbean markets as well as capital to invest in bound labor demonstrated an early interest in enslaved Africans. Lord Baltimore, for example, lost little time in seeking to provide his new Maryland property with laborers as well as livestock, requesting in 1637 that Richard Kemp, secretary of the Virginia colony, purchase "fforty neate Cattle, ten Sowes, fforty Henns and Ten Negroes to be Transported to St. Maryes."[14]

The proprietor's attempt to procure slaves in Virginia reflects the limited availability of enslaved workers during most of the century. Few ship captains transported Africans to the region, and those who did were likely to sell their entire cargo in the lower bay, with no need to extend their voyage to Maryland. Direct trade with slavers—ships engaged primarily in the slave trade—played only a minor role during the mid-seventeenth century. Selling slaves was so profitable in the Caribbean islands, where intensive production of sugar consumed an appalling number of coerced laborers, that captains of slavers rarely bypassed the islands to visit the Chesapeake market. Instead Virginians and Marylanders developed Caribbean trade routes by shipping foodstuffs and lumber products to the islands and exchanging them for sugar and slaves. In April 1671, for example, Virginian Thomas Jarvis acquired molasses, rum, and "three negroe men and one negroe woman" in Barbados, pledging that within ninety days he would supply an equivalent value "in goods of the growth of Virginia" to Barbadian merchant Thomas Jolley.[15]

Trading connections also played a key role in enabling some Maryland gentry to acquire workers bound to lifetime service. Robert Slye, a wealthy justice and delegate for St. Mary's County, likely acquired the fourteen enslaved Africans he held when he died in 1671 as part of his trading activities both with Caribbean islands and at New Amsterdam (present-day New York City), where Dutch slavers periodically delivered human cargo. Slye in turn provided enslaved workers for his Maryland neighbors, as in 1661 when he sold "one Negro man Called by the name of sampson and an Negro woman Caled Maria" to Francis Pope.[16] Reports to England's Board of Trade in 1708 confirmed the importance of the Caribbean market for both colonies. As Edmund Jennings, Virginia's acting governor, stated, "before the year 1680 what negros were brought to Virginia were imported generally from Barbados for it was very rare to have a Negro ship come to this Country."[17]

For much of the mid-seventeenth century, slaveholding remained highly concentrated among the relatively few wealthy, elite planters who also filled most provincial and county offices. Between 1635 and 1660, for example, officeholders accounted for roughly 80 percent of those who claimed headright land in Virginia for importing enslaved blacks. These men owned enough land to employ additional workers profitably, had sufficient capital or credit to afford the purchases, and enjoyed connections that provided access to island markets. Local officials, such as justices and sheriffs, generally held only a few bondspeople. Substantial investment in enslaved labor occurred most often among the smaller pool of provincial officeholders, who frequently held as many as ten slaves; a few had holdings that exceeded twenty. When Colonel John Carter died in 1659, his labor force included not only thirty-four indentured servants but also forty-three enslaved men, women, and children.

Through the 1650s, the status of black workers was not defined by legislation in either colony. Some, like John Baptista, came as indentured servants and successfully completed a limited term of service. The lack of precedents in common law defining the status of imported Africans and their offspring afforded some blacks, particularly those of mixed parentage, the opportunity to challenge their bondage. Yet in most instances, even if Africans were not explicitly identified as slaves, they and their descendants were not treated as servants. Wills bequeathed ownership of blacks as property, just as inventories clearly valued some blacks based on lifetime service.

The lack of statutory definition ended in 1662, not long after a young Virginia woman named Elizabeth Key successfully sued for her freedom. Key was the daughter of an enslaved woman and Thomas Key, a Virginia planter, member of the House of Burgesses, and master of Elizabeth's mother. By English common law, children inherited their father's status and therefore Elizabeth should have been a free woman. But after fulfilling nine years of service, for which she was bound out by her father, Key was listed as enslaved property in the estate of Colonel John Mottrom. In addition to suing for her freedom on the strength of her father's status, Key argued that she had been baptized and therefore should be free because she was a Christian. Key finally succeeded in securing her freedom in 1656 by an appeal to the legislature.

Beginning in 1662, however, the two Chesapeake assemblies created a legal framework for slavery, in the process closing off the avenues that Key had used to become free. A Virginia statute of 1662 declared that a child inherited legal status—enslaved or free—from his or her mother, contrary to English precedent. Children of mixed race, designated in both colonies as mulattoes, henceforth enjoyed free status only if born to free women; any child of a white man born to an enslaved woman was a slave for life. Maryland delegates echoed the Virginia law in a 1664 act stipulating that "all Children born of any Negro or other slave shall be Slaves."[18] In 1667, a second Virginia statute declared that conversion to Christianity could not be used to achieve freedom, and a comparable Maryland act passed four years later. In 1669, the Virginia legislature gave masters extensive authority to manage and discipline slaves without outside interference. A fourth Virginia statute, passed in 1672, committed the colony's government to policing slaves, with authority, for example, to take up runaways or suppress riots. The act provided compensation to masters of any slaves killed by these "corrective" actions. This law placed an enslaved person's status as property well above his or her status as a human being: in such cases the killing of a slave was no longer considered an act of manslaughter, but rather a crime against property.

Chesapeake assemblies enacted statutes that provided the basic legal foundation for hereditary, racially defined slavery at a time when ownership of enslaved workers was both uncommon and highly concentrated. In Virginia in the 1660s, for example, there were only about two thousand blacks (about 7 percent of total population) who were largely held by elite planters, not evenly dispersed across Virginia's settled areas. In Maryland, where slaves accounted for no more than 1 percent of population until the 1690s, ownership was even more concentrated in a small group of wealthy officials. By mid-seventeenth century, these elite Chesapeake men were firmly committed to slavery as a labor system. The statutes they enacted to regulate enslavement provided legal and physical security for their expensive investment. Hereditary slavery that could be revoked only by masters on a voluntary, individual basis protected their property rights; broad authority to discipline workers, backed by the colony's government, allowed masters and officials to deal swiftly and effectively with any threats to personal or public safety.

Although this early commitment to enslaved labor ultimately had profound effects on the Chesapeake region, it was the characteristics of the immigrant English population that powerfully affected the region's social and political development in the seventeenth century. At any given time during the period from roughly 1625 until about 1675 most independent householders were former servants, men and women who had traveled from England with little in the way of possessions or reputations. In this society of newcomers, characterized by high mortality and a continual influx of immigrants, few men arrived with widely recognized claims to authority or experience in governance. As civil war broke out in England and spilled over into the Chesapeake region in the mid-seventeenth century, the fragility of political power in Virginia and Maryland became all too evident.

WAR IN ENGLAND: TIDEWATER CONSEQUENCES

During the 1620s and 1630s, Chesapeake settlers took up land, acquired laborers, and set about the business of cultivating tobacco. In England during these same decades, tension between Charles I, England's monarch, and leaders of Parliament, the country's legislature, escalated to the point that by the early 1640s both sides were preparing for armed conflict.

The struggle between England's king and parliament emerged from economic troubles, religious disputes, and the complexities of European geopolitics. England's participation in conflicts between Catholics and Protestants that ranged across most of Europe played a role, as did attempts by Charles I to exert political and religious authority in Ireland and Scotland. Involvement in the affairs of other countries was expensive, and Charles could not raise revenue to pursue his goals without support from Parliament, which controlled taxation. The two sides were engaged in a perpetual battle over money. Members of Parliament wishing to limit monarchical power pressed demands for broad changes in English government, finally insisting that the king yield all control over the military, the judicial system, and the Church of England. Not surprisingly, Charles I refused to accept such drastic reductions in royal authority. Supporters of each side accused the other of fomenting treasonous plots, while gathering their own soldiers and arms in preparation for battle. Minor skirmishes escalated into civil war in the summer of 1642.

Trying to follow the course of events from afar, Chesapeake colonists gleaned information from each vessel making its way to the region. First they learned of a series of inconclusive battles between royal forces and Parliament's army, then an alliance between parliamentarians and the Scottish army in 1643, followed by decisive defeats of the royalists in 1644 and 1645. The situation became even more tangled when Charles I surrendered to the Scots in 1646. For more than two years, the various sides argued, changed partners, and traded proposals, but could not find any stable solution. Out of the chaos, Oliver Cromwell, a parliamentary army officer, emerged in 1648 with the reins of government in hand but only a shaky claim to constitutional authority. For roughly a decade he managed to hold the country together, first in uneasy partnership with Parliament (which charged Charles I with treason and executed him in 1649) and then as sole commander, with the title of lord protector. But in 1658, after a period of ill health, Cromwell died. His son Richard succeeded as lord protector but could not muster sufficient support to retain power. The country threatened to descend once more into chaos until, early in 1660, one army faction forced election of a new Parliament, which promptly proclaimed Charles Stuart, eldest son of Charles I, as the restored monarch, Charles II.

Turmoil in England raised very serious problems for Chesapeake colonists. By seizing control and usurping royal authority, Parliament jeopardized the legitimacy of colonial government. Lord Baltimore's Maryland proprietorship was a direct grant from the king to Cecilius Calvert and his heirs; whether the proprietor could hold his territory after Charles I lost power was an open question, particularly given the animosity toward Roman Catholics among Parliament's Puritan leaders. Similarly, the power of William Berkeley, Virginia's royally appointed governor, explicitly depended upon the king's authority; without that authority any action taken by him or his council could be deemed illegal.

English civil strife also had less abstract repercussions. During the period of warfare preceding the king's surrender, both parliamentarians and royalists tried to achieve military victories at sea by issuing documents, known as letters of marque, that authorized supporters in the merchant marine to seize enemy vessels if opportunity arose. Rival political and religious interests thus reinforced economic competition to set London shipmasters and merchants, who tended to favor Parliament, against those of western ports, particularly Bristol, who remained loyal to the king. This rivalry spilled over to Chesapeake waters, where Londoners dominated—but did not completely control—the tobacco trade, with fateful consequences for both colonies.

A ship captain and tobacco trader named Richard Ingle played the leading role in the opening episodes of the midcentury conflicts. Ingle's story weaves together several strands running through the region's seventeenth-century history: the pivotal role of religious belief; alliances that shifted as events challenged religious convictions, political loyalties, and economic self-interest; the fragile nature of colonial governance; overlapping involvement of key individuals in affairs of both colonies; and the influence of English events and policies.

Ingle's trading activities in the late 1630s and early 1640s attracted little attention, but in February 1643, while entertaining Virginia planters on board his ship, Ingle quarreled with several who favored the king's cause. Enraged, he set sail with such haste that at least a dozen planters received free passage to Maryland. Witnesses later testified that Ingle, while in Maryland, declared "that King Charles was no King"—words taken as "intending & conspiring the death & destruction" of the monarch.[19] Despite these statements, Ingle went about his business and presently sailed back to England with a hold filled with tobacco. Neither individual planters nor Maryland authorities allowed religious or political loyalties to jeopardize an opportunity to sell the year's tobacco crop. If they refused to deal with Ingle, there was no guarantee that another trader would visit their landings looking for tobacco. Moreover, with little local knowledge of the current situation overseas, it would be risky to act decisively in favor of either side.

When Ingle returned during the winter of 1643/44, Leonard Calvert was in England. Giles Brent, the acting governor, had quarreled with Ingle over at least two business transactions in previous years, creating friction that may have influenced subsequent events. In January 1644, Brent heard an accusation that Ingle was a traitor for proclaiming support of Parliament, based on the statements Ingle allegedly made the preceding year but that had met with no official action at the time. Brent responded by issuing warrants for Ingle's arrest on charges of high treason and for seizure of his ship as an enemy vessel. Within hours, Thomas Cornwaleys, a member of the governor's council, and others persuaded the captain of the guard to remove his men from Ingle's ship and return Ingle's weapons. Ingle then continued to trade with Maryland planters—including Brent—for their tobacco. In April 1644, after Ingle and Cornwaleys posted bond for Ingle's appearance if called to answer further charges, the two men sailed freely to England.

In the same month that Ingle left the Chesapeake Bay, a pair of enterprising London ship captains attacked an anchored Bristol vessel near the mouth of the James River, using Parliament's letter of marque as their authority. Taking advantage of the incoming tide, the Londoners anchored on either side of the Bristol ship, raised Parliament's flag, and fired broadsides from their cannon that caused several casualties. The Bristol vessel escaped by cutting her anchor line and riding with the tide into a nearby shallow creek, where the larger London ships were unable to follow.

The consequences of this brief engagement were both dire and unexpected. For many years relations between English settlers and the Powhatan had simmered with intermittent hostility but had not flared into warfare, despite continual pressure exerted by land-hungry Virginians on Native American villages and seasonal use of broader territories. Shortly after the London-Bristol battle, this relative peace evaporated. Opechancanough, observing that the English "began to go to war among themselves," launched his second major effort to repel the invaders.[20] The Powhatan leader had again lulled colonists into thinking he accepted their presence. Virginia's officials regarded the status quo as an enduring truce, but Opechancanough likely viewed the situation as a temporary arrangement that could be renegotiated given the right opportunity. The divided loyalties and political confusion of the English civil war provided that opening. Powhatan warriors replicated the strategy of 1622 by attacking English settlements early in the morning and killing more than five hundred colonists before Berkeley and his council could organize their defense.

Virginians, caught off-guard that April morning in 1644, needed some time to gather resources for retaliation. By the middle of 1646, however, the Virginia militia had achieved decisive victories against Powhatan warriors, reintroducing a military strategy that emphasized burning Native American cornfields and villages. Opechancanough was captured by Berkeley's soldiers, one of whom murdered the Powhatan chief. In October, the Virginia General Assembly ratified a treaty with Necotowance, successor to Opechancanough. For the first time, Virginians succeeded in turning military dominance into political dominion. The colonial government recognized Necotowance as "king of the Indians," but relegated him and his successors to a subordinate, tributary status. In exchange for an annual payment of twenty beaver skins, the assembly pledged to protect Necotowance "against any rebells or other enemies whatsoever," but stated that he held "his kingdome from the King's Ma[jes]tie of England" and required that his successors be "appointed or confirmed" by the colony's governor.[21] In addition, the treaty limited the territory the Powhatan could inhabit and restricted their movements among English settlements.

As the Virginia militia was beginning campaigns against the Powhatan late in 1644, Richard Ingle returned to the Chesapeake Bay on his annual trading voyage, bringing cargoes of goods ordered by Maryland planters, including Thomas Cornwaleys, who remained in England. Ingle also carried a letter of marque authorizing him to seize vessels trading from ports hostile to Parliament. When Ingle stopped at Jamestown, he learned that Leonard Calvert had also returned, carrying a royal commission that gave him authority to seize any parliamentary ships in Chesapeake ports. Should Ingle sail to Maryland in search of tobacco and to deliver the goods he carried, he risked loss of his ship and renewed accusations of treason.

Ingle chose instead to persuade his men to sail to Maryland on "a man of war voyage" to seize any vessels found trading there.[22] Maryland itself, by virtue of Calvert's letter of marque, was now the enemy, not just royalist ships. Meanwhile, William Claiborne, still intent on regaining his former trading post, journeyed to Kent Island in an unsuccessful attempt to persuade its residents to attack Giles Brent's plantation. Although Ingle arrived in Maryland waters explicitly intending to treat its rivers and creeks as enemy "ports," he started trading as usual for tobacco. According to later testimony, however, he also sent confidential letters to prominent Maryland Protestants, telling them of his parliamentary commission to rid the colony of all "Papists" (a derogatory term for Catholics) and to seize their property.

After learning of Claiborne's failure to gain support on Kent Island, Ingle sailed briefly back to Virginia to recruit more men. Upon returning to Maryland, Ingle first seized a competitor, a Dutch ship trading near St. Mary's City. He also captured Giles Brent, who was on board the ship and who remained Ingle's prisoner for the conflict's duration. Ingle next attacked the Maryland settlement, plundering the estate of any settler—Catholic or Protestant—who refused to take an oath acknowledging Parliament's authority. His men burned fences and slaughtered or scattered livestock. Looted houses included that of Thomas Cornwaleys, Ingle's former associate. Plunderers first took the silver, trade goods, and tobacco, but later returned for all the household items, not stopping until they had taken the window and door hardware. On Kent Island, Ingle's supporters looted Brent's plantation and burned his mill. Ingle also struck directly at proprietary power by destroying government records and smashing the great seal, symbol of the proprietor's authority. Ingle captured the Jesuit priests and plundered their property as well, ending their mission to Native Americans. Yet through this period, Ingle still adhered to tobacco's calendar, and in April 1645, he sailed back to England with his cargo and the captured Dutch ship. His passengers this time included prisoners, among them two Jesuit priests and Giles Brent.

During the chaos of the plundering time, many Maryland colonists, fearing loss of life as well as property, sought shelter in Virginia. Leonard Calvert crossed the Potomac into Virginia, where he recruited an armed force of about twenty-eight men composed of displaced Maryland colonists and Virginians hired on promise of payment when Calvert regained control. Late in the fall of 1646, Calvert succeeded in reestablishing proprietary authority in Maryland, but his position was insecure because Ingle's plundering left Maryland's treasury with no money to pay the hired troops. At this perilous juncture, Leonard Calvert succumbed to a sudden illness and died in June 1647, having time only to appoint Thomas Greene, a Catholic planter, as governor and to name Margaret Brent as his executor. Calvert's untimely death threatened to unravel his success, but Brent's sale of the proprietor's property to pay the men forestalled renewed chaos and secured—at least for the moment—Lord Baltimore's hold on his colony.

As the 1640s drew to a close, officials in both colonies had reestablished a modicum of control after episodes of significant instability, but in each case without resolving underlying sources of trouble. In Virginia, Berkeley succeeded in rallying colonists after the devastating Powhatan attack. Despite efforts of colonial officials to negotiate with Necotowance as leader of a broad alliance of Native American groups, however, the 1646 treaty resolved relations only between Virginia and groups at the core of the Powhatan chiefdom. The perception of peace ushered in a new phase of expanding English settlements, thus setting the stage for conflict with other Native Americans in decades to come. Underlying sources of trouble in Maryland were similarly unresolved. Ingle's success in rallying support exposed a significant fault line within the English population, one that divided a privileged, elite minority, comprised mainly of Catholic gentlemen, from a larger body of outsiders, primarily Protestants who had arrived in Maryland as indentured servants. Religious conflict thus intersected with issues of status and access to power. Lord Baltimore regained control of his colony, but religion remained a significant source of instability. Events in England soon precipitated new challenges to colonial rulers and extended the period of civil unrest.

TOLERATION AND RESTORATION

By the late 1640s, Parliament and its army, led by Cromwell and his Puritan allies, were gaining the upper hand and preparing to bring their imprisoned king to trial for treason. Because the volatile political and military situation could shift dramatically long before news reached Chesapeake colonies, both settlers and officials had to act cautiously. Virginia's royalist governor, William Berkeley, had to negotiate warily between his own commitment to the monarchy and the support for Parliament exhibited by some prominent Virginians and shared by many merchants trading to the colony. In Maryland, as colonists returned and began the task of rebuilding their homes and polity, Lord Baltimore recognized that Parliament's ascendancy posed an even more serious challenge to his proprietorship than had Ingle's attack.

Beginning in August 1648, the proprietor took a number of steps to deflect Puritan hostility. First, he replaced Thomas Greene, Maryland's Catholic governor, with William Stone, a Protestant and a Virginian (but taking care to instruct Stone, formerly an associate of Richard Ingle, never to pardon "that ungrateful villaine").[23] Stone's commission mandated that Stone would "procure five hundred People . . . to Come from other places and plant and reside within our said province"; any settlers recruited by Stone most likely would be Protestants.[24] As added incentive for immigration to replace population lost during the plundering time, Lord Baltimore increased the headright from fifty acres per person to one hundred acres.

In April 1649, following the proprietor's instructions, the Maryland assembly passed "An Act concerning Religion," pledging that no Christian would be "any waies troubled, Molested or discountenanced for or in respect of his or her religion nor in the free exercise thereof."[25] The statute, one of the earliest legislative efforts to guarantee religious freedom, gave the force of law to the policy the Calverts had followed from the first. By removing religion from the public sphere and endorsing toleration, the proprietor and legislators hoped to preserve civic peace while encouraging settlement to expand the colony's population and restore its economic health.

Earlier actions to foster toleration in Maryland had sought protection for Roman Catholics. Now the act's language was also intended to reassure dissenting Protestants (known as Separatists, Congregationalists, or Independents), to strengthen connections with men sympathetic to Parliament and to counter allegations that Maryland actively supported England's Catholic enemies. In addition, the proprietor wanted to encourage prospective migrants from Virginia, where Governor Berkeley upheld the Church of England's privileged position with requirements for church attendance and payment of tithes. The forbidden "reproachfull" and unacceptable terms listed in the act therefore included a number that applied to dissenters, including "heritick, Scismatick, . . . puritan, Independant, Prespiterian . . . Lutheran, Calvenist, Anabaptist, Brownist, Antinomian, Barrowist, Roundhead, [and] Sepatist."[26] Dissenters summoned to answer charges in Virginia's courts could be confident of toleration if they settled in Lord Baltimore's colony.

Finally, in 1650, Maryland legislators created a new county, Anne Arundel, on the western shore north of St. Mary's County. Virginia planters harassed for their separatist views and behaviors had begun surveying land along the bayside and waterways from the Patuxent to Patapsco Rivers. By forming a new county encompassing these settlement areas, the assembly ensured that dissenters could elect their own representatives and be governed by county justices appointed from among their members. Two representatives of Providence, the dissenters' name for their new home, already sat in the assembly that designated the area as a county.

Events of the next decade severely tested Lord Baltimore's effort to keep religious belief and practice a private matter. In the fall of 1649, while Stone was visiting his Virginia plantations, news reached Maryland that Parliament had executed Charles I. Thomas Greene, who was serving as acting governor, on 15 November declared Charles II king as successor to his father. Greene quickly retracted his pronouncement, but the damage was done. The proprietor's enemies hastened to inform parliamentary leaders that Maryland's governor had openly expressed royalist support.

Greene's proclamation helped draw the English Parliament's attention to problems posed by the Chesapeake colonies. Throughout the 1640s, William Berkeley, Virginia's governor, had remained unswerving in his support of the institution of monarchy. As long as he could act in the king's name, the governor negotiated the difficult political terrain by serving Virginia's best interests in ways that neither violated his royal commission nor provoked Parliament. For its part, it had been expedient for Parliament to ignore Berkeley's royalist views until English circumstances became more stable. But when Berkeley received official notice of the king's execution, he promptly denounced Parliament's action and proclaimed Charles II as king of England and Virginia's ruler.

Thus, both Chesapeake colonies, by acknowledging Charles Stuart as king, placed themselves in opposition to Parliament, which moved to discipline the wayward sisters by forming a special commission authorized to take control of the two colonies, backed by warships and British soldiers in case of resistance. The five commissioners, men familiar with the region but loyal to Parliament, included three members of the Virginia Council of State: William Claiborne, Thomas Stegge, and Richard Bennett, who was also a leader of Maryland's dissenting Protestants. The other two, Edmund Curtis and Robert Dennis, were ship captains engaged in the tobacco trade.

The fleet left England late in 1651 with commissioners and soldiers but suffered the loss of a vessel and two commissioners, Dennis and Stegge, in a storm en route. As the remaining ships made their way up the James River early in 1652, Governor Berkeley prepared to meet the three surviving commissioners with a show of strength. Calling upon the militia for support, Berkeley gambled that the men would rather negotiate a peaceful surrender than shed blood to seize control. His act of bravado won concessions, most notably Parliament's confirmation of colonists' rights as "free-born people of England" and recognition of Virginia's General Assembly (with an upper house, the Council of State, and a lower house, the House of Burgesses) as the colony's legislative body.[27] In addition, Berkeley secured amnesty for himself and other colonists who had supported the king but were willing to profess loyalty to Parliament (or at least to refrain from explicitly rejecting its authority). Berkeley then retired to his Green Spring plantation and tended his personal affairs, maintaining a discreet distance from politics but keeping abreast of developments in Jamestown and London.

By the time the commission turned its attention to Maryland, only two members remained: Richard Bennett and William Claiborne, both hostile to Lord Baltimore's interests. Bennett and Claiborne named a council of Protestant settlers to govern the colony, but left Stone in office, creating a conflict of political authority between the proprietor's governor, with his allies in St. Mary's City, and the commissioners' councilmen, mostly dissenting Protestants originally from Virginia but now living in Providence. For two years the rival parties struggled for control until Providence settlers persuaded Bennett and Claiborne that Stone himself was disloyal to Cromwell. On 22 July 1654, the two men, now serving as governor and secretary of Virginia, commissioned a ten-man executive body to govern Maryland on behalf of Parliament. Once in control, the group called for a new assembly and barred Catholics not only from serving as delegates but also from voting in the election. The resulting Commonwealth Assembly in October 1654 rescinded the 1649 "Act concerning Religion" and prohibited Catholics from public celebration of mass and other religious ceremonies. The assembly also challenged Lord Baltimore's authority by removing the requirement that landowners take an oath of fidelity to the proprietor.

For a time, each side pressured English officials to settle the conflict in its favor. Lord Baltimore called upon influential Protestants to support his proprietorship, while his opponents emphasized not only his Roman Catholicism but also perceived flaws in a charter that granted "king-like" privileges and territory that some considered to be part of Virginia. Impatient with the slow pace of decision making in England, Lord Baltimore reappointed Stone as governor and urged him to reassert proprietary control. When the Providence leadership again rejected Lord Baltimore's authority, Stone assembled a small force of perhaps two hundred men who sailed to the Severn River, where they landed on 24 March 1655. The next day, Stone's troops came under fire from a larger group of armed men on shore and from the guns of the *Golden Lyon*, a ship trading in the river. About a dozen of Stone's men were killed and most of the others wounded, with only five avoiding capture. Protestant leaders condemned ten prisoners to death and executed four before heeding appeals for mercy. Verlinda Stone, the governor's wife, wrote to Lord Baltimore that "Sentence was passed upon my Husband to be shot to death, but [he] was after saved by the Enemies owne Souldiers, and so the rest of the Councellors were saved by the Petitions of the [Providence] Women."[28]

An uneasy peace settled on Maryland, while in England a war of pamphlets followed as Lord Baltimore's supporters and opponents continued to challenge and defend his rule. Two years passed with no resolution as Cromwell opposed any further use of force and directed various committees and councils to settle the dispute. The continued delay at last persuaded the two sides to reach their own agreement. On 30 November 1657, Lord Baltimore and Richard Bennett framed a settlement of the conflict that restored proprietary control by confirming Lord Baltimore's right to the territory granted in the 1632 charter. Providence settlers who wished to remain in Maryland could do so, but only by accepting Lord Baltimore's authority. For his part, Lord Baltimore promised that the 1649 "Act concerning Religion" would be reinstated and never repealed. The proprietor granted amnesty for actions taken since December 1649, while the Admiralty Court in London resolved lingering conflict from the plundering time when it denied Richard Ingle's claim to the Dutch prize ship.

The 1657 agreement resolved Maryland's crisis of colonial governance by upholding the Calvert family's charter. But Virginia soon experienced its own crisis when the sudden death of

Samuel Matthews, the colony's third governor since 1652, left a vacancy that coincided with uncertain leadership in England, where Cromwell's son had abdicated as lord protector. Thrust once again into a constitutional quandary, the colony's Council of State decided to select an interim governor until matters were settled in England. With few suitable candidates, William Berkeley emerged as the only viable choice. In the spring of 1660, Berkeley accepted the council's nomination to serve as governor, just months before Charles II accepted Parliament's restoration of the English monarchy.

These restorations echoed the situation before the civil war in England, with a Stuart king named Charles, William Berkeley as Virginia's governor, and Maryland's proprietor in control of his colony. In significant ways, however, circumstances in 1662 were different from those of 1642. Substantial growth in the non-Indian population by the early 1660s spread tobacco-producing plantations across the landscape. Expansion of settlement outward from Jamestown and St. Mary's City spurred the transfer of local judicial and administrative functions from the provincial government to county courts under the leadership of justices of the peace selected from county elites. But as colonists gained more authority over local affairs, they lost a measure of control over their own economic development when imperial authorities in London began to regulate colonial trade more rigorously.

Disruptions in English shipping during the civil war had provided an opening filled during the 1640s by other nations, particularly the Dutch, who began to profit from the carrying trade through freight charges and other fees associated with transporting goods from one location to another. With the end of warfare in England, Parliament passed a series of Navigation Acts to counter the Dutch. This legislation limited foreign trade following the logic of mercantilism, the economic theory that a nation should maximize its exports to other countries while minimizing its imports. The first act, passed in 1651, permitted only English ships with predominately English crews to carry commodities to and from the colonies, thus excluding foreign ships from the carrying trade. The act of 1660 designated "enumerated commodities," including tobacco, which could be exported only to England or other English colonies, even if the ultimate market lay elsewhere, as was the case for some Chesapeake tobacco. The

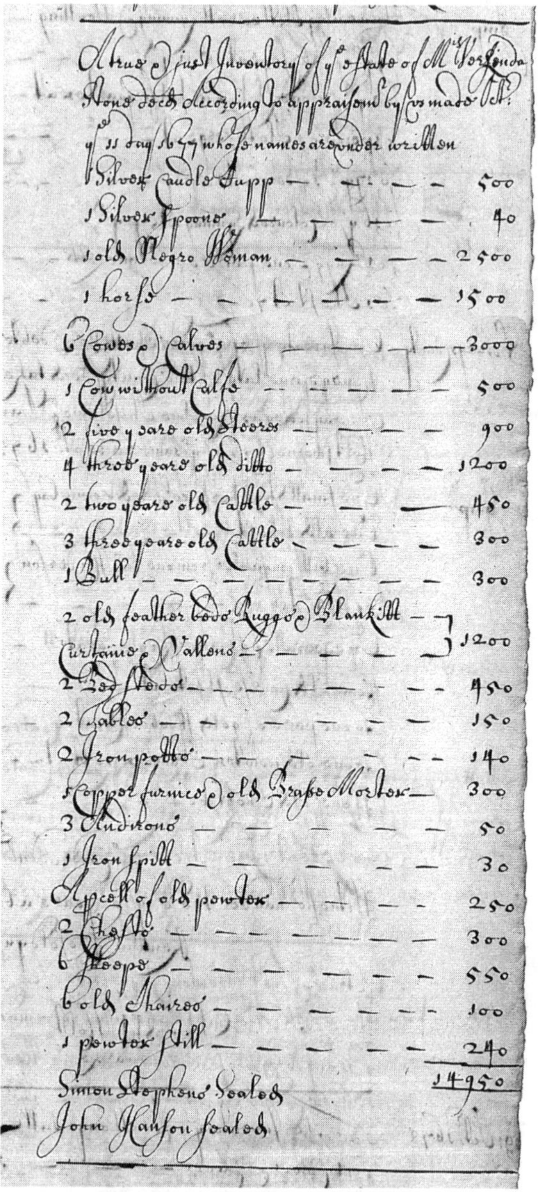
A true & just Inventory of ye Estate of Mrs Verlinda Stone deced According to appraisment by us made the ye 11 day 1677 whose names are under written

1 Silver Caudle Cupp	500
1 Silver Spoone	40
1 old Negro Woman	2500
1 horse	1500
6 Cowes & Calves	3000
1 Cow without Calfe	500
2 five yeare old Steeres	900
4 three yeare old ditto	1200
2 two yeare old Cattle	450
3 three yeare old Cattle	300
1 Bull	300
2 old feather beds Ruggs & Blanketts Curtains & Vallens	1200
2 Bedsteeds	450
2 Tables	150
2 Iron potts	140
1 Copper furnice & old Brass Morter	300
3 Andirons	50
1 Iron Spitt	30
A pcell of old pewter	250
2 Chests	300
6 Sheepe	550
6 old Chaires	100
1 pewter Still	240
	14950

Simon Stephens Sealed

John Hanson Sealed

Inventory of Verlinda Stone's Property. When Stone died in 1678, appraisers listed the personal property that she owned at death. As a widow, she was legally a *feme sole* and held property in her own right. Collection of the Maryland State Archives, ff. 354–55, MSA S536-6

A true and just Inventory of ye estate of Mrs Verlinda Stone decd According to appraisemt by us made Octr: ye 11 day 1677 whose names are under written

1 Silver caudle Cupp — — — — — — —	500
1 Silver spoone — — — — — — — —	40
1 old Negro Woman — — — — — — —	2500
1 horse — — — — — — — — — — —	1500
6 cowes & calves — — — — — — — —	3000
1 cow without calfe — — — — — — —	500
2 five yeare old steeres — — — — — —	900
4 three yeare old ditto — — — — — —	1200
2 two yeare old cattle — — — — — — —	450
3 three yeare old cattle — — — — — —	300
1 Bull — — — — — — — — — — — —	300
2 old feather bede Ruggs & Blankitt curtaine & Vallens — — — — — — —	1200
2 Bed steds — — — — — — — — — —	450
2 Tables — — — — — — — — — — —	150
2 Iron potts — — — — — — — — — —	140
1 copper furnice & old Brasse Morter —	300
3 Andirons — — — — — — — — — —	50
1 Iron spit — — — — — — — — — —	30
A pcell of old pewter — — — — — — —	250
2 chests — — — — — — — — — — —	300
6 sheepe — — — — — — — — — — —	550
6 old Chaires — — — — — — — — —	100
1 pewter still — — — — — — — — —	240
	14950

Simon Stephens Sealed

John Hanson sealed

Navigation Act of 1663 required that European or other foreign goods could not be shipped directly to a colonial port, but must be transshipped through England. Collectively these restrictions raised revenue for the English government through customs duties and other charges and increased profits for English merchants by restricting foreign competition. For Chesapeake planters, the Navigation Acts brought lower prices for tobacco, higher prices for imports, and discouragement of local manufactures. Faced with the dual pressure of reduced household income and higher expenses, colonists sought to increase their returns from agricultural production by bringing more land into cultivation.

HOMELANDS

Despite the political and economic turmoil associated with the English civil war, settlers continually migrated into Native American territory during the mid-seventeenth century. English colonists pursued a European ideal of land use—permanent, private ownership by individuals—that inevitably brought them into conflict with Indians. Native American understandings of land ownership were more fluid, with an emphasis on communal and productive relationships with the environment. Indian groups possessed land while they were using it, but land that had been vacated (left fallow to regain fertility, for example, or abandoned to follow the shifting habitat of deer) could be put to use in the future by the same or another group. Productive use of land, not fences placed to mark territory, served to indicate ownership for Native Americans.

Waves of immigration and relocation dictated that the Chesapeake colonies had multiple frontiers, from the hinterland of Jamestown in the 1620s on through the bay's eastern peninsula in the 1650s, the Potomac River valley in the 1670s, the Shenandoah Valley in the 1720s, and eventually to the Allegheny Mountains by the end of the colonial period. In the history of each successive frontier, the same basic story unfolded. A trickle of settlers moving into an area established homesteads that overlapped territory Native Americans used seasonally for cultivation, hunting, or foraging. An initial period of relatively peaceful coexistence gave way to one of small-scale conflict (usually involving boundaries and livestock), followed by a period in which Indians rapidly became displaced through a combination of warfare, migration, and disease. Colonial officials tried different strategies to claim territory out of Native American homelands, such as negotiating alliances, obtaining permission to settle specific areas, or purchasing land—agreements that often held little meaning in day-to-day life, when hogs strayed into a cornfield or recently freed servants tramped upstream in search of vacant land. At the same time, Indians tried different strategies to preserve their communities. The histories of particular groups of Native Americans illustrate variations that occurred within the broad narrative of English expansion and Indian displacement.

On Virginia's Eastern Shore, for example, Native Americans developed largely peaceful relationships during the earliest phases of contact with English settlers and generally tried to adapt to colonial expansion without engaging in large-scale violence. Two main groups of Indians, the Accomac and the Occohannock, inhabited the lower peninsula at the time of Jamestown's founding and were loosely united under a paramount chief, Esmy Shichans, whose chiefdom included a number of subordinate groups. Although allied with the Powhatan during the first decade or so of English settlement, the Accomac and Occohannock took no part in the violence of the 1610s and ended their Powhatan alliance with an explicit refusal to participate in the 1622 attack on English colonists. By the 1630s, Esmy Shichans and lesser chiefs at the southern end of the peninsula were gifting and selling land to the English, precipitating an expansion of English landholding that quickly displaced the Accomac from their territory along the bayside creeks. Indians moved east to new fields and used seaside marshes for fishing and foraging; with this relocation they began identifying themselves as Gingaskin, rather than Accomac. Soon, however, colonists began claiming seaside land as well. To protect Indian territory from competing claims by settlers, the provincial government set aside fifteen hundred acres of fertile land, a grant that survived until 1813.

Virginians began claiming land on the colony's upper Eastern Shore about a generation later by a process that occasionally involved purchases but more frequently saw Native Americans displaced when county and provincial courts upheld patents of allegedly vacant land. Unlike the Gingaskin, many of whom tried to preserve their community by using the Virginia legal system to secure property and civil rights, the Occohannock largely left

Virginia to join stronger Algonquian groups in Maryland whose territory in the late seventeenth century was still remote from English settlements.

The Piscataway on Maryland's lower western shore followed a different course. Kittamaquund, the Piscataway tayac who took control in 1636, needed English support to maintain his leadership. Kittamaquund's position was weak, partly because he had seized power by killing his brother and partly because traditional enemies of the Piscataway, Iroquoian groups from farther north and west, were moving closer to his people's homelands. Kittamaquund therefore welcomed the Jesuit mission, entered into an agreement giving the Maryland government the right to appoint his successor, and positioned the Piscataway as a loyal and protected subordinate tribe. For decades, the Piscataway had extensive official and informal contacts with colonists, replaced Indian-made objects with English goods (particularly muskets), and experienced the occasional disputes over marauding animals and land boundaries.

The Piscataway story could be read as one of decline, resulting partly from realignments within Native American groups and partly from displacement by the English, but a shift in perspective offers a different view. Maryland officials nominally controlled selection of Kittamaquund's successors as tayac, but only to the extent of ratifying Piscataway choices that followed traditional patterns of kinship-based succession. Burial practices, the most lasting evidence of religious beliefs, suggest that the Jesuit mission's influence was superficial, as burials showed no significant changes over the century. Like the Accomac/Gingaskin and Occohannock on the Eastern Shore, the Piscataway never engaged in large-scale military conflict with English settlers. The Maryland council laid out a reservation in 1668 to protect some territory from English settlement, but most Piscataway continued to farm and hunt on historic tribal lands; Maryland officials did not forcibly move any Piscataway to the reserved lands. The tayac continued to exercise control over his chiefdom; when his control weakened later in the century, it did so primarily because Susquehannock and Seneca raids from the north scattered some groups and slaughtered others. For nearly sixty years, the Piscataway succeeded in ignoring some aspects of English culture and incorporating others that served their own purposes, while maintaining their traditional subsistence economy, thereby avoiding dependence on European goods or depletion of resources.

The Piscataway achieved some success in preserving their communities in part because their leadership pursued a mutually advantageous alliance with the English who governed the Maryland colony. Native Americans inhabiting the territory along Virginia's Middle Peninsula, between the York and Rappahannock Rivers, and the Northern Neck never secured meaningful support from Virginia's governor and council, necessitating alternative survival strategies. The Rappahannock, who drew their identity from their attachment to the river bearing their name and made remaining near the river their paramount goal, tried an approach of nonengagement. When settlement activity reached Rappahannock territory late in the 1640s, the group sold roughly one-third of its land on the river's north shore and withdrew to secluded places within their homeland: along the banks of freshwater creeks, in higher, wooded elevations unsuitable for tobacco fields, and near marshes of little value to Virginians.

The Patawomeck, whose territory lay along the Potomac River on the Northern Neck, faced a similar flood of English migrants early in the 1650s, led by Giles and Margaret Brent, who filed patents for thousands of acres of Native American lands. The Patawomeck appealed to Virginia's governor, council, and assembly repeatedly, first to enforce restrictions on patenting Indian land, then for justice after Giles Brent and three other Virginia magistrates framed their werowance for murder, and finally for intervention when Brent and his allies led a military expedition against them. Settlers responded with persistent accusations that the Patawomeck and other Native Americans inhabiting the Rappahannock and Potomac river valleys were conspiring with Iroquoian raiding parties to attack outlying settlements, transforming initial tepid support from provincial authorities into explicit enmity. In 1666, Governor Berkeley and his council granted permission for local militias to attack Indian villages. Although extant records contain little information about actual campaigns against Native Americans, evaporation of provincial support for Indian interests and continual migration of settlers into the region pressured more Indian groups to leave. As these "neighbor" Indians withdrew from the river banks to more remote territory, they left a void into which northern groups like the Doeg and

Susquehannock moved. Thus by their implacable hostility toward nearby Indians in pursuit of acquiring land, Virginians succeeded in making themselves more vulnerable: English settlers distrusted the new "foreign" Indians and felt more threatened by them, with dire consequences for "foreign" and "neighbor" Indians alike when large-scale conflict broke out again in the 1670s.

Three threads run through the history of Virginia and Maryland during the 1640s and 1650s and into the 1660s. Both colonies dealt with the repercussions of political and religious conflict originating in the mother country. Colonial governments understood the necessity of avoiding premature commitment to Crown or Parliament during England's civil war, but the conflict nevertheless spread across the Atlantic and embroiled both colonies, particularly Maryland, where animosity between Roman Catholics and Protestants threatened its very survival. Throughout the midcentury period, both colonies also absorbed thousands of immigrants, some as enslaved workers, more as free persons, and most as indentured servants. Most free and servant migrants regarded producing tobacco for profitable sale in overseas markets as their best chance to secure a living. And in both colonies, the relentless need to acquire land on which to grow tobacco created a continually moving frontier that pressed upon occupation and use of those same lands by Native Americans. Particularly in Virginia, where officials controlling land patents were local men for whom acquiring acreage was a source of profit and power, many colonists perceived Indian communities as inconvenient obstacles or dangerous impediments. Not all Native American groups responded to pressure on their lands with violence, but throughout the tidewater region, the process of encroachment and displacement eroded their territory.

The midcentury troubles of the Chesapeake colonies eased when restoration of the monarchy ended England's civil war. Yet the underlying sources of instability all persisted, including the fragility of local government in colonial settlements, the insecurity of an economic system built around a single crop and dependent upon intensive importation of labor, and the fundamental tension between Native American and European cultures. These issues continued to disrupt the Chesapeake region during the next several decades. Controversies over Indian policy and colonial governance threw Virginia into its own brief civil war during the 1670s, while a new constitutional crisis in England with overtones of religious conflict once more threatened the Maryland proprietorship in the 1680s. The destabilizing conditions that plagued the tobacco coast during the time of troubles surfaced again in this late-century period of violence and turmoil.

THREE

Transformations

Born in 1674 in Somerset County, Maryland, Betty Denwood grew up surrounded by aunts, uncles, and cousins as well as her parents and three siblings. Denwood was a granddaughter of Levin Denwood, an Englishman who migrated to Virginia's Eastern Shore in the 1630s. Several branches of Betty Denwood's extended family were among groups of Quakers and other nonconforming Protestant Virginians who moved up the peninsula into Maryland in the 1670s and 1680s. Her grandfather is credited with erecting the first Quaker meeting house on Virginia's Eastern Shore, while her father, also named Levin Denwood, and her uncle, Nehemiah Covington, were among the founders of Somerset County's Monie Meeting.

Marriages among members of Denwood's family reflect the Eastern Shore's religious diversity during the century's last quarter. Betty Denwood's aunt Mary, although likely raised as a Quaker, married an Anglican named Roger Woolford, while Denwood's cousin, Priscilla Covington, married Robert King, described by one chronicler as an "uncompromising" elder of the Presbyterian Church.[1] By creating a colony where religious affiliation remained a private matter, Lord Baltimore had opened colonial doors not just for his fellow Roman Catholics but for a variety of Protestant dissenters as well. During a resurgence of Anglican orthodoxy following the restoration of English monarchy in 1660, dissenting Protestants from England and Virginia migrated to Maryland, where their religious practices did not invite persecution.

About 1704, Betty Denwood herself married a member of the Anglican Church. George Gale, son of a Whitehaven merchant and brother of a prominent London tobacco merchant, had captained ships trading between the Chesapeake region and his family's home in England. His marriage likely furthered an existing mercantile association with the interrelated Denwood and Covington families. Aided by connections to English merchant communities and ties to local gentry, Gale soon assumed a leading role in the county. By 1707 he served as a major in the local militia, in 1708 was elected an assembly delegate, and in 1709 became a county court justice. Recommended for a place on the governor's council, Gale died before being appointed.

In his will, written in the summer of 1712, George Gale stipulated that his four children, all sons, be "educated & brought up according to the Profession of the Church of England."[2] Because Quakers refused to swear oaths required for holding public office, Gale may have meant to ensure that his sons could continue his role in political affairs. Three of the sons followed their father's example and held county offices; the eldest, Levin Gale, served on the provincial council from 1738 until his death in 1744. The Gale-Denwood marriage, joining individuals of different faiths, benefited the aspirations of each: for Gale, marriage to Denwood placed him within an influential local network of planters and merchants; for Denwood, the marriage ensured that her children could inherit that influence and take part in civic life.

When George Gale died, he named his wife as executor of his estate, a position that gave the widowed Betty Denwood Gale an integral role in the local economy. She inherited outright more than £1,000 in household goods, servants, slaves, and merchandise. During her sons' minority, furthermore, Gale controlled the residue of her husband's estate, including thousands of acres of land and shares in four merchant ships. Because of her wealth and age, she escaped the pressures to remarry that poorer and younger widows experienced, especially those with young children to support. Had she remarried, under English common law Gale's status as a *feme couvert* (a "covered woman"; that is, covered by her husband's authority) would have transferred ownership of her property and management of her children's estate to her new husband. With ample wealth and experience to support her sons and herself, Gale chose not to marry and thus remained a *feme sole*, keeping legal control over the property she inherited and managed. Because the youngest child was an infant when George Gale died, Betty Denwood Gale's guardianship lasted for decades. As an exceptionally wealthy widow, Gale was positioned to participate fully in Somerset's economic life through such activities as buying land, selling tobacco and surplus crops, extending credit to neighboring planters, witnessing legal documents, and acquiring bound labor.

Betty Denwood Gale came of age during transformative years in the colonial Chesapeake region. The seventeenth century's last three decades encompassed significant free white population growth, with newcomers like George Gale settling among native-born colonists like Betty Denwood, her siblings, and her cousins. The last decade also witnessed dramatic black population growth, primarily fueled by an upsurge in the forcible transportation of Africans, but also by children born to women imported in earlier decades. Among Native Americans, however, the period after about 1660 was primarily one of decline, as decades of warfare, migration, and disease substantially reduced the numbers who persisted in their tidewater and Piedmont homelands.

The first twenty years of Gale's life also spanned a period of renewed political and religious upheaval for Chesapeake inhabitants. Both colonies experienced significant disruptions in government, first during Bacon's Rebellion in Virginia and then during the Protestant Revolution in Maryland. In the aftermath of these tumultuous events, English authorities exerted more control over colonists' economic and religious undertakings. In a number of critical ways, the cultural life of Chesapeake planters became more closely aligned with English trends. An increasing reliance on enslaved labor, however, marks one fundamental respect in which Virginia and Maryland did not resemble Great Britain. Investment in slaves became essential to the economic, social, and political position of families such as the Gales, who held ten slaves when George died. By the 1730s, when the youngest son came of age, at least thirty-five enslaved men and women labored on Gale land. At the end of the seventeenth century, nearly all elite planters like the Gales profited from the coerced labor of Africans and African Americans—by far the most consequential transformation of these pivotal years.

During the second half of the seventeenth century, the labor system that supported Chesapeake plantation society experienced significant changes. The flow of indentured servants from the British Isles diminished in the century's last quarter, while the small trickle of enslaved Africans that began in 1619 increased to a steady stream of imported laborers by midcentury and became a wide river in the 1690s. As the century drew to a close, Virginia's black population numbered between eight and ten thousand, representing 10 to 13 percent of a non-Indian population of seventy-five thousand. In Maryland, about three thousand Africans and African Americans accounted for about 10 percent of the colony's population of some thirty thousand. Through a combination of natural increase and importation, moreover, black population had begun to increase exponentially, a trend that continued into the early eighteenth century. Maryland's black population nearly tripled in the century's first decade, reaching almost eight thousand by 1710. The numbers also climbed rapidly in Virginia, approaching twenty thousand by 1710. A decade later, people of African ancestry represented roughly 25 percent of the Chesapeake region's non-Indian population.

The precise timing, mechanisms, and motivations for the transformation from a labor system primarily based on short-term indentured servitude to one that relied heavily on lifetime chattel slavery are the subject of debate among scholars, but several key variables are well understood. One element of the shift was a significant decline in the availability of servants in the century's last decades. Severe overcrowding and depressed economic conditions in England had eased, leading fewer people to migrate; those who did more commonly bargained for passage to newer colonies, such as Carolina or Pennsylvania. The price of servants accordingly rose to the point that enslaved Africans, although still expensive, became a rational economic choice for planters who needed workers and had cash or credit to invest.

Direct participation of English merchants in slaving ventures after 1660 provided another contributing factor. Charles II granted a monopoly over trade in slaves to the joint-stock Company of Royal Adventurers and its successor, the Royal African

Company. Although the tobacco colonies were always a secondary market compared with the more lucrative trade with Caribbean sugar islands, the numbers of enslaved workers offered for sale increased dramatically as a result of direct English trade between Africa and North America. Scholars estimate that English ships arriving from Africa carried somewhat more than seven thousand Africans to the region between 1670 and 1700. During the same years, between six and seven thousand Africans arrived through transshipment from Caribbean islands. These numbers illustrate both the substantial contribution of direct trade, which more than doubled the number of imported Africans during the period, and the continued importance of indirect trade, which brought small numbers of enslaved workers from the islands year in and year out.

In addition to economic factors of supply and demand, cultural attitudes supported both the general concept of slavery as a labor institution and the specific shift toward use of enslaved Africans. There was no comparable form of permanent bonded status in England, but systems of slavery existed elsewhere in Europe and in Mediterranean cultures with which Europeans had traded for centuries. Historical and biblical precedents similarly underscored slavery as an abstract idea compatible with the fundamental English belief in hierarchical social organization. The first colonists who ventured to North America considered slavery an acceptable labor system and anticipated conscripting Native American workers. Practical considerations, however, made enslavement of Indians difficult until late in the century, when warfare in frontier areas of southwestern Virginia and the Carolinas supplied large numbers of captives. Following the general policy that "all Indians taken in warr [would] be held and accounted slaves dureing life," the majority of war captives were shipped from Charleston to the Caribbean, but Virginia planters purchased a significant number and consigned them to work in tobacco fields alongside enslaved Africans.[3]

Although colonists did not fully articulate a racial ideology for slavery during the seventeenth century, from the time of initial Chesapeake settlement English migrants regarded Africans as different from and inferior to themselves. This attribution of "otherness" helped justify purchase of enslaved workers for the often-menial tasks of building farms and cultivating tobacco.

Slave codes enacted in the 1660s linked cultural and economic factors explicitly by codifying slavery as a system of perpetual bondage determined by racial heredity. Slavery became not only the status of an African individual during his or her lifetime but also the status inherited by children, ensuring that the labor of successive generations would benefit owners of enslaved workers. Slavery expanded the pool of workers in another significant way: planters did not perceive any cultural reasons to exempt African women from field work. Planters did not expect their wives and daughters to cultivate crops of tobacco and corn, and generally did not employ female servants in the fields either. As Robert Beverley later observed, "a White Woman is rarely or never put to work in the Ground, if she be good for any thing else."[4] But neither corn nor tobacco required exceptional physical strength for cultivation, and in the absence of any cultural proscription against the practice, enslaved women worked alongside enslaved men.

The relative importance of economic and cultural factors in decisions to purchase slaves remains open to debate, but their effects are easy to discern: by the end of the seventeenth century, slavery emerged as the dominant labor system in the Chesapeake colonies. In the longest-settled counties, wealthy planters with Caribbean connections had been heavily invested in enslaved laborers for decades. Throughout both colonies, slaves appeared at least as often as did servants in the inventoried property of men and women who owned bound labor when they died, and in some areas slaves dramatically outnumbered servants. Inventories compiled during the 1690s in York County, Virginia, for example, list nearly twenty-five enslaved Africans and African Americans for each indentured English laborer. In areas where the wealthiest tobacco planters profited from the best tobacco soils, labor force composition shifted decisively from a majority of short-term, indentured servants to a majority of permanently enslaved workers. Grandees—planters with large holdings of land worked by dozens or more bondspeople—became a distinctive element within colonial society well before the seventeenth century ended, foretelling the future direction of Chesapeake development.

The vast majority of enslaved workers imported during the late seventeenth century either arrived directly from Africa or spent only a brief period in the West Indies to recuperate from the arduous trans-Atlantic passage before being carried on for sale to tobacco planters. Rather than arriving as a heterogeneous collection of individuals commingled on the African coast by their captors, cargoes tended to be made up of men, women, and children taken from contiguous areas along the coastline. The largest slavers called at African harbors big enough to accommodate their ships and able to provide full cargoes; in turn, they transported their cargoes to the strongest Chesapeake market, the sweet-scented tobacco area between the James and Rappahannock Rivers. This trading pattern provided one benefit for Africans brought to Chesapeake shores: shared geographic origins increased the likelihood that a shipload of bondspeople would speak the same or a related language and share a similar culture. The probability of common origins among clusters of imported slaves improved the chances of retaining elements of African culture, particularly if a number of shipmates were purchased as a group by one master or by men with plantations in the same neighborhood.

This modest benefit, however, barely registers against the stark deterioration in status that Africans and African Americans experienced during the late seventeenth century. Building upon the legal framework established in the 1660s, colonial legislatures renewed and expanded laws that withheld rights from enslaved men and women. Although planters now lived with the threat of resistance and rebellion from enslaved workers, their decision to treat slaves as property rather than as people permitted extensive controls and punitive measures. Denied basic civil rights that protected English servants, enslaved Africans and African Americans had no legal standing and no redress to local courts for any amelioration of their condition.

LOCAL GOVERNANCE

The shift from indentured English to enslaved Africans brought devastation to the lives of hundreds of thousands of people held in lifetime bondage on the region's plantations. Yet for elite planters, the transition brought certain advantages. The change solved the labor-supply problem created by the decreasing pool of potential servants. Purchasing slaves instead of servants solved a social problem as well. Developing a labor force perpetually in bondage eliminated any obligation to provide economic opportunities or political rights to successive waves of new immigrants.

After 1670, only free, male owners of land or significant personal property could participate in civic or political life. No woman could vote or hold office regardless of status, although wealthy and well-connected women like Betty Denwood Gale wielded considerable economic and social power. Male tenants might aspire to civic roles once they accumulated enough capital to purchase land and establish themselves as freeholders. Neither indentured servants nor enslaved laborers were able to vote or hold office, with the key distinction that male servants held some expectation of moving a place or two up in the hierarchy that ran from servant to tenant to freeholder to officeholder.

From mid-seventeenth century to the end of the colonial period, counties formed the backbone of local Chesapeake society. They provided political and religious organization, official sanction for the spread of white settlement, and the everyday setting for vital events in colonists' lives. In both colonies, the governor commissioned a small group of men from among each county's local elite to serve as justices of the peace. County courts held jurisdiction over moral offences, orphans' estates, land grants, shipping matters, and crimes not punishable by loss of life or limb (these cases were referred to a higher court in Jamestown or St. Mary's City). County justices also had a range of administrative duties that included setting annual taxes, registering servants' ages, providing poor relief, maintaining highways and bridges, supervising legislative elections, and overseeing relations with those Native Americans who continued to live within county boundaries.

Surviving records testify to the courts' broad jurisdiction and extensive responsibilities. Justices met a minimum of four times per year, with sessions usually lasting three to five days. Each court meeting encompassed an array of business that ranged from criminal cases to minor administrative matters and always included a substantial number of civil prosecutions. In August 1688, when justices in Maryland's Somerset County included Roger Woolford (Betty Denwood's uncle by marriage), the majority of cases before the bench involved debts that county residents owed each other. Thomas Jones successfully sued Peter Whaples for nine hundred pounds of tobacco, for example, and widow Elizabeth Stevens settled an account with Simon Perkins, who owed Stevens for such goods as rum, corn, wheat, sugar, nails, a frying pan, and a cow. Justices handled a number of criminal cases as well. Three female servants confessed to bearing illegitimate children, while a jury of twelve men found John Ellis guilty of stealing three hogs from John Culhoone but cleared William Baker from a charge of breach of Sabbath when "Noe Evidences nor proofe" appeared against him.[5]

As part of their administrative duties, county courts collected taxes to pay for services and purchases as well as each county's share of provincial expenses. Constables maintained an annual list of each household's taxable labor, which consisted of all able-bodied men and enslaved women age sixteen and above. Officials calculated the tax rate by dividing total expenses by the number of taxables (also called tithables, particularly in Virginia, where expenses included tithes to support the established Anglican Church); each household head then paid the total due for the household's taxables. Administrative matters heard by the August 1688 court included appointing Roger Burkum as the sheriff's assistant, authorizing repairs for three of Somerset's numerous bridges, and correcting the annual tax list because Roger Cattlin had been "charged in the list for 5 Thythables," instead of two, and James Ingram had been charged "with an Indian that belongs to Tondotank Towne."[6] Justices also looked after the welfare of orphans, binding out the five children of Jenckin and Margaret Morris and taking a bond from Thomas Gordon for administration of their estate.

In theory, the county court system resolved problems of local governance by replicating familiar English practices to promote political stability and civility. In practice, the process was not always smooth. Extant records are replete with evidence of men (and not a few women) jockeying for position in a fluid and far from polite society. Colonists who succeeded in securing not only financial success but also a measure of political and social status were protective of their gains and quick to respond to any challenge to their right to rule. Thus when John Robinson of Middlesex County, Virginia, claimed that justice Matthew Kemp was drunk during court in 1705, Kemp not only denied the accusation but felt compelled to defend his honor and history of public service. Kemp reminded county residents that he had been repeatedly deemed worthy not only of his post as a justice but also of "considerable Commissions of Trust and Reputation" and that the county's freeholders had "thought him fitt" for election as a burgess. In each of these arenas, Kemp asserted, he had worked "faithfully and honestly" and dispensed "Justice and Right to every person to the best of his Judgment."[7] Such incidents of defamation and rebuttal reflect the fragility of political and social status throughout the seventeenth and early eighteenth centuries. Colonists had established the outlines of a civil society, but the details of who exactly merited a position of authority were still open to debate.

REMAKING THE LANDSCAPE

The men jockeying for political and social position and the diverse population over which they sought authority took part in a process of reshaping the natural environment to earn a livelihood. Each new householder faced the same challenges, whether a newly freed servant, a tenant meeting the terms of his lease, a free immigrant establishing himself and his family, or even a wealthy landowner starting cultivation on a new tract. Land needed to be cleared for buildings and for crops. At a minimum, any household needed a place to live and storage for harvested tobacco and corn. Other tasks included building fences, planting orchards, and making provision for livestock. Although colonists used the term *planting*, when they carved a working plantation out of forested land their activities constituted *farm building*. Men and women invested their labor in improvements that earned income for themselves and their descendants in future years.

The first steps required clearing enough land to grow tobacco and corn crops, build dwelling and tobacco houses, and plant a kitchen garden and orchard. When Robert Cole arrived in Maryland in the early 1650s with his wife, four young children, and two servants, for example, he acquired three hundred acres along a navigable creek in St. Mary's County. Cole and his workers first needed to clear fifteen acres or so of land, a task that took about three months but required no tools other than an axe for cutting trees. The men removed trees completely from the half acre intended for buildings, which provided wood for housing, fencing, and heating, but those on cropland were only girdled. Six acres planted in corn supplied enough grain for the household;

any surpluses could be sold to newcomers or fed to livestock. The three hands—Cole and his servants—could also tend six to seven acres planted in tobacco. In time, a one-acre orchard of seventy fruit trees provided cider for drinking. Purchase of a sow and pigs, chickens, and a cow or two from established planters provided the foundation for Cole's livestock herds.

Each step seemingly replicated circumstances of rural English life, but resulted in a landscape bearing little relation to the one English migrants left behind. Because tobacco could be grown in unplowed fields, settlers had no need for draft animals (oxen or horses) and no need to clear tree stumps before planting. Because labor was in short supply, Chesapeake planters used fences sparingly, generally opting for worm fences, or split rails laid in a zigzag pattern that did not require the time or resources demanded by traditional English fencing. Viewed together, scattered fields dotted with dead or dying trees and irregular wooden fences, surrounded by woods and thickets, bore little resemblance to an English farm's cultivated fields, neatly bounded by hedgerows or stone fencing.

Livestock practices represented another dramatic change. In addition to grasses for grazing, animals raised in fenced pastures need a regular supply of food—hay and water for cattle; oats, too, for horses. Chesapeake planters had no spare labor to clear, plant, and harvest hay and oats or to build barns for storing fodder. Instead, colonists adopted free-range animal husbandry, putting fences around crops and allowing livestock to roam freely in search of food. Planters did not fear that livestock would run away because domesticated animals did not generally stray far from the humans who tended them. Planters registered livestock marks, generally patterns of notches in the ear, to settle ownership disputes. When John Ellis was convicted of killing hogs in 1688, for example, the indictment specified that the animals "were Cropt and Slitt in the left yeare and Swallow forke over bitt and under bitt in the right Eare which is the proper marke of John Culhoone."[8]

Free-range husbandry dictated that much plantation land had to remain forested. A single cow needed five acres in summer months and at least three times that in winter months. Even a tenant or small farmer with no more than a dozen cows and a similar number of hogs needed access to one hundred and fifty acres of forested land for his animals. If an area was not too densely settled, planters could use adjoining tracts of unpatented land for their livestock. Generally plantations had twice as much woodland as arable; Ralph Wormeley's Rosegill plantation in Virginia, for example, had two thousand cleared acres and four thousand still forested to supply forage for five hundred animals.

Free-range husbandry also contributed to a different mix of animals than in rural England. Wolves preyed on sheep, making vulnerable any that roamed freely, while thickets and brambles snagged their wool. Sheep did not become common until bounties on wolves and denser settlement reduced the predators' threat. Colonists initially imported goats in large numbers, but there were few by midcentury. Goats ate the bark of apple trees, and cider was more valued than goat milk. Because tobacco and corn did not require plowed fields, oxen remained uncommon, used mainly for hauling timber and other heavy loads. Nor were there many horses until the 1660s, although most households owned one or two for transportation. Planters did raise cattle, but primarily for meat rather than for dairy products. Poorly nourished and sensitive to summer heat, Chesapeake cows produced less milk than English cows, and their milk made inferior butter and cheese that spoiled quickly in the hot summers. Just as critical, many Chesapeake households had no mistress or older daughter or female servant to supervise the dairy, traditionally a woman's role. Together these circumstances shaped livestock herds focused on swine and beef cattle, adaptations so successful that Chesapeake residents likely consumed more meat in their diet than did their English counterparts.

The Chesapeake diet underwent other modifications from the English model. The primary grain crop was Indian corn, planted in fields prepared by girdling, rather than wheat or secondary grains like oats or rye, which required plowed fields. The English drank beer, but barley from which beer was brewed also grew in plowed fields and few planters were willing to allocate labor for plowing. Because apple and other fruit trees needed little attention once planted, colonists drank cider and other fruit beverages such as perry, fermented from pear juice, and mobby, made from peaches, from summer through early winter. Milk was commonly consumed during spring and fall. For the remainder of the year, spring or well water was the most likely substitute for those who could not afford imported spirits, wines, or beer.

Free-range animal husbandry and an emphasis on tobacco cultivation affected the Chesapeake landscape in still another way. In England, where land rather than labor was in short supply, farmers carefully fertilized fields with manure to maintain soil productivity. In the Chesapeake colonies, planters had better uses for the labor required to grow fodder and muck manure out of pens. As a result, planters maintained soil quality by planting tobacco for several years, followed by a few years in corn, and then allowing fields to lie uncultivated for about twenty years to restore nutrients. Fallow land undergoing a slow process of reverting to woodland presented an unkempt appearance to observers accustomed to cultivated English fields. Travelers often reviled Chesapeake planters as slovenly farmers because their practices diverged so sharply from methods employed in the mother country.

Nor were observers impressed by most Chesapeake homes. Traditional English housing required skilled craftsmen and time-consuming techniques to make bricks, construct brick chimneys, saw planks from felled trees, and craft complex mortise-and-tenon joints to build an elaborate wooden frame. Instead, colonists experimented with various simplified techniques, finally settling on a mix of adaptations known as the Virginia house. They framed houses around a series of roughly fashioned posts placed directly in the ground and secured by nails to horizontal framing. Clapboards, short overlapping slats of split oak or chestnut fastened to the frame with nails, created a light but durable surface that could be weatherproofed with a pine-tar coating. Clapboards or shingles replaced thatch and tile as roof covering; a wooden chimney, easily pushed away from the house if it caught on fire, completed the structure.

Typically these houses were one or two rooms of sixteen feet by twenty feet, perhaps with a loft or lean-to shed for additional storage or sleeping space. Floors might be covered with planks, but often they were left as beaten dirt. Greater comfort came from plastering the inside with clay, closing gaps in the sheathing to keep out rain and cold winter drafts. These houses were not elegant or durable; they tended to rot quickly because posts were set in the often-damp ground. But they conserved scarce

Godiah Spray Plantation. The large building to the left is the tobacco barn of the reconstructed mid-seventeenth-century plantation at Historic St. Mary's City. The smaller building to the right is the family's dwelling house. Split-rail fences protect crops from foraging animals. 1984-DRT-0666s, The Colonial Williamsburg Foundation

resources of labor and money for more important purposes. Only at the upper levels of society did planters build brick homes, but even these tended to be relatively small and no longer-lasting than wooden structures. The most common outbuilding was a tobacco barn that could be moved or replaced as cultivation shifted from one field to another. Middling planters might also have a separate cabin for enslaved workers. Wealthier planters housed their slaves in one or more cabins, some near the "great house" and others in quarters closer to outlying fields. Outbuilding construction used the same simplified methods of earth-fast construction, light framing, and nails rather than joinery.

Because most planters cultivated holdings of at least two hundred acres, home sites continued to be scattered; few Chesapeake families lived in sight of another household. Neighborhoods took shape slowly, as networks of roads and paths began to link home sites together and provide access to gathering places such as the court, parish churches and meetinghouses, ordinaries (places that served fixed-price meals and beverages), and workshops of rural artisans. None of these neighborhoods, however, brought together all the functions that contemporaries recognized as forming a town. Writing to the Lords of Trade in England in 1678, the third Lord Baltimore observed that "wee have none That are called or cann be called Townes. . . . [I]n most places There are not ffifty houses in the space of Thirty Myles."[9] Conditions did not alter much in the next twenty-five years. Robert Beverley commented in 1704 that "to this Day, [Virginians] have not any one Place of Cohabitation among them, that may reasonably bear the Name of a Town." Beverley noted the "Advantage of the many Rivers, which afforded a commodious Road for Shipping at every Man's Door."[10] With a staple crop that could be processed for export on the plantation where it grew, "a Road for Shipping" at the door, and most overseas trade controlled by English merchants, the Chesapeake economy provided scant encouragement for seventeenth-century urbanization.

For areas with marginal tobacco land, a similar landscape often had a different economic focus. Settlement of Virginia south of the James River, for example, began in 1635 with a grant to Adam Thoroughgood of 5,320 acres on the Lynnhaven River. This area produced poor tobacco, but became the center of a thriving livestock industry, using pasture land created by fencing off necks of land that extended between smaller rivers and creeks. Trading vessels called not for tobacco but for beef, pork, and naval stores of potash, tar, and turpentine extracted from the pine forests. Rapid settlement led to creation of New Norfolk County in 1636 and its division into Upper Norfolk and Lower Norfolk a year later. By 1659, Virginians were moving south to the west bank of Albemarle Sound, in what later became North Carolina. Because the sound lacked a suitable harbor, they continued to look toward Virginia for trading purposes. Ships traveled to the West Indies and mainland colonies laden with cargoes of oak and cypress shingles and plank, casks of pine tar and pitch, livestock and salted meat, hides and furs from the Carolina Indian trade, wheat and corn, peas and beans, butter and cheese, and some tobacco.

Whether they focused on tobacco or produced a more diverse array of goods for trade locally and overseas, Chesapeake planters engaged in similar processes of farm building and contributed to the region's gradual transformation into settled English communities. Within a decade of his arrival, for example, Robert Cole had created a successful plantation worked with three servants. He was not rich, but was comfortably off. His plantation was somewhat larger than the area's 250-acre median, and he had more personal property than most planters. Cole and his servants produced between five and seven thousand pounds of tobacco each year and garnered additional income through sales of meat, tallow, hides, butter, cheese, and occasional surpluses of cider and corn. Established plantations like Cole's found a ready market for these products as continued demand for tobacco brought in new settlers who needed food and resources as they began the farm-building process.

Three of Robert Cole's male servants eventually succeeded in becoming landowning householders after completing their terms of indenture. Of the three, Robert Gates had arrived in 1655, and both Joseph Alvey and John Johnson arrived in 1657. Once free of their obligations to Cole, they lived in the colony long enough to acquire land, marry, father children, and accumulate some wealth. Each of the three may have spent a few years as a tenant on someone else's land while saving enough to pay fees and other costs for the land he eventually patented. For freedmen, tenancy was the first step toward land ownership. For owners with surplus land, tenancy offered an immediate source of income and potential for greater future profits. When leases ended, landowners had a working plantation to sell to a newly arrived settler, rent at a higher price, or pass on to children.

Thomas Gerard, for example, owned a large tract in St. Mary's County, Maryland, known as St. Clement's Manor. In the early 1650s, Gerard turned a profit by selling some tenant-developed land as freehold. As Gerard began to consider his children's future, he started preparing plantations for their eventual ownership. Gerard put servants to work clearing land, building houses and workers' cabins, making fences, and planting orchards. At the same time, he increased his livestock herds and poultry flocks. When Gerard's son Justinian turned twenty-one in 1664, he began adult life with a five-hundred acre plantation, a furnished dwelling house, farming and dairying tools and equipment, six male servants, small stocks of cattle, hogs, and sheep, two horses, a flock of chickens, corn to feed his servants for a year, and casks to pack the first year's tobacco crop.

Other planters began dividing their workforce into smaller units placed on pockets of good tobacco land. These individual quarters, or outlying work units, might contain as many as a dozen working hands each. In the 1680s, for example, John Carter housed his laborers on six quarters on his Corotoman plantation, where they raised tobacco and corn and tended cattle and hogs. George Plater, a lawyer and planter, migrated to Maryland in his early twenties and accumulated substantial landholdings on the western shore. Plater divided his twenty-eight slaves among four quarters; on each quarter, he placed an indentured servant to oversee the workers. As slaveholdings expanded during the eighteenth century, quarters like these spread across the region's tobacco-growing areas, accelerating the changes that farm building brought to the land.

SPIRITUAL MATTERS

In the same way that Chesapeake settlers reshaped physical landscapes and refashioned political institutions, they also faced the challenge of revitalizing religious communities in the aftermath of the English civil war. In England, restoration of the Stuart monarchy also restored the Church of England to its prewar status as the established church, with severe penalties for anyone not taking communion as part of that church. A group of between one and two thousand dissenting clergymen, comprised of Puritans, Presbyterians, and others, lost their positions for refusing to use the Church of England's revised Book of Common Prayer. They and their followers, known as nonconformists, were forbidden to hold office, attend universities, or assemble for worship in groups larger than five. Penalties enacted against dissenters contributed to an influx of nonconformist immigrants to the Chesapeake region, particularly to Maryland with its policy of toleration for all Christian beliefs. The expanding and vibrant religious community in which Betty Denwood grew up reflected this migration.

At the same time, the growth of thriving congregations of nonconformists highlighted the difficulties Anglicans experienced, particularly in Maryland, where the church received no public financial support. For thousands of Chesapeake residents who desired Anglican worship, lack of clergy and weak institutional support characterized seventeenth-century religious life.

Anglicans constituted a majority of the non-Indian population, but they struggled to maintain churches and parishes even as dissenting congregations formed in both colonies. Attracting suitable ministers posed a perennial problem for Virginia's Anglican churches, despite being the colony's established church. In the early 1660s, when about twenty-five thousand English settlers lived in Virginia parishes, no more than a dozen ministers worked among them. By the end of the century, when population exceeded sixty thousand, fewer than half of the fifty parishes had resident clergymen. For immigrants arriving from England, where rhythms of worship shaped and structured community life, the precarious state of the Church of England was a source of distress, particularly in comparison with the growing presence of dissenting congregations.

English authorities and colonists, who worried that without adequate clergy Virginia's settlers were "grow[ing] wilde in that Wildernesse," found even more cause for alarm in Maryland, where Lord Baltimore had carefully refrained from establishing any denomination as a state-supported church.[11] In doing so, he put Anglicans on equal footing with Roman Catholics, Quakers, Puritans, and a variety of other nonconforming Protestants. Each group could organize itself for worship, but none received government support. Catholics and non-Anglican Protestants embraced their freedom to build churches and communities, activities they were accustomed to pursue without public assistance. Immigrant Anglicans, who had worshipped within a church supported by public funds and public policy, found the burden of creating a religious community unfamiliar and unwelcome. Erecting church buildings proved relatively easy, with as many as fifteen or twenty constructed during midcentury, but as in Virginia the challenge lay in attracting and retaining clergymen. Only sixteen Anglican ministers resided in Maryland before the century's end, and never more than three or four at any one time. Without financing from government taxes, Anglican congregations could not guarantee any significant salary to their ministers, who likely would have to purchase land and grow tobacco for support. In both colonies the dispersed pattern of settlement provided an additional disincentive, obliging clergymen to travel constantly to tend their far-flung parishioners. As Mary Taney of Calvert County advised the archbishop of Canterbury in 1683, without more churches in convenient locations, a minister would "ride 10 miles in a morning & before he can dine 10 more and from house to house in hot wether [which] will disharten a minester if not kill him."[12]

In contrast to Anglicans, dissenting Protestants customarily supported themselves in adverse circumstances and traveled long distances for their faith. Quakers, for example, not only endured intense persecution in England but also expected members to travel extensively to proselytize. Founded in England at midcentury, members of the Society of Friends held that all individuals, male and female, could commune with God directly by drawing upon the innate spark of divinity, or inner light, that each person possessed, without ministers or priests as intermediaries. Quaker theology thus threatened both church elders and government officials in England's hierarchical society, for the logic of Quakerism argued that any man or woman could wield authority and influence through this individual connection with God. Female missionaries, who preached throughout England, Europe, and the colonies, were an expression of Quaker beliefs that appalled members of traditional churches, while refusal to swear oaths, serve in militias, or signal deference to authority by removing hats in court provoked widespread distrust.

Quaker missionaries made numerous visits to both colonies and found a ready audience among settlers who lacked churches and clergy to tend their spiritual needs. The Quaker message that divine truth could be found through individual reflection and without reliance on a trained ministry appealed to colonists struggling with the absence of community worship. Marylanders responding to Quaker missionary efforts included a significant number of the dissenting Protestants who had settled in Anne Arundel County in the early 1650s. At least five and perhaps as many as eleven of the men serving on the Protestant Council became Quakers. Their prominent participation in a government opposing the proprietor likely contributed to a brief period of harassment after the Calverts regained power in 1658, when legislation ordered that "vagabonds & Idle persons knowne by the name of Quakers. . . . be apprehended & whipped from Constable to Constable untill they shall be sent out of the Province."[13] Lord Baltimore found Quakers' refusal to take oaths of allegiance particularly unacceptable during a time of political instability, but as proprietary control became more secure, policy shifted significantly. The confirmation of freedom of worship for Christians laid out in the "Act concerning Religion" clearly extended to Quakers, whose theology derived from Christ's teaching. The refusal to swear oaths continued to be a problem, but political considerations prompted the Calverts to be accommodating in the 1660s, when Virginia's expansion posed a greater threat.

By 1660, Virginia colonists had begun pushing their Eastern Shore settlements farther north. With good cause, Lord Baltimore and his council suspected a new effort to encroach upon territory granted by his charter. In a move calculated to secure the peninsula, Maryland governors once again welcomed dissenting Protestants who suffered persecution in Virginia. Those accepting Maryland's invitation included Betty Denwood's father and uncle, and migrants like the Denwoods formed the nucleus of initial settlement on Maryland's lower Eastern Shore. Other Quakers forced out of Virginia relocated farther north in Talbot County and across the bay in Anne Arundel and Baltimore counties.

Diversity of religious faith increased late in the 1660s when a handful of Presbyterians settled on Maryland's lower western shore. Matthew Hill, a minister ejected from the Anglican Church for nonconformist beliefs, reported to his patron in London that Presbyterians who lived along the Patuxent River ("where the people and the plantations are thickest") enjoyed "a great deal of freedom" and recommended that church elders sponsor "itinerary preachers" to proselytize.[14] Additional Scottish and Irish Presbyterians settled on the Eastern Shore in the 1670s in sufficient numbers that an Anglican magistrate, William Stevens, petitioned the Presbytery of Laggan in Ireland to send a minister for their benefit. In response, Francis Makemie, widely regarded as the founder of organized Presbyterianism in North America, arrived in Somerset County, Maryland, in 1683. Additional Presbyterian ministers followed and assisted in establishing three congregations in that county alone. Makemie used Somerset as a base for missionary work throughout the North American colonies before purchasing a plantation in Accomack County, Virginia, where he lived until his death in 1708.

Other dissenting Protestants included a number of Puritan groups scattered throughout the region, as well as a few small sects like the Labadists, followers of French cleric Jean de Labadie, who established a commune in northern Maryland in the 1680s. The presence of these nonconformist Protestant congregations offered a variety of alternative spiritual homes for English colonists who were neither Roman Catholic nor Anglican. Maryland records also document the presence of a few Jewish immigrants, like the physician Jacob Lumbrozo of the Netherlands, but neither colony attracted Jewish communities as sizeable as those found in colonial cities like New York, Philadelphia, and Newport, Rhode Island.

Other non-Christian beliefs also endured in the Chesapeake region. Although Native American groups occasionally absorbed Christian teachings into their pantheistic cosmology, very few Indians fully converted to a Christian faith. Traditional religious practices of Native Americans persisted throughout tidewater and Piedmont areas. The growing population of enslaved Africans added another layer of religious diversity. Slavers brought cargoes drawn primarily from Africa's western coast, from the Senegambia region down to Angola, an area that encompassed a wide variety of religious belief systems. Some of the populations were monotheistic, including both Muslims (particularly in the Senegambia region) and Roman Catholics (in Portugal's colony of Angola), but others shared a pantheistic cosmology. For many West Africans brought to the Chesapeake colonies, spirits exercised power associated with specific places or objects within the natural world. Particular places could be made holy by events that associated them with gods who once lived there; items collected from such places gave power to charms. Individuals could also call upon clan ancestors to invoke their spirit power for aid or protection. Aspects of these West African belief systems endured in the Chesapeake region, surviving alongside persistent elements of European popular culture that similarly invoked the supernatural through magic and worship of pre-Christian deities.

The religious and spiritual practices of the region's inhabitants affected attitudes toward work, time, family ties and obligations, man's place in the natural world, expectations of an afterlife, and many other aspects of individual and communal values. At the same time, the presence of these overlapping and frequently incompatible spiritual belief systems contributed to the seventeenth century's cultural and political battles, either as an explicit cause of conflict (as in Maryland's Catholic-Protestant struggles) or as a secondary source of discontent bound up in broader disputes over governance.

REBELLION

During the late seventeenth century, settlers in both Chesapeake colonies experienced periods of upheaval that brought provincial government to a standstill. In Virginia, Bacon's Rebellion in 1676 escalated from a disagreement over Indian policy to an uprising of planters and servants that compelled Governor Berkeley to flee Jamestown for several months. In Maryland, a series of events generally known as the Protestant Revolution forced the Calverts to surrender the colony's government to the English Crown for more than two decades. In both cases, struggles over authority and public policy resulted in relatively little loss of English life or property, but had disastrous consequences for some Native American groups.

Deteriorating relationships with Native Americans along the upper reaches of Virginia's rivers in the early 1670s provided the spark that triggered Bacon's Rebellion. The spark flared into armed conflict between groups of colonists on this occasion because it fed on resentments and rivalries that had festered over nearly two decades. Population growth and continual movement of settlers west and north seeking new tobacco land not only brought Virginians into conflict with Indians but also fostered political instability. County formation did not keep pace with increased numbers, leaving a limited supply of political offices for ambitious men in frontier areas. Moreover, officials too often viewed their positions as opportunities for personal gain, not as places of trust to be used for the common good. Because few men could claim a right to rule based on inherited status, insecurity bred infighting and jousting for position. Concerns of small planters struggling to support families, tenants hard-pressed to pay rent and taxes, and indentured servants facing an uncertain future took second place, if they registered at all, to the needs of elite officeholders.

Economic troubles exacerbated these problems. During the second and third Anglo-Dutch wars, raiders attacked Virginia in June 1667 and again in March 1673, burning tobacco ships each time despite an expensive fort built at the mouth of the James

River. The Navigation Acts placed imperial concerns for regulating trade ahead of colonial desires for unfettered shipping and direct access to foreign markets. Forced to send all tobacco to England, planters often found markets saturated and prices too low. Governor Berkeley's ambitious plans to diversify the economy beyond tobacco raised taxes but produced no results. Further complicating the struggle to earn a living, from the mid-1660s to the early 1670s planters experienced a series of violent hurricanes, extensive droughts, destructive early spring storms, and epidemic diseases that posed continual threats to their economic and physical survival.

For years, English settlers and Native Americans in frontier areas had engaged in sporadic episodes of raids and counterattacks. Relations were unstable in part because English officials in Jamestown and St. Mary's City did not fully grasp the migrations and diplomatic alliances that pressured Native Americans in this period. In particular, Maryland officials valued an alliance negotiated with the Susquehannock in 1652 because it removed the threat of attack if settlers took up territory on the colony's Eastern Shore. They did not comprehend the chain reaction that followed. Native American groups inhabiting territory upriver along the Potomac did not have diplomatic or trade relationships with the Susquehannock, but the peaceful relations they enjoyed with the Maryland government associated them with the Susquehannock, Maryland's new allies. At the same time, the Maryland-Susquehannock alliance freed the latter group to wage war against their traditional enemies among the Five Nations. The chain of alliances now effectively made the Piscataway and other groups enemies of the Five Nations.

In the 1660s, raiding parties from the north began to penetrate the territory of the Susquehannock and their presumptive allies. Reports filtered back to government officials of attacks by Seneca and Iroquois warriors along the frontier of each colony, threatening both settlers and native groups. In 1674, as the conflict between the Five Nations and Susquehannock turned against the latter group, Governor Calvert invited the Susquehannock to take refuge in Maryland, where they settled at a fortified town on Piscataway Creek in Charles County. Calvert's invitation provoked hostility not only from frontier planters but also from

Piscataway, Mattawoman, Nacotchtank, and Pamunkey groups who did not welcome the Susquehannock as neighbors. In these unsettled conditions, colonists, observing escalating violence among Native Americans in addition to the incidents of Indian-English hostility that were common along the frontier, feared that worse was to come.

In July 1675, a party of Doeg and Susquehannock crossed from Maryland to Virginia and appropriated some hogs to settle accounts with Thomas Mathews, a Stafford County planter, precipitating a series of raids and counterattacks back and forth across the Potomac River. The escalation of hostility continued during the summer and fall and into the early months of 1676, particularly after a joint colonial force besieged the Susquehannock's fortified town in September and then murdered five Indian leaders who came out to parley during a period of truce. Numerous attacks along the fringes of colonial settlement melded with news of similar unrest in New England colonies to raise fears of a widespread, coordinated Native American effort to destroy English settlements up and down the eastern seaboard. Nathaniel Bacon, a recent arrival in Virginia, member of the Council of State, and kinsman of Governor Berkeley's wife, described frontier settlers' anxiety as "the feare of Generall Combination."[15]

Although initially drawn into the fighting by the Doeg and Susquehannock raid, Lord Baltimore's settlers had not yet spread far enough westward to create chronic conflict with neighboring Indians and therefore remained on the fringe of subsequent warfare associated with Bacon's Rebellion. Along the more-settled Virginia frontier, however, panic approached the level of hysteria and settlers increasingly pressured Berkeley for authority to move decisively against Native Americans. Frontier residents lobbied not only for military action against groups participating in raids on settlers but also measures against tributary Indians, the remnants of the Powhatan confederacy who lived in reserved territory scattered among Virginia's counties.

Berkeley withheld this authority and instead persuaded the assembly to sanction only banning weapons sales to tributary Indians, restricting other Indian trade to a handful of licensed colonists, and building a series of forts, a measure that meant new taxes. The assembly deferred to the governor on these issues, not least because some of them would greatly benefit from trading licenses and as land speculators in areas designated for forts. But in outlying counties, where Native American attacks were taking the greatest toll, and among small planters throughout Virginia who could ill afford new taxes, Berkeley's plans provoked outrage. According to English officials, small planters felt that "the erecting of [forts] was a great Grievance, Juggle and cheat [and] meerly a designe of the Grandees to engrosse all [the planters'] Tobacco into their owne hands."[16]

Restless men gathered in April 1676 along the James River's upper reaches to express enthusiasm for an expedition against Indians. The group had plenty of volunteers and weapons but lacked a leader with status until Nathaniel Bacon, who came to investigate the gathering, took charge. Over the next six months, the situation remained volatile as Berkeley and Bacon challenged one another for control. Bacon demanded permission to lead his men against any and all Indian groups, but Berkeley advocated caution with respect to the colony's allies and resented Bacon's efforts to seize authority. Berkeley suspended Bacon from the council, declared him a rebel, captured him, then pardoned and reinstated him to the council. Berkeley fled to the Eastern Shore for a time, returned to Jamestown, and fled again, while Bacon took an armed force to Jamestown on three occasions and burned the capital on his last visit in September.

While awaiting Berkeley's response to Jamestown's destruction, Bacon began to lose control of his followers. Drawn away from their primary goal of reducing the threat of Indian attacks and kept idle while Bacon pondered his options, many seized the opportunity to plunder both Native American villages and estates of planters who declined to endorse their rebellion against the governor. In October 1676, when Bacon died after suffering a "Bloody flux" and "a Lousey Disease," many erstwhile rebels quietly returned to their homesteads, hoping a low profile would spare them retribution.[17] The timely appearance of tobacco merchants' ships, conveniently armed with cannon for their own protection, enabled Berkeley to commandeer their firepower to defeat the remaining rebels. In January 1677, a squadron of British vessels and troops arrived to quell the rebellion, inquire into its causes, and dispatch the governor back to England to account for the colony's disarray. The commissioners responsible for

Sir William Berkeley (1605–1677). Virginia's longest-serving governor, Berkeley held office from 1641 to 1652 and from 1660 to 1677. Wearing military dress of the early 1660s, he holds a baton of office in his right hand. By Sir Peter Lely, c. 1662. With grateful thanks to the Berkeley Castle Charitable Trust, Berkeley Castle, Gloucestershire

these tasks found the rebels sufficiently quelled: many had been executed, and Berkeley had encouraged his supporters to plunder estates of leaders and followers alike.

At first glance, Bacon's Rebellion appears to have collapsed without achieving much in the way of discernable goals; indeed, goals were in short supply apart from the fervent wish to annihilate Native Americans. Bacon issued two statements that presented his dubious justification for the uprising—primarily, his argument that action was necessary to protect the king's loyal subjects not only from Indians ("tho[se] barborous Outlawes") but also from Berkeley's cronies ("unworthy Favourites and juggling Parasites").[18] Other than listing grievances and demanding that Berkeley and his supporters surrender, however, Bacon's manifestos did not advocate any reform program or promote any change in governmental structure. It is unlikely that corruption had motivated Bacon except insofar as he had been denied a share of the spoils, but the English commissioners found considerable evidence that Berkeley permitted councilors and burgesses to advance their own interests in ways that burdened small planters with excessive taxes and fees. The governor was removed from office and sent back to England. But little substantive change followed; various reforms were proposed and some measures enacted, but they were either disallowed or ineffective.

In the period after the rebellion, Virginia's great planters—many of whom lost considerable property during the turmoil—became wary of unleashing the anger of the lesser sorts, but their main challenge came from England. Officials in London concluded that Virginia's governor and assembly had been granted too much freedom for too long, a conclusion that squared neatly with recent interest in developing more coherent governance for all of England's colonies. The king and his ministers wanted to maximize the economic benefit of colonial enterprises. They certainly did not want civil war in Virginia to disrupt the tobacco economy, which generated a significant share of royal revenue. Governors who succeeded Berkeley were chosen to promote the Crown's interests, setting the stage for decades of struggle between the Virginia General Assembly and England's government.

Native Americans experienced the greatest change during the rebellion and its aftermath. Panic over the threat of a pan-Indian uprising against all English colonies (coupled with a large dose of desire to appropriate Native American homelands) overruled the distinction Berkeley and his predecessors had drawn between Native American groups that threatened colonists and those "as are amongst us in peace."[19] By the fall of 1676, colonists who were unable or unwilling to distinguish between friends and enemies had inflicted heavy losses on numerous native villages throughout the region. In the years following the rebellion, English authorities tried to establish diplomatic alliances with Native Americans in the Piedmont area to guard against further incursions from northern Indians. In addition, the royal commissioners renegotiated the colony's relationship with Indians remaining in the tidewater region. The Treaty of Middle Plantation, signed in 1677 and expanded in 1680, clarified the status of signatory tribes as subjects of the English king. Although the treaty agreements contained measures to protect territory for Native Americans, the provisions also limited Indian travel and trade in ways that demonstrated the enduring inability of English settlement to coexist with Indian patterns of land use. The resulting loss of sovereignty and continued disruption of traditional economies played into a significant reconfiguration of Native American alliances and the migration of several key groups, especially the Susquehannock, who abandoned the Potomac River valley, moved north to their traditional homeland, and allied with the Five Nations.

Bacon's Rebellion has loomed large in the history of Virginia and the English colonies, spawning a considerable quantity of scholarship and a wide variety of interpretations. Scholars generally agree that the rebellion proved to be a pivotal event in colonial history, but disagree about its larger significance. Interpretations range from those stressing personal conflict between Berkeley and Bacon to those highlighting the event as a spontaneous uprising of small planters too long oppressed by a corrupt elite. Others place the rebellion within a larger history of backcountry vigilante movements or stress elements that foreshadowed the American Revolution. Among the most influential analyses are those emphasizing the current of racial hatred running through Bacon's justification for attacks on Indians and evidence that Virginia's elite responded to small planters' unrest by promoting racial solidarity among whites to mask growing disparity in economic status. The variety of interpretations and vigor of scholarly discussion surrounding them reflect the disorder of the event itself. Bacon's Rebellion provides scope for debate because so many different threads of colonial history—relations with Native Americans, divergent interests of tidewater and frontier areas, tensions between small planters and the governing elite, and conflict within the governing elite over political control to further personal enrichment—became intertwined during the summer of 1676.

REVOLUTION

Unrest in Virginia exposed differences in outlook between elite men who governed from Jamestown and small landholders and former servants along the frontier who rallied to protest Indian policy and administrative practices. A similar fissure occurred in Maryland, roughly a decade later—this one along fault lines of religion as well as status. In Virginia, the name Bacon's Rebellion gives primary cause to the actions of a single individual and identifies the outcome as a disruption of government, but not an overthrowing of one regime in favor of another. In Maryland, by contrast, events of the late 1680s are generally called the Protestant Revolution, highlighting both the collective nature of the uprising and its political success in removing Catholics from the colony's government.

As in Virginia, many sources of Maryland's unrest had deep roots. Hostility toward powerful Roman Catholics expressed during the plundering time in the 1640s continued to fester even after Lord Baltimore's authority was reconfirmed in the late 1650s. On several occasions, Protestant men who achieved economic success in Maryland but failed to obtain high political or military offices tried to incite rebellion against the proprietor and the small circle of his friends and relatives who reserved lucrative and powerful positions for themselves. When Cecilius Calvert died in 1675, his son Charles inherited the proprietorship. Unlike his father, Charles lacked the ability to navigate successfully between threats to his charter in England and threats to his authority in Maryland, being both less sensitive to Protestant fears and antipathies and a much poorer judge of character when making critical appointments. An influx of Anglicans who migrated to the colony in the 1680s combined virulent anti-Catholicism with demands for the state-supported church that Maryland notably lacked, exacerbating the situation.

A series of acrimonious sessions of the province's General Assembly marked the 1670s. Attacks by the Seneca, pursuing Susquehannock enemies who had sought refuge on Maryland's Potomac shore, raised contentious questions about whether settlers or the proprietor would bear the expense of defending outlying households. Delegates and Lord Baltimore also fought over measures to improve the tobacco trade. Declines in tobacco prices adversely affected planters in both colonies, making effective action appear to depend on intercolonial cooperation to limit production. Virginia's Governor Berkeley sought Maryland's agreement on a stint, or one-year moratorium on growing tobacco. After considerable negotiation, including a visit by Berkeley to St. Mary's City, both colonies passed stint legislation in 1666—only to have Lord Baltimore veto Maryland's law. Lord Baltimore and the lower house also argued over the conflict between proprietary authority, on the one hand, and English law, on the other. Delegates tried to invoke English law as a check on the proprietor's power, particularly after Cecilius placed property qualifications on voting in 1670 and Charles reduced each county's delegation from four to two in 1676.

Underlying all of these issues lurked a persistent concern that the extensive powers exercised by Lord Baltimore and his largely Catholic council undermined traditional English rights and liberties. Virginia's assembly had expanded its powers during the civil war period, but Maryland's lower house had not been similarly successful. The preoccupied and fractured English government had essentially left provincial and local affairs in the hands of the Virginia elite for the better part of two decades, fostering the assembly's evolution from an advisory council into a bicameral body reserving broad legislative powers for itself. In Maryland, however, Lord Baltimore's attentive oversight of colonial affairs limited development of the lower house as a self-governing institution. In particular, the proprietor's unrestricted authority to veto legislation greatly weakened delegates' power. His unwillingness to grant an explicit provision transferring all applicable English laws and customs to the colony also limited legal safeguards in the courts (where, significantly, there was no channel for appeal to courts in England).

Complaints by leading Protestants that the proprietor reserved all important provincial offices for a small circle of Roman Catholics and relatives surfaced again early in the 1680s, when six of the eleven men appointed to the council were Catholic and two of the Protestants were married to Lord Baltimore's Catholic stepdaughters. To compound the problem, council members frequently held plural appointments to many of the most important positions, controlling the land office, militia leadership, and the provincial court. Protestants noted with unease that three council appointments in 1683 and a fourth in 1685 all went to Catholics related to the proprietor. At the time, the colony's population numbered about twenty thousand; the small minority of no more than three thousand Catholics thus exercised political power quite out of balance with its size. Lord Baltimore's goal may have been to solidify upper house support at a time of challenges to his prerogative power, but Protestants who felt excluded from prestigious and lucrative offices saw the proprietor's choices as ominous. At best, they felt that Catholics held more power than was reasonable; at worst, they contended that Catholics conspired to deprive Protestants of their rights and liberties.

Charles Calvert, the third Lord Baltimore, was the first proprietor to live in the colony, but in 1684 he sailed to England to defend Maryland's boundaries against New York (which claimed former Dutch settlements on the upper Eastern Shore) and Pennsylvania (which claimed territory that lay within the borders of the Maryland grant). Lord Baltimore commissioned council members as deputy governors and awarded the post of acting chief executive to his Catholic cousin, George Talbot. Colonists, already suspicious of the predominantly Catholic council, were scandalized just months later when Talbot murdered Christopher Rousby, a royal customs collector, during a quarrel. Talbot escaped from custody and fled to Virginia. The council's failure to bring Talbot to justice and other acts of maladministration further eroded public trust.

In 1688, Lord Baltimore tried to rectify the situation by sending a new council president, but his choice of William Joseph proved to be a grave error. Not only Roman Catholic but also outspoken and authoritarian, Joseph quickly alienated assembly delegates when he railed against them for their sins and lack of allegiance to the king, James II, who had succeeded his brother Charles II in 1685.

In the aftermath of Joseph's intemperate behavior, rumors began to reach Maryland about renewed political and religious conflict in England. Partly in response to this news, the active members of the council (all Catholics) issued an order to call in for repair all weapons distributed to local militias. The location of provincial arms and ammunition had long been a bone of contention, with the council advocating a central magazine to keep weapons in better repair and the assembly arguing that they should remain in the counties in case of Native American attacks or other alarms. Now the council required militias to deliver their arms to St. Mary's City, citing the need to ready the province in "a posture of defence against the Enemies of our King and Country."[20] But because the English king and the Maryland council were both Catholic, many saw the council's order as a pretext for disarming non-Catholics. Sporadic raiding by northern Indians still threatened outlying settlements, and the recall fit easily into pervasive fears that English Catholics were conspiring with the Five Nations and French colonists in Canada to destroy Maryland Protestants.

In the midst of this turmoil, events in England precipitated a new challenge to Maryland's stability. As in the 1640s, the English crisis reverberated so strongly because it revolved around the constant Catholic-Protestant conflict. That an openly Roman Catholic individual, James II, had succeeded to the English throne despite Parliament's efforts to limit the English monarchy to Protestants was bad enough. When his second wife gave birth in 1688 to a male heir who took precedence over the Protestant daughters of James II's first marriage, the prospect of a lengthy succession of Catholic rulers precipitated revolution. After complex negotiations, James's eldest daughter, Mary, and her husband William, stadtholder of the Dutch provinces (and a grandson of Charles I), accepted the English throne as joint monarchs. In November 1688, William, fully supported by Dutch warships and regiments, took command in England without resistance, while James II fled to France. Maryland's Protestants greeted this news with relief and anticipated orders from Lord Baltimore that would officially recognize William and Mary as sovereigns of England. But the proprietor's messenger died before sailing and duplicate orders, if they existed, never arrived. Already suspicious of their proprietor's motives and allegiances, some among Maryland's Protestants put the worst possible interpretation on the delay.

In the spring of 1689, another round of rumors that Native Americans were gathering in large numbers along the frontier coincided with the council's decision to postpone calling an assembly session. Neighboring colonies had proclaimed the new king and queen, but still no word arrived from Lord Baltimore. In the absence of council action, John Coode, an outspoken Protestant critic of the government, took matters into his own hands, with support from a number of influential men who shared his objections to Catholic rule and fear of an imminent Iroquoian attack. Gathering together weapons and men, Coode advanced toward St. Mary's City. In an action reminiscent of Bacon's effort a decade earlier in Virginia, Coode and seven fellow Protestants issued a statement to clarify their purpose. They emphasized their earnest wish to proclaim their loyalty to the new king and queen and outlined their dread of a Catholic-French-Indian conspiracy. Unable to muster enough support to counter Coode's growing army, the council abandoned St. Mary's City in July 1689. Council members regrouped to the north at Mattapany with supporters of the proprietary government, but were quickly outnumbered and besieged by Coode's forces. To avoid bloodshed and destruction of property, the council agreed to articles of surrender.

Having successfully routed the despised Catholic council, Coode and his allies (a group subsequently known as the Associators) were left with no clear purpose or path. After sending the proclamation of allegiance to England's new monarchs, many Protestants were willing to wait for a royal response before taking further steps. In mid-August, however, the Associators issued a call for election of a provincial assembly. Although a number of prominent Protestants protested that Coode and the Associators had no authority to do so, the Associators' Convention met for fourteen days to consider management of the colony's affairs. The convention clarified that non-Catholics should continue in office, issued petitions to the Crown seeking approval of their seizure of power and requesting a Protestant government, and assigned committees to set taxes and investigate rumors of Native American–Catholic conspiracies. Not surprisingly, the latter committee promptly asserted that the leaders Coode characterized as Maryland's "late popish Gov[ernou]rs" had endeavored "to betray their Majestie's Protestant Subjects of this Province to the French, Northern and other Indians."[21] As the existence of a plot was the uprising's rationale, any determination that no plot existed would have recast the Associators' actions as treasonous.

For several months, the government remained in limbo, with Coode taking on a self-appointed role as commander-in-chief.

County courts continued to meet with a reasonable facsimile of normalcy to consider routine business and activities. In January, another murder of a royal customs collector by Catholics bolstered support for the Associators but also exposed the weakness of their position. When the men responsible fled to Virginia, Coode's repeated requests for their return were coolly denied by Francis Nicholson, Virginia's newly arrived governor. But Nicholson did forward to Maryland the long-awaited response from England's new rulers. Protestant supporters were relieved to learn that the monarchs requested the Associators to continue administering the colony's government pending a review of Lord Baltimore's charter. The royal orders did specify that the proprietor should receive land rents and his share of customs revenue, but in all other respects his authority was, for the moment, suspended. For the next two years, the Associators oversaw a scaled-down provincial government, with assemblies that met twice a year and a committee to oversee executive functions. Throughout this period, the general stability of political life testifies to the evolution of the county court system and the leadership of elite men able to command respect in local communities despite the ambiguous position of the provincial government.

Although the change to Protestant rule was not official until appointment of a royal governor in the summer of 1691, in essence the die was cast as soon as William and Mary indicated that they would not regard the actions of Coode and the Associators as a treasonous rebellion. Over the objections of Lord Baltimore, the Crown and the Privy Council decreed that authority in Maryland would descend solely from the monarchs to the governor. Lord Baltimore continued to own the colony's land and remained entitled to quitrents and customs, but all political powers and authority were withdrawn. For all practical purposes, Maryland became a royal colony.

The shift in governance had significant repercussions for the region's Native Americans. Charged with the dual task of extending royal control over the North American seaboard and increasing royal revenues generated by export duties on tobacco and other commodities, governors sent to both Chesapeake colonies supported efforts to expand English settlements with little regard for Indian sovereignty. Recognizing that the Algonquian groups that persisted in their tidewater and Piedmont homelands had been greatly weakened by decades of conflict with Iroquoian and Siouan enemies, colonial governors became increasingly heavy-handed in diplomatic negotiations. The shift in attitude contributed to a new phase of Native American migration and realignment. In 1697, for example, the Piscataway responded to unfavorable negotiations with Francis Nicholson, now serving as Maryland's governor, by relocating across the Potomac River to territory on the northern edge of Virginia settlements. When relations with their new neighbors quickly soured (in part because Nicholson became Virginia's governor in 1698), the Piscataway sought alliances with William Penn, Pennsylvania's proprietor, and the numerous Native American groups who lived within his colony. Willing to yield a measure of sovereignty in exchange for new homelands, the Piscataway migrated north to the Susquehanna River, where they identified themselves as the Conoy and entered into peaceful association with their former enemies, the Susquehannock (now known as the Conestoga) and the Five Nations.

For Maryland colonists, however, transition to royal control brought little change to daily life. The rights of freeholders to elect an assembly, the assembly's role in crafting legislation, the county court system, and general outlines of provincial administration all persisted. In two essentials, however, the royal period marks significant change. First, with royal government came the long-desired establishment of the Church of England. The first royal assembly in 1692 passed an act mandating financial support and dividing the province into Anglican parishes. Physical construction of churches and successful recruitment of clergymen took time to achieve, but vestries formed in all parishes during the 1690s. Second, royal government removed Roman Catholics from any significant role in Maryland politics. In keeping with English practice and law, officeholding required taking an oath of supremacy (acknowledging the king as head of the church), effectively barring Catholics from any public office and jury duty (although they could still vote). After sixty years of struggle, Maryland's existence as a land where Roman Catholics could openly practice both religion and politics came to an end.

As the seventeenth century drew to a close, new migrants to England's Chesapeake colonies, like George Gale, entered a tidewater landscape dramatically transformed from the one first encountered by Jamestown's founders. Although tobacco fields, worm fences, and Virginia houses appeared untidy and ramshackle to English eyes, they nevertheless marked the boundaries of settlement, distinguishing colonial areas from native ones in unmistakable ways. The transformations of the late seventeenth century included intangible changes as well, with emergence of native-born families like the Denwoods, the flourishing of local governance in county courts and provincial assemblies, and accumulation of capital in the form of plantations and laborers. Successfully planted by the 1630s and nurtured through the political and religious tempests of midcentury, England's Chesapeake colonies found their footing in the 1680s and 1690s, as significant population growth and steady dispossession of Native Americans decisively shifted the demographic equation. At the brink of the new century, Virginia and Maryland finally had the pieces in place—a degree of political maturity, a more stable social order, and a multifaceted economy with a reliable source of workers—to anticipate a future of expansion and prosperity.

FOUR

Coming Together, Moving Apart

A YOUNG ENGLISHMAN named Robert Peake arrived in Maryland sometime in the 1640s or 1650s, most likely as an indentured servant to planter John Hall of Anne Arundel County. When Hall died in 1660, his assets included a debt owed by Peake, now a free man. Hall also left a widow, Mary Parker Hall, and a young son, John Jr.; within a year, Robert Peake had married Mary Hall, become stepfather to her son John, and assumed administration of Hall's estate. Peake prospered for a time, but falling tobacco prices during the 1670s plunged him into debt. At his death in 1681, Peake held only a modest tract of land and had scant personal property to leave to his only child, a five-year-old boy named Aquila. After Robert's death, John Hall Jr. moved himself, his half brother Aquila, and their mother north up the bay to land he purchased in Baltimore County. Along the frontier of settlement, a talented individual might prosper, even if starting with few tangible goods. Such proved to be the case with Aquila Paca (as his surname was now written), who came of age in 1697. Through planting and mercantile activity over the next two decades, Paca accumulated fifty-four hundred acres of land and £4,800 in personal goods, including four indentured servants and forty-two slaves. When he died in 1721, his six surviving children shared the estate that had made Aquila Paca one of the wealthiest men in the area.

John Carter, another Englishman, was born in London, emigrated as a free man, and settled in Virginia in the late 1630s. The father of six children by five wives, when he died in 1669 Carter was survived by a daughter and three sons. John, the eldest son, and Elizabeth were adults when their father died, but Robert, son of Carter's fourth wife, was only about six years old and, like Aquila Paca, was raised by his half brother. As the eldest son, John Carter Jr. inherited nearly all of his father's extensive landholdings and much of the moveable property; Robert received one thousand acres of land and a share of the personal estate. But because John Jr. left no male heirs when he died in 1690, Robert inherited the much larger estate that had originally passed from his father to his elder brother. With this fortuitous legacy and an advantageous marriage of his own, Robert began the career that eventually led him to be known as "King" Carter. When Carter died in 1732, his five sons and five daughters, surviving children of two marriages, shared his vast estate, which reportedly exceeded three hundred thousand acres of land and one thousand slaves.

No contemporary matched Robert Carter's success as a tobacco planter, but several circumstances of his life paralleled those of Aquila Paca. Each man was the son of an immigrant, had few or no full siblings, lost his father while still a child, was raised by an older sibling with whom he shared only one parent, and inherited a relatively modest estate. Each of these native-born men married women who were also native-born and raised much larger families of their own. Through these births, deaths, and marriages, the lives of Carter and Paca capture the experiences of many individuals who came of age in the late seventeenth and early eighteenth centuries. Together Carter and Paca illustrate the key demographic shift of the colonial period, from an immigrant society to one dominated by the native born, also known as creoles.

The transition to a native-born majority occurred first among white settlers but became evident among enslaved workers as well after importation rates began to decline. In both populations, creole women tended to be healthier and longer-lived than immigrants and to begin childbearing at younger ages, contributing to exponential growth with each succeeding generation. Accelerated population growth generated opportunities for economic diversification at the same time that it created pressures for geographic expansion. As settlement became denser in older

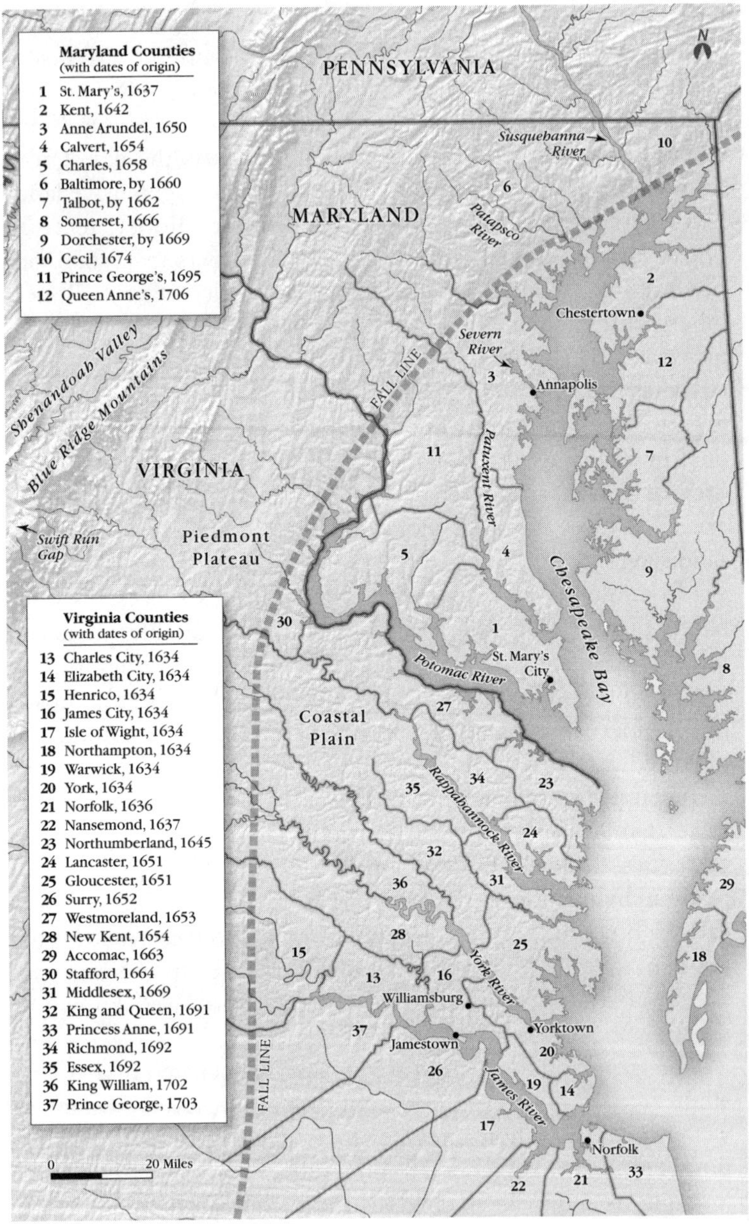

The Chesapeake region, c. 1715, with colonial county locations and dates of origin to illustrate expansion of settlement. Map by Robert Cronan, Lucidity Information Design, LLC

areas, demand increased for locally produced merchandise and foodstuffs as well as for a wide range of imported goods, from basic tools marketed by resident merchant-planters to exotic cloths and spices traded by factors, the local representatives of British merchants.

But increased population also created competition for resources, especially land, and fueled efforts to extend settlement into the Piedmont area and on toward the Appalachian valleys. Geographic expansion perpetuated conflict with Native Americans, who continued to pursue varied survival strategies, such as accepting settlement on reserved lands, relocating to join Indian allies in other colonies, or withdrawing to the fringes of white settlement. Natural increase among enslaved workers, which was economically beneficial to planters, had mixed consequences for Africans and African Americans. An expanding population fostered opportunities to form families and communities, but larger labor forces also enabled planters to transfer slaves from tidewater plantations to new quarters on Piedmont land, often forcibly separating individuals from familiar environments and kin. As discussed in chapter 5, the Chesapeake region's black population experienced complex cultural changes during the eighteenth century.

This chapter focuses on the white colonists in Virginia and Maryland, and for them, too, the consequences of demographic change and population growth were mixed. On the one hand, the presence of a predominantly native-born population encouraged political and social stability. When native-born fathers and mothers lived long enough to raise sons and daughters to maturity, those children had significantly better odds of entering adulthood with enough property to form new households. Sons also gained training and experience to prepare them for their roles in colonial civic life. On the other hand, transfers of wealth and power through established families limited opportunities for newcomers. During the seventeenth century, strategic marriages had linked freed servants like Robert Peake with propertied widows like Mary Hall, and free immigrants like George Gale with established families like the Denwoods. But native-born sons and daughters were increasingly likely to marry each other rather than newly arrived immigrants or freed servants. Marriages among the native-born gradually wove complex kinship networks that solidified status for those within the network but created barriers to advancement for those outside.

Social and political changes resulting from growth of a native-born white population had a further, paradoxical effect. The majority of Anglo-Americans had no direct experience of life in England, but the colonial elite increasingly looked to London as its model for genteel tastes and behaviors to declare and affirm its affluence. Earlier leaders had often been ambitious to return to the old world with a fortune made in the new, but creole elite men rarely contemplated relocating to England; rather, they wished to improve the society in which they lived, so as to improve their standing in the eyes of their English counterparts. Chesapeake leaders built new capital cities; fostered urban development elsewhere in the region; founded a college and schools; modeled their provincial assemblies more closely on Parliament; and encouraged a vigorous established church. In pursuit of these goals, creole planters often had the support of royal governors seeking to align colonies more closely within the British Empire, itself given shape by the 1707 Act of Union that united England and Scotland as the Kingdom of Great Britain. As colonists drew upon the same cultural sources for refashioning their societies, Virginians and Marylanders moved closer together, creating and sharing an identity as British Americans. But the white population was also moving apart—both physically, with growing geographic distance from the oldest tidewater plantations to the newest settlements at the Piedmont's western edge, and economically, with a diversifying economy and increasing stratification along lines of wealth and status.

A CREOLE SOCIETY

For much of the seventeenth century, Virginia and Maryland were immigrant societies that grew through the continual arrival of laborers like Robert Peake. But as several generations of immigrants and children of immigrants married and reproduced, the Chesapeake region's white population became predominantly native-born. Like Aquila Paca and Robert Carter, members of the first creole generation might lose one or both parents before reaching the age of majority and might be raised by siblings or stepparents, but they had advantages not shared by immigrants. Because the native-born ratio of men to women was more balanced, fewer native-born men had to postpone or forego marriage. Because native-born children did not experience indentured servitude, they could marry at an earlier age. Because they were native-born, creole children did not experience seasoning, and so generally lived longer, healthier lives. As a result, their marriages produced more children: seven for Aquila Paca and his wife, rather than the one surviving child of his parents' marriage; ten for Robert Carter's two marriages in contrast to the four survivors of John Carter's five marriages. At the same time, the general standard of living improved for native-born households. Successive generations of planter families needed to invest less income in establishing plantations, leaving a surplus for improvements in living conditions.

Creation of a creole society brought greater security and comfort for the free white population as a whole, but it came at the price of a society in which wealth and position were more likely to be inherited than achieved, where poor men found fewer opportunities, and where the social structure developed a much clearer hierarchy. Colonies that had offered opportunity for indentured servants increasingly reserved their rewards for individuals who inherited parental property and position. In addition, the gentry became much wealthier relative to the rest of the population. Although there had always been winners in the seventeenth century, the gap between those at the top of free society and those at the bottom had not been insurmountable (witness Aquila Paca) and wealth had been distributed more equitably than it would ever be again.

Rising land prices, triggered by growing population density, contributed to stratification of white society. Older and more settled counties did not have enough unclaimed land for freed servants or younger sons of small planters who were reaching adulthood to establish plantations of their own. Many chose to migrate out of tidewater communities, settling in areas farther from the Chesapeake Bay or moving on to newer colonies, such as Pennsylvania and North Carolina. Others, who elected to remain within the web of connections formed during servitude or childhood, did so by working as overseers for large slaveholders or renting land from owners needing tenants. In Virginia's Surry County, for example, on the south side of the upper James River, 40 percent of householders rented their land. Circumstances were little different in Maryland, where tenants in three counties on the western shore (Prince George's, Charles, and St. Mary's) accounted for nearly one-third of all householders in 1705, a threefold increase in tenancy since 1660.

As another important consequence, development of a creole society fostered the formation of a stable ruling elite. Because creole parents were more likely to survive to see at least some children reach adulthood, both status and wealth could be transferred to the next generation with greater likelihood that children could use their inheritances as the foundation for further advancement. Officeholding, for example, became increasingly restricted to the native-born. An adult son could move into office upon the death of his father, rather than leaving an opening to be filled by a newcomer. When Aquila Paca came of age, circumstances in sparsely settled Baltimore County were sufficiently fluid that he served in the lower house, as sheriff, and as justice of the peace. When the next generation reached maturity, talented newcomers found opportunities to display their merits more severely restricted. Even for an immigrant arriving as a free man, exemplary service as juror or constable rarely led to a seat on the justices' bench.

As population density burgeoned within each county, service in local offices effectively became the right of well-established members of the gentry, whose numbers made it unnecessary to seek capable men beyond their circle. Across the region, a small number of families tended to dominate local officeholding over several generations. Immigrants were never totally excluded from public office, but as a rule those who acquired office, such as George Gale, arrived already favored by connections to the local elite through marriage, kinship, or trade. In addition, some county dynasties cemented their position through marriages across county lines and even provincial boundaries. Members of these extensive Chesapeake-wide kinship networks, chosen for the influence they wielded at the local level, dominated provincial officeholding.

By the early 1710s, Maryland's new ruling elite had formed the intricate network of familial relationships necessary to gather and keep wealth and power in its own hands. In Virginia, where settlement began a generation earlier, the early-eighteenth-century web was even stronger. Wealth became concentrated in the hands of a small group of politically powerful families, made up of current officeholders and descendants of earlier officials. These families owned nearly two-thirds of the estates with two thousand or more acres of land. In the five richest Virginia tobacco counties, located between the James and Rappahannock Rivers, one-quarter of the area's households owned nearly three-quarters of its land. At the head of the York River, in King and Queen County, the wealthiest 10 percent of households owned more than one-half of the county's acreage. Across the longest-settled tidewater areas, the foundations for most of the eighteenth-century's leading families were well-established when the century began.

The native-born could pass more than political power and social connections from one generation to the next. If at least one son were of age when the father died, a family's wealth faced a much smaller risk of loss through mismanagement by greedy or indifferent stepparents or guardians. When an adult son inherited an established plantation, its maintenance required a smaller share of his profits from tobacco and other products than a new plantation consumed. Native-born planters thus could use household income in ways that shaped future development of tidewater society. Families had a variety of choices for disposable income, ranging from immediate, short-term gratification to strategies for ensuring prosperity for subsequent generations.

An increasing availability of consumer goods that enhanced daily comfort and enjoyment of life offered one possibility. Another option prepared sons and daughters for their adult roles. Elite planters hired tutors for their children or sent sons to school overseas, usually in England or, for Catholic children, on the Continent. Middling and small planters could have a child educated by a local schoolmaster or arrange an apprenticeship in a trade or craft. Local opportunities to generate new income offered another choice. A planter whose landholdings included a likely stream, for example, might choose to construct a mill as a new source of household income. In addition, landowning families at all levels might buy land to hold in reserve for the next generation. In their wills, middling planters frequently divided land to leave each heir a viable plantation currently being worked by a tenant. Colonial families generally pursued several strategies, purchasing consumer goods for a more comfortable life and making investments that had long-term benefits for themselves and their heirs.

Most critical for the direction of development, Chesapeake planters with available capital or credit invested in slaves. The higher price of slaves (compared with indentured servants or workers hired for short terms of service) put these lifetime laborers out of reach for many small planters, but for those with land to put into production, credit or capital for the purchase, and connections providing market access, buying enslaved workers was a prudent gamble. That it was a gamble can be seen from the experience of men like Jacob Rice, who kept an ordinary in Middlesex County, Virginia, where neighbors and travelers could obtain food and lodging. Rice purchased an African woman and her infant child in 1720, but both soon died. At the sale of his estate seven years later, Rice's property brought only £39. With no inherited bondspeople and no resources with which to buy any, Rice's son never escaped poverty before his own death in 1763. Had the elder Rice's female slave lived and given birth to more children, Rice might have left his son positioned to make a favorable marriage or use the slaves as collateral for acquiring land.

Middling planters who fared better than Rice were those with slaveholdings large enough to absorb the loss of a worker or two and with enough women and children to provide inheritances for the next generation. Among elite planters, those with the largest slaveholdings in the early eighteenth century generally had benefited from an earlier generation's successful risk taking because they inherited enslaved descendants of the Africans acquired by parents and grandparents. These grandees reinvested income produced by their inheritances in a combination of additional purchases of African workers, entrepreneurial activities, and the consumer goods that signified a genteel lifestyle. With their wealth and their command over the labor of others well in hand, they increasingly turned their efforts to improving their colonial society.

CAPITAL CITIES

Population growth and the imperative to maintain an adequate supply of fertile land for each laborer spurred continual movement of colonists into new territory and replication of local government in new counties. The area of colonial settlement thus spread along both shores of the Chesapeake Bay and up its many tributaries. In Maryland, this process made St. Mary's City, the original capital, increasingly remote from most of the colony's population. After the establishment of royal rule in the early 1690s, Francis Nicholson arrived in Maryland in 1694 as the second royal governor. He soon persuaded the assembly to approve relocating the capital to Arundell Towne, a more centrally located settlement near the mouth of the Severn River. The shift brought the added benefit of moving the seat of government from the area with the highest proportion of Catholic residents to one dominated by Protestants. Nicholson renamed the cluster of houses Annapolis in 1695 to honor Princess Anne, future queen of England and Scotland, and gave the town its distinctive baroque plan of circles, squares, and radiating streets.

With Nicholson's encouragement and financial support, the legislature in 1696 established King William's School in Annapolis. Maryland's first publicly supported school, King William's offered instruction in Greek, Latin, writing, and other subjects that would prepare male students to enter the newly founded College of William and Mary in Virginia, an institution Nicholson also had helped to establish. In addition, the legislation authorized creation of a school in each county when funds permitted, although another generation of children grew to adulthood before that goal began to be realized.

The colony's Anglican Church provided another focal point for Nicholson's energy. The deplorable state of the Church of England in Maryland had been a major grievance against Lord Baltimore's rule and one of the first areas addressed by the royal assembly that convened in 1692. Acting upon direct instructions from the Crown, legislators authorized division of the colony into parishes, provided for election of vestries by parish freeholders, required county sheriffs to collect taxes for parish support, and instructed each vestry to use the funds to build churches and chapels. All colonists, regardless of personal religious beliefs, now paid taxes to support the established Church of England.

Despite this encouragement, at the time of Nicholson's arrival Maryland had only three clergymen properly ordained and fully inducted in office. By contrast, there were seventeen weekly meetings of the Society of Friends; eight Roman Catholic priests;

and a number of active Presbyterian congregations, particularly on the lower part of Maryland's Eastern Shore. Nicholson moved to strengthen the Anglican Church beyond simply encouraging the establishment legislation. He offered a contribution of £5 to each parish that built its minister a house and allocated land for his support, and enlisted the bishop of London's aid to supply the thirty parishes with suitable clergymen and to organize parish libraries.

The long delay in creation of an established church meant that Maryland's vestries never exercised the full range of powers that Virginia's Anglicans transferred from English practice. The county court continued to hold authority over such varied areas as poor relief, moral transgressions (including drunkenness, profanity, slander, and adultery), and determination of land boundaries. Maryland vestries occasionally called parishioners to account for moral infractions, generally involving adultery or cohabitation without marriage, but lacked the power to impose meaningful sanctions and frequently found their summonses ignored. Should the relationship result in pregnancy and an illegitimate child, the county court, not the vestry, oversaw prosecution and punishment. While Virginia vestries had the power to set an annual tax for parish expenses and to collect tobacco as payment, Maryland's establishment legislation set the rate and authorized sheriffs to make the collection.

Nicholson's tenure as governor of Maryland lasted only from 1694 to 1698 and ended amid quarrels and acrimony between the legislators and their governor. Nevertheless, Nicholson left behind a capital city that bore the imprint of his efforts and for which contemporaries awarded him the credit: "Governour Nicholson hath done his endeavour to make a towne. . . . There are in itt about fourty dwelling houses, . . . seven or eight whereof cann afford good lodging and accomodations for strangers. There is alsoe a Statehouse and a free schoole built with bricke which make a great shew among a parscell of wooden houses, and the foundation of a church laid, the only bricke church in Maryland."[1]

Maryland's predominantly rural tidewater landscape now had the beginning of its first town of consequence. A dozen years after Nicholson's departure, Annapolis received a royal charter that provided for an elected municipal government. Substantial growth, however, awaited the colony's return to Lord Baltimore's control in 1715. After renouncing Catholicism and raising his children within the Church of England, Benedict Leonard Calvert, who became the fourth Lord Baltimore when Charles Calvert died in 1715, lobbied successfully to regain control of Maryland. Benedict Leonard died less than a year after his father, leaving his son Charles, the fifth Lord Baltimore, to assume the proprietor's rights and privileges. [Because Charles was only fifteen when his father died, a guardian acted on his behalf until he came of age in 1720.] Following the return of political control to the Calvert family, the establishment of a proprietary bureaucracy, designed to maximize the proprietor's income from his overseas possession, stimulated Annapolis's development. The increasing need of a growing population to do business with officials in Annapolis as well as greater use of the provincial court system eventually provided the impetus for urban growth.

Francis Nicholson returned to Virginia as governor in December 1698 and again oversaw relocation of a colonial capital to a new town of his design. As early as 1677, residents of the area along the ridge between the James and York Rivers had petitioned commissioners investigating Bacon's Rebellion to move the capital to their settlement of Middle Plantation. The request was rejected out of hand, although the General Assembly did meet in Middle Plantation that fall because Bacon's burning of Jamestown left no state house in which to convene. In 1693, the legislature designated Middle Plantation as the site for the newly chartered College of William and Mary, locating the college near the existing Bruton Parish Church. When the Jamestown state house burned for a third time in October 1698, Middle Plantation's day had come, aided by support from Nicholson and from an Anglican minister, James Blair, founder of the college. In May 1699, students from William and Mary lobbied the legislature to move the capital to Middle Plantation. They noted that the settlement already contained "a Church, an ordinary, several stores, two Mills, a smiths shop a Grammar School, and above all the Colledge," located in a "good neighborhood of . . . substantial Housekeepers." The "housekeepers" to whom they referred included Thomas Ludwell, the colony's secretary; John Page, a local merchant and member of the House of Burgesses; and James

Bray, a merchant-planter who later sat on the governor's council—all elite men with interests and influence in the debate over relocation.[2]

Nicholson laid out Duke of Gloucester Street, a mile-long avenue, to connect the college at one end with the proposed capitol at the other. Construction of the H-shaped capitol building began in 1701 and reached completion in 1705. In that year, Governor Edward Nott obtained authorization from the assembly for a governor's residence, placed at the end of a broad plaza running north, perpendicular to the main avenue. Construction began in 1706, moved ahead in fits and starts, and concluded after considerable public expense in 1722. Although not as large in square footage as the college building, the Palace, as it was known, was the most impressive and architecturally fashionable house in the Chesapeake colonies when it was built, requiring a staff of about twenty-five for its operation. It provided a fitting residence for a royal governor and a standard for the region's gentry households to emulate. Middle Plantation itself ceased to exist, being renamed Williamsburg in honor of the English ruler. Unlike Maryland's change of capital, however, Virginia's relocation did not entail a major geographical shift, just a move up the James to the peninsula's interior. Only at the end of the century did Virginia's capital migrate westward to the falls of the James River to provide easier accessibility for the greatly expanded area of settlement.

EXPANSION WESTWARD

Beyond this movement of capital cities, geography shaped significant differences in the development of the Chesapeake region's two colonies. Virginians living in the tidewater area looked west toward a vast hinterland with great potential for future expansion. Not only was the territory large, but the rivers of Virginia's western shore penetrated deeply into those undeveloped lands. Colonists settling along navigable waters below the fall line knew they could export tobacco and other crops easily by ship. Maryland settlers, on the other hand, looked west and saw the Potomac River's northwestward course confining the area of future development to a narrowing band between the waterway and the Pennsylvania border. Within this broad picture, further differences between the two sisters that shaped settlement along the westward-moving frontier included the process of distributing vacant land, access to capital for developing new landholdings, and perceptions of the western land's fertility.

As settlement moved westward to accommodate a population growing through continued immigration and natural increase, the creation of new counties ensured that colonists had convenient access to courts and local officials. Two Virginia counties, Henrico and Stafford, straddled the fall line by 1664, and two more, Spotsylvania and Brunswick, reached across the north and south passes through the Blue Ridge Mountains by the early 1720s. Maryland, in contrast, added two Eastern Shore counties in 1706 and 1742, but did not make any alterations to the political subdivision of its more slowly settled western territory until the creation of Frederick County in its western Piedmont area in 1748.

Population growth did not provide the only spur to development of land along the frontier. Virginians with influence, connections, and political power sought to acquire as many acres as possible to capture the profits to be made by combining land with tobacco and laborers. The vast expanse of undeveloped soil offered the prospect of eventual riches, either through rent or sale to second parties or through legacies to provide estates for offspring—as long as the land came without heavy annual expenses. In both colonies, land owners owed quitrents—annual payments that replaced older feudal obligations of service—to the titular owner of the land. Virginia's settlers owed their payments to the king, while Maryland quitrents enriched Lord Baltimore, but the Crown exercised much less careful oversight than did Maryland's proprietor. For much of the seventeenth century, Virginia officials did not collect quitrents with regularity or efficiency. Even when governors began to exercise greater supervision, influential planters successfully argued that the levy should be collected only on productive land and not on acreage held for future cultivation or sale. Clerks (who were among the colony's elite) allowed speculators (also members of the elite) to lay claim to land but delay the paperwork that made property liable to quitrents until the claimants were ready to utilize the acreage. Various royal governors and other British officials tried to reform the system to prevent speculation and to increase revenue, but they lacked sufficient power to thwart the colonial leadership's vested interest in the status quo.

In exploiting its undeveloped western territory, Virginia continued to face the problem of managing relations with Native Americans. Governor Alexander Spotswood in the 1710s adopted a policy of defensive pacts with friendly nearby Indian groups to act as buffers against more hostile Indians in the Carolinas. Spotswood supplemented this program with military assistance to Carolina settlers, first against the Tuscarora in 1712 and then during the Yamasee War in 1715. In 1721, shortly before the end of his tenure in office, Spotswood obtained an agreement from northern Iroquois groups not to move through settled parts of Virginia when traveling south to the Carolinas to attack the Catawba, their traditional enemies. Spotswood also endeavored to control trade with Native Americans through creation of the Virginia Indian Company, giving it a twenty-year monopoly over trade south of the James River. He hoped to reduce grievances, and thus a basis for conflict, by eliminating the worst abuses of unregulated trade. In return for its monopoly, the company took responsibility for Fort Christanna, a trading post on the Meherrin River built to protect the area's tributary groups and the southwestern frontier. The company's efforts were short-lived, however, as its support became an issue of contention between Spotswood and the House of Burgesses. When Spotswood's administration ended, the company lost its primary supporter and faded in significance.

Efforts to monopolize the market in land also occurred in the Piedmont plateau and the valley of the Shenandoah River. Following reports, by rangers patrolling the western frontier, of a pass that cut through the Blue Ridge Mountains, Governor Spotswood led a company of fourteen rangers, four Indians, twelve gentlemen, and thirty-three attendants on an exploratory expedition. In September 1716, the troop, known as the Knights of the Golden Horseshoe, crossed through the pass that later settlers called Swift Run Gap. After fording the Shenandoah, the leaders claimed the west bank for King George I. The day's festivities concluded, as colonial celebrations generally did, with numerous toasts accompanied by consumption of "Virginia red wine and white wine, Irish usquebaugh, brandy, shrub, two sorts of rum, champagne, canary, cherry, punch, water, cider, &c."[3]

The journey dramatized the opening of the westernmost area of Virginia expansion. Authorities hastened to secure this new region before the French challenged Virginia's claim to the territory. The imperative to establish a buffer against the French and their Native-American allies provided impetus for erecting Brunswick and Spotsylvania Counties in 1720. To encourage settlement by colonists loyal to Virginia and the Crown, the legislature offered subsidies for military supplies and for construction of a church, courthouse, and prison in each county. The new counties also provided ample scope for land speculators, particularly as the governor requested that payment of quitrents be suspended for ten years. Those claiming land could thus hold it, virtually without cost, until there were settlers interested in renting or buying or until adult children needed land. On the last day of the session that created the counties, the council approved grants of one hundred thousand acres, of which forty thousand went to Spotswood.

Unlike their counterparts in Virginia, Maryland colonists paid quitrents to proprietary agents, even during the period of royal government (1689–1715). Because quitrents constituted the private income of the lords Baltimore, their agents diligently collected revenues owed on all surveyed land. From 1716 (when the Calvert family regained full control of Maryland's government) until 1733, the Calverts accepted a duty of two shillings per hogshead of exported tobacco in lieu of quitrents. During this period, it still behooved proprietary officials to keep a firm hand on the land office because undeveloped land held for speculation or inheritance did not produce tobacco; no tobacco meant no proprietary income. Lord Baltimore's appointees handled the process of issuing warrants, recording survey certificates, and confirming patents for new land. Too much leniency on behalf of colonists could result in an official's dismissal from a profitable position.

Because the proprietor exerted greater control over the land system, Maryland planters had less incentive and opportunity than Virginians to acquire vast tracts that could lie undeveloped for many years. Moreover, doubts about the fertility of Piedmont land discouraged its early development. Not until the 1740s, when settlement moved into the area that eventually became Frederick County, did wealthy individuals acquire tens of thousands of acres. Only a few men patented holdings of that size, however, and even they still found their acreage dwarfed by the estates of contemporary members of Virginia's elite. Maryland's richest planters eventually amassed between forty and fifty thousand acres, but their Virginia counterparts held one hundred to three hundred thousand acres. Smaller landholdings translated into smaller investments in enslaved labor: one hundred bondsmen for the wealthiest Marylanders, but five hundred to one thousand for the comparable stratum of Virginia planters. Profits from sweet-scented tobacco continued to provide the financial and political power that underwrote Virginia's dynasties.

The inexorable push of settlement north, south, and west onto new land carried with it a potential problem for all planters, whether large or small, tidewater or Piedmont. As tobacco production expanded, it outstripped existing markets, contributing to the long-term decline in prices that followed the end of the tobacco boom of the early 1600s. Improvements in packing and shipping sustained profits for a time, but eventually they too fell. Both colonies tried various remedies to stem the decline, including limits on production and destruction of inferior leaves, without notable success or compliance.

Competing interests made it difficult to achieve political consensus. Both the Crown (for Virginia) and the proprietor (for Maryland) levied a tax on exported hogsheads and thus favored quantity over quality. Large planters, who cultivated the best land and prided themselves on their skill in producing superior crops, favored quality, coveting the higher prices good tobacco could command. Small planters, who worked inferior land with limited labor, favored quantity and opposed inspection for fear that much of their tobacco would be rejected and burned. Feelings on the issue could be intense. When Maryland's assembly proposed a bill in 1726 to require burning all inferior tobacco, Charles Carroll of Annapolis favored the measure so strongly that he challenged James Hollyday of Talbot County, a delegate in opposition, to a duel. Hollyday accepted the challenge, but the lower house intervened before the two came to blows. The legislation finally passed in 1728, but proprietary objections led to its repeal without ever being enforced.

In Virginia, difficult economic conditions during the 1720s coupled with skilled leadership by Governor William Gooch resulted in passage of an inspection act in 1730. At public warehouses, inspectors examined all tobacco shipped overseas; leaf that did not meet standards was burned immediately to prevent its export. Planters whose crops passed inspection received receipts that circulated as legal tender, providing a form of paper money as substitute currency for unwieldy and perishable tobacco. Although the system initially met with violent resistance in some areas, higher prices brought by smaller crops in 1732 and 1733 dampened opposition. The system remained in force and marked the beginning of a twenty-year rise in price for Virginia tobacco. The improvement in tobacco prices played a key role in financing the vigorous expansion of tobacco cultivation into the Piedmont region.

Despite Virginia's success, Maryland colonists argued for seventeen additional years before passing their own inspection act in 1747. Planters recognized that elimination of trash tobacco could bring higher prices, as it had in Virginia, but insisted that payments to government officials and clergymen, set by law at fixed quantities of tobacco, be adjusted downward to compensate for the expected increase in tobacco's value as currency. Proprietary resistance to any fee adjustment resulted in stalemate until repeated letters from Daniel Dulany the Elder, himself a proprietary official, persuaded Lord Baltimore of the impossibility of passing the needed legislation without adjustment of fees. The resulting act, which created an inspection system and included instructions for setting new fees, brought the same improvement in prices for Maryland planters as Virginians had experienced nearly two decades earlier.

Geography combined with the proprietor's interest in controlling land distribution fostered a relatively more egalitarian social order within Maryland by depriving its political and social elite of the extensive opportunities for land engrossment, speculation, and endowment of future generations that Virginia's leading families exploited. In both colonies, free society developed as a hierarchy capped by a small number of elite households that exercised power at the provincial level. A somewhat larger group of gentry families dominated county government, followed by a lower, middling group of landowners without significant status, and a bottom tier of small planters and tenants, including a small number of households headed by free blacks. The gap beneath the very top level of the social hierarchy and the next tier, however, was greater in Virginia than in Maryland, and the wealth of the elite Virginia group, in land and slaves, exceeded that of its

Maryland counterpart. The two colonies became more alike in many ways during the eighteenth century, but the vastly different potential of their respective western territories contributed to significant differences in wealth and social structure.

REGIONAL VARIATIONS

The shift from immigrant to native-born society occurred in the context of a changing economic climate and increasing regional variation. While the Chesapeake tidewater may conveniently be seen within colonial British North America as a relatively homogeneous whole, it nonetheless consisted of several smaller areas that differed from one another in soil quality, accessibility to markets, trading networks, and saleable commodities. These differences in turn affected the distribution of wealth and investment in enslaved labor both within and among areas. These distinct subregions, labeled for convenience as sweet-scented, oronoco, and provisioning, became apparent as early as the mid-seventeenth century.

The most prosperous tidewater area encompassed the two peninsulas between Virginia's James and Rappahannock Rivers plus a swath of land on the Northern Neck along the Rappahannock. Only in this subregion could planters cultivate the sweet-scented tobacco that enjoyed the highest demand in the British domestic market. This was the first Chesapeake area to import slaves in large numbers and it remained the tidewater's center of wealth and power for the duration of the colonial period. The concentration of wealth created the region's largest and most active slave market, drawing ships that carried hundreds of Africans below decks to landings along the rivers. Elite planters in this area began acquiring slaves in the 1630s and 1640s, using mercantile connections with the West Indies. As the supply of Africans brought directly to the Chesapeake Bay increased later in the century, wealthy planters bought in quantity and paid with sound bills of exchange drawn on established London tobacco firms (in effect, checks written on the planter's balance or credit with the firm), or more rarely with gold or silver coins. As a result, the western shore grandees bought most of the slaves shipped to Virginia in the first quarter of the eighteenth century, when the great planting families consolidated their places in society. Planters in this subregion purchased a majority of the nearly fifty thousand Africans brought into the colony before 1745.

Larger slavers generally avoided the remaining tidewater areas. Because fewer planters could afford to buy even small numbers of slaves, a large shipment or arrival of more than one ship might glut the market. Planters in these less-prosperous areas also offered less attractive forms of payment, including inferior tobacco, long-term credit, and less-reliable bills of exchange drawn on smaller London firms or on merchants in other English or Scottish ports. Virginia planters on the Potomac side of the Northern Neck, for example, grew oronoco tobacco, generally lacked strong trading ties with firms dealing in slaves, and only gradually accumulated enough wealth to invest heavily in enslaved labor. Consequently, the area remained a minor destination for slavers, particularly early in the eighteenth century. Maryland's western shore and upper Eastern Shore, also oronoco-producing areas, were likewise less attractive markets than the sweet-scented area, with few potential buyers in any given locale and only a small number of planters able to buy in quantity. Larger slavers often needed to peddle their cargo along more than one river before selling all the Africans they carried. Planters outside the sweet-scented and oronoco areas—the south side of the lower James River, Virginia's Eastern Shore, and the lower part of Maryland's Eastern Shore—all worked land with little soil suitable for tobacco and had minimal connections with the tobacco trade. Many residents of these areas earned their living by producing provisions, such as foodstuffs and lumber products, that could supply merchant and navy ships, be sold locally, or be exported to coastal and overseas markets. Fewer than one thousand enslaved workers entered the provisioning region between 1698 and 1730, and most arrived in small lots on ships engaged in West Indies trade, not directly from Africa.

Elite planters who lived outside the sweet-scented area used a variety of methods to develop their workforces. In addition to buying Africans whenever their accumulation of sufficient capital coincided with a ship's arrival, they imported some slaves from the West Indies, acquired seasoned Africans and African Americans through marriage or inheritance from kin, and increasingly bought slaves locally as an internal market developed. Large planters with a surplus of enslaved children and debtors in need of cash or credit to settle accounts, for example, sometimes offered to sell slaves on more generous credit terms than international traders granted. In addition, owners who could not provide full employment for all of their enslaved property sometimes opted to hire out all or part of the workers' time, thus retaining legal title but transferring the direct benefit of that labor to other planters.

Following the accession of William and Mary in 1689, England, now governed by Protestant rulers, engaged in two decades of warfare with Catholic France, ruled by Louis XIV, first during King William's War (1689–97) and then during Queen Anne's War (1702–13). This extended period of military conflict brought hardship to some parts of the tobacco coast and windfall profits to others, further accentuating the regional differences. Enemy warships and privateers added new hazards to transatlantic shipment of the annual tobacco crop. These disruptions to trade and countermeasures taken to safeguard the tobacco fleet brought increased profits to sweet-scented producers, but gave planters in marginal areas further incentive to turn away from tobacco in favor of local markets, coastal trade, and West Indies outlets.

To preserve trade, and thus the Crown's revenue from customs fees and duties, the royal government instituted measures to protect the tobacco fleet and other British traders during the prolonged period of warfare. Restrictions on the number of seamen employed by trading fleets increased the pool of sailors available for the navy's ships and limited the trading fleets to a size the navy could protect. Limiting the tobacco fleet's size effectively capped the number of firms engaged in the trade, favoring larger firms, which had political clout, over smaller. Control of the trade thus became concentrated in the hands of fewer, bigger merchant firms, which tended to be those firms trading with the sweet-scented areas.

Armed naval escorts protected the tobacco fleet on its voyages to the Chesapeake Bay. Once ships had filled their holds with tobacco, the Virginia council, in coordination with customs collectors and naval officers, made arrangements for the return trip, setting the timetable for sailing and then informing Maryland authorities of the date. The fleet gathered at the mouth of the

James River until the convoy was ready to sail in late June or July. Consolidating shipping and limiting the size of the fleet discouraged tobacco production outside the sweet-scented area and reduced the size of the Chesapeake region's export crop. This system created a symbiotic relationship between the largest London traders and elite Virginia planters, to the great benefit of both. The convoy system raised tobacco's price on the London market, to the planters' advantage, and at the same time decreased costs and risks of overseas trade during a time of warfare, to the merchants' advantage.

Planters in the oronoco and provisioning areas did not reap as great a share of the convoy system's bounty. Oronoco tobacco grown in most of Maryland and on Virginia's Potomac River plantations found its market not in England but on the European mainland. With England and France at war, tobacco could not easily be transshipped from England to its continental market. The shortage of supply raised oronoco prices on the Continent, but not to the benefit of Chesapeake planters; rather, it encouraged cultivation by Dutch and French peasants. The market for Chesapeake oronoco did not rebound until after peace was declared in 1713. Maryland's oronoco-growing planters also suffered because the Virginia Council of State controlled the outbound convoy. The need to coordinate collection of Maryland tobacco with a timely arrival at the convoy's assembly area near the Capes did not encourage English merchants to send their ships north for tobacco if the smaller fleet of ships could fill its holds in Virginia. The prolonged period of warfare both accentuated regional differences within the two colonies and contributed to the erosion of tobacco's central place in the regional economy. Settlers in oronoco and provisioning areas increasingly pursued opportunities in crafts, services, and alternative ways to produce marketable exports.

ENTREPRENEURIAL PURSUITS AND A DIVERSIFIED ECONOMY

Throughout the Chesapeake region, the efforts of individual colonists to produce marketable goods and services outside the sphere of tobacco cultivation contributed to an increasingly diverse colonial economy. Entrepreneurial men, with resources to invest and a willingness to take risks, pursued economic opportunities that emerged both within the Chesapeake region and in the broader Atlantic economy. As new markets developed in the West Indies, the Atlantic's Wine Islands, and southern Europe, men with connections and capital assembled and shipped cargoes of foodstuffs and lumber products to these destinations. As planters began to grow wheat and other grains in addition to corn, entrepreneurs erected mills, engaged sawyers and coopers to supply barrels for shipping flour, and built the ships needed to carry it to market. As Britain experienced shortages of wood for smelting iron or building ships, colonists with access to local resources of iron ore and timber moved to fill the gap by building ironworks and setting up shipyards. Officeholding facilitated these activities, while financial success in capitalizing on new opportunities in turn improved the chances of being considered for additional lucrative offices.

Pursuit of entrepreneurial activities enabled men like John Tayloe to establish successful elite dynasties. Tayloe was the son of William Tayloe, a Londoner who moved to Virginia by the 1680s and married Anne Corbin, daughter of a wealthy Middlesex County planter. When his father died in 1710, John, who was about twenty-three, inherited an estate consisting of three thousand acres of land, twenty-one slaves, and more than £800 in personal property, including store goods. Three years later Tayloe married widow Elizabeth Gwynn Lyde, whose inheritance from her first husband included one thousand acres of land and ten slaves. Tayloe engaged in a variety of mercantile activities, such as investing in an ordinary, acting as local factor for British merchants, and participating in the slave trade. In addition, Tayloe profited from renting his Northern Neck land to tenants and from operating a number of gristmills as local production of grains increased. In 1724 Tayloe obtained permission from Richmond County justices to buy land for a gristmill; by the 1740s he had at least four mills on his Northern Neck properties.

After a decade or so of local service, including a term as sheriff and a commission as county justice in 1714, Tayloe received a seat on the council in 1732. Tayloe used his council membership to good effect in 1737, when he began to develop the Neabsco Ironworks on the Potomac River's south shore. Tayloe had sufficient timber on his Virginia land for iron production, but it lacked adequate ore supplies. To solve the ore problem Tayloe bought ore-bearing land on Maryland's Patapsco River and then persuaded his council colleagues to exempt the Maryland ore from Virginia's duties on imports. Tayloe also had ships built to transport his ore from Maryland to Neabsco and the iron to England. In addition to the shipyard, the Neabsco property included at least one blast furnace, as well as gristmills, sawmills, and a blacksmith's shop that brought additional profit by providing services to neighboring planters.

When Tayloe died in 1744, he left his son John Tayloe II an estate greatly enlarged from the one inherited in 1710. Landholdings expanded from three thousand to more than twenty thousand acres in two colonies, and the enslaved workforce grew from twenty-one to more than three hundred. Tayloe's slaves produced tobacco, corn, wheat, oats, peas, and beans and tended livestock herds of hogs, cattle, and horses. Tayloe built up his estate, one of the largest in the colony and worth between £33,000 and £44,000, through participation in the early eighteenth century's diverse array of economic activities.

Maryland's elite did not have comparable opportunities for land accumulation, but they, too, made the most of the resources and connections they did enjoy. In his early twenties, Dr. Charles Carroll arrived in Maryland from Ireland about 1715, settled in Annapolis, and married well. After practicing medicine for a few years, he turned to mercantile activity that complemented his role as a substantial planter. Carroll collected tobacco from neighboring small planters and shipped it with his own crops on consignment to several British tobacco firms. Over time, he extended his network of contacts to the West Indies, southern Europe, and the Atlantic wine-producing islands of Madeira and the Azores. Carroll directed agents to assemble cargoes of grain, lumber, staves, pork, and other foodstuffs to fill vessels on their outward Caribbean voyages. In return, Carroll collected shipments of sugar and molasses or acquired bills of exchange for purchase of English goods. Grain and lumber products like barrel staves and headings found markets in the Wine Islands and southern Europe. Imported grain helped feed a growing population; staves and headings made casks for wine. Some wine-filled casks came back to Carroll as payment for his shipments. Carroll's interests also included a Patapsco River shipyard that built shallow-draft shallops and deeper-draft vessels for bay and Caribbean voyages. In

Principio Furnace. Pickering's photograph shows the furnace of the Principio Iron Works in Cecil County, Maryland. The ironworks was started in 1719 by the Principio Company with funds from a group of British investors. This furnace produced pig iron for export to Britain. E. H. Pickering, 1936. HABS MD, 8-PRINF,1-1, Historic American Buildings Survey, Library of Congress, Prints and Photographs Division

addition, Carroll bought shares in larger ships delivering Chesapeake tobacco to England. Return voyages brought cargoes of English manufactures for sale to smaller planters whose tobacco crops did not merit the personal attention that English merchant houses gave to requests from men like Carroll for the latest and most fashionable goods.

With Daniel Dulany, Benjamin Tasker, and two Carroll cousins, Dr. Charles Carroll was a founder of the Baltimore Ironworks in 1731. The Baltimore firm emerged as one of the industry's most successful operations. Plentiful iron deposits littered the company's land along the Patapsco; charcoal from local hardwoods provided fuel for furnaces and forges; and the river's flow powered its mills. By the 1740s, ships leaving nearby Baltimore Town for England carried pig and bar iron along with hogsheads of tobacco. Eventually, the company's operations encompassed several furnaces, three forges, 150 enslaved workers, and thirty thousand acres of land. Carroll also speculated in western land, acquiring more than twenty-five thousand acres in Baltimore and Frederick Counties that he subdivided and sold at a profit when settlers moved into the Piedmont area. Carroll recognized, from his own experience and that of others, that if one wished to become rich, "Planting will not do without some other Business or Professions" to provide additional income.[4]

Across the region, planters continually pursued new markets and new products, whether to keep bound workers fully productive, to exploit natural resources, or to maximize returns from small plantations with marginal land. The net result was an increasingly diversified economy, an expanded range of occupations, and a society that more and more resembled that of the mother country except in its commitment to the use of enslaved labor. As the economy expanded beyond tobacco cultivation, new crops and new industries required an array of trained artisans, setting in motion further economic diversification.

Even in the seventeenth century, when the tidewater was a region of plantations strung out along waterways with few towns or market centers, some inhabitants combined planting with the practice of a craft skill. Well before the end of the century, skilled artisans included carpenters, coopers, sawyers, tailors, weavers, shoemakers, blacksmiths, ship carpenters, and bricklayers. Some, like carpenters and blacksmiths, shoemakers and tailors, supplied

essential products like buildings, ironware, shoes, and clothing. Others created necessary goods from locally abundant raw materials, such as lumber from wood, bricks from clay, cloth from sheep's wool, and leather from the hides of the livestock slaughtered every fall for winter food. Although initially their numbers were small and their presence uneven, by the early eighteenth century the variety of skilled trades and the proportion of settlers engaged in their practice mirrored patterns found in rural English villages.

The proliferation of trades within the region did not, however, result in a self-sufficient Chesapeake economy. Rich and poor alike depended heavily on imported goods for most of the manufactures they consumed. Colonists could not import their houses and outbuildings, but wealthier households ordered much of their furniture directly from British merchants, leaving few customers for specialized woodworkers like joiners and cabinetmakers. Blacksmiths derived much of their work from repairing ironware originally imported new from England. Shoemakers turned local leather into shoes, but merchants and ship captains also brought in cargoes of shoes, boots, and small leather goods such as gloves, at prices that made local production by specialized leatherworkers unprofitable. Weavers produced cloth from local wool and flax (spun into yarn by local women and girls) but supplied only a small amount of any household's fabric needs. Imported fabric clothed the bodies of slaves and masters alike, and for most colonial households imported cloth was a major expenditure. Earthen tableware and drinking vessels arrived in Chesapeake households by ship from manufacturers as far away as China, despite the presence of suitable local deposits of clay. No more than a handful of Chesapeake men may ever have tried to earn their living as potters during the eighteenth century. Local producers of earthenware, gloves, hats, handkerchiefs, and other inexpensive manufactures could not compete with imports so easily carried in the empty holds of ships arriving to collect tobacco. By the same token, very expensive goods, such as carriages that carried gentry families on their social rounds, also arrived by ship. There were too few colonists able to afford such an expensive purchase to provide adequate patronage for local carriage makers until late in the colonial period.

Nor did individual plantations make the investments in tools and labor necessary for self-sufficiency. Planters may have owned basic woodworking or shoemaking tools, but they possessed neither the skills nor the tools to construct buildings, make casks, weave cloth, tailor clothes, bake bricks, and build a shallop. Even slaveowners generally utilized enslaved workers in a limited number of trades, employing them mainly as carpenters, coopers, shoemakers, and, occasionally, blacksmiths. William Byrd II chose to write of himself as "Like one of the patriarchs, [with] my bond-men and bond-women, and every soart of trade amongst my own servants, so that I live in a kind of independence on every one, but Providence," but more likely Byrd was projecting a wished-for ideal rather than describing his or any slaveowner's true circumstances.[5]

Chesapeake artisans generally sold their products only within limited, local markets because the nature of colonial trade discouraged self-sufficiency, but there were exceptions. Colonial ironworks, for example, found a ready market for their pig and bar iron in the mother country and received financial and legislative encouragement because Britain lacked sufficient charcoal to manufacture adequate supplies. The Maryland legislature provided additional support, beginning with a 1719 "Act for the Encouragement of an Iron Manufacture within this Province" that made acquisition of a suitable site easier and exempted up to eighty workmen from taxes.[6] The Baltimore and Neabsco ironworks were two early examples of colonial entrepreneurs responding to Britain's shortage of wood. By 1750, there were at least six furnaces (producing pig iron) and five forges (supplying bar iron) in Maryland, and nine furnaces and four forges in Virginia. By the end of the colonial period, iron products ranked third in value behind tobacco and wheat among the region's exports, with Virginia and Maryland holding roughly equal shares by value of shipments to Britain. Moreover, three-quarters of locally produced iron may have remained in the colonies for use in shipbuilding, wagon construction, barrel making, fabrication of locks and hinges for new buildings, and a myriad of other domestic uses.

Shipbuilding was another income-producing activity that expanded during the colonial period as Chesapeake merchants

The Spencer Shipyard, Gray's Inn Creek. This painting is the earliest-known view of a Chesapeake shipyard. It shows a small yard on Maryland's Eastern Shore, where sawyers are using whipsaws to cut timber and carpenters are building two vessels. In the foreground, the artist has depicted the variety of vessels found in Chesapeake waters. Unknown artist, c. 1760. 1900.5.1, courtesy of the Maryland Historical Society

and craftsmen responded to developing markets. From the earliest days of settlement, the region's waterways provided passage for goods carried by canoes, flat-bottomed barges, and a variety of small sailing vessels, such as pinnaces and shallops, most of which were built locally. By the 1690s, at least four major shipyards operated on Maryland's Eastern Shore; these shipyards, like similar operations throughout the tidewater region, not only constructed small craft for local trade but also built larger vessels to carry cargo to New England and the Caribbean. For the latter trade, with its threat of pirates but lure of smuggling, Maryland shipbuilders developed distinctive, single-masted sloops and two-masted schooners that were fast and maneuverable enough to evade predators at sea and to slip into secluded coves in the islands and at home. When shortages of suitable wood for masts and spars led to rising shipbuilding costs in Britain, Chesapeake shipyards also began producing larger, more traditional ships for the tobacco trade, such as "the good Ship Hanbury," advertised in 1754 as a "new Vessel, built at Annapolis, staunch, strong, and well fitted."[7] These ships might carry tobacco to England on the maiden voyage and then be sold to British firms. The expanding shipbuilding industry not only generated demand for skilled shipwrights and blacksmiths but also fostered development of local centers of ship chandlery, particularly in Annapolis, Chestertown, and Norfolk, where vessels could be supplied with rope, canvas, pumps, blocks, and other gear for repair and refitting.

The movement away from tobacco monoculture to a broader array of economic activities provided income sources to supplement or replace earnings from tobacco. Diversification had the effect of smoothing out fluctuations in income that were an inevitable part of reliance on a staple crop. It also provided a variety of employment opportunities for men and women who did not own land, including independent artisans, housekeepers, craft workers on large plantations, overseers of quarters, managers of ironworks and shipyards, and tutors and schoolteachers. Profits from sectors other than tobacco production helped maintain per capita income even as the average size of households increased, with first white and then black native-born populations producing more children. Economic diversification played a significant role in enabling a broad range of colonists to enjoy an improved standard of living.

STANDARDS OF LIVING

Throughout Virginia and Maryland, most colonists succeeded in satisfying their immediate requirements for shelter, clothing, food, furnishings, and plantation buildings. This was particularly true in longest-settled areas, less so on the frontier where householders were not as well-established; however, newly settled areas developed rapidly and soon reached a similar level of sufficiency. All but the poorest creole households had some discretionary income once basic needs were met. Thus, families not just at the top but further down the social scale began to buy amenities that made life more comfortable. The fortunate households at the top of the economic and social hierarchy could also indulge in luxuries that became increasingly available during the eighteenth century.

Estate inventories recorded in Maryland in the 1730s provide insight into the standard of living achieved by the second quarter of the eighteenth century. The value of inventoried property ranged from just under £0.50 to nearly £6,000, or from abject poverty to vast wealth. These inventories bear witness to economic stratification: roughly one-half of the estates were valued at less than £65, but each of the wealthiest 5 percent of decedents—seventy men and six women—held at least £600 in moveable property. These seventy-six men and women together owned 38 percent of the colony's inventoried wealth, while the bottom 5 percent—seventy men and eight women—owned barely one-thousandth of 1 percent of the total. To use a different but equally stark measure, the moveable assets of the top 5 percent equaled the total wealth of the bottom 85 percent. Virginia's surviving probate records do not permit a similarly broad comparison, but if such a study were possible, it would likely demonstrate an even greater degree of inequality.

What did the abstract numbers mean for the men, women, and children who lived in these families? The poorest decedents owned almost nothing, but they were often unmarried adult children who lived with parents or other family members. Because these individuals died at an early age, their inventories do not fully reflect their resources and expectations. All of the poorest decedents had little personal property, but rarely lacked shelter, clothing, or food. One did not have to move too much farther up the social scale, moreover, to live comfortably. Roughly one-half of decedents owned less than £65 in moveable property but most of these individuals had been household heads, living in modestly furnished homes and generally relying on family labor, with perhaps a servant or young slave as an extra hand, to work their land.

A relatively small increase in the size of one's estate represented a noticeable increase in the number and variety of possessions. John Steward, for example, resided in southern Anne Arundel County with his wife Sarah and their two sons. Steward likely rented the land on which he raised crops of tobacco and corn, but also earned additional income through his skill as a ship carpenter. His livestock included nineteen head of cattle, forty-nine hogs, and ten sheep—more than enough animals to supply the family with meat and dairy products as well as a surplus for sale. When Steward died in 1734, appraisers valued his total estate at £129, well below those of the wealthiest planters. Yet the family's property included purchases that had improved their lives over time, from six good Russia leather chairs to the writing desk to the parcel of old books and a large Bible. The best bed had a feather mattress, curtains and valance to enclose the bed for warmth and privacy, and coverings of blanket, counterpane, and a pair of sheets. The family ate off pewter plates and owned earthenware and ceramics as well. Implements of iron, copper, brass, and pewter lined Sarah's kitchen shelves, and a small looking glass hung on one wall. Steward also owned an assortment of agricultural tools and a parcel of ship carpenter's tools.

The Steward household included five additional persons besides John, Sarah, and their children. Three apprentices assisted Steward as they learned his craft, and he also owned an enslaved woman named Dinah, valued at £28, and a one-half interest in a boy named Tom, at £7 10s. Steward, still a relatively young man when he died, had already achieved a comfortable position; with land of his own in addition to the plantation he rented, two slaves, and a craft skill, he had the potential to move up the social ladder had he lived longer.

All householders, no matter how poor, considered beds and cooking pots essential furnishings. A few chests and trunks for storage, a table, and some benches completed the minimal possessions needed for eating, sleeping, and holding personal goods —and probably filled the available space in the poorest settlers' small, one-room houses. For a total expenditure of about £3, a planter could supply his family with two beds (simply straw- or flock-filled mattresses), two iron pots and pot hooks for his wife to prepare meals over the hearth, a few pewter and woodenware serving pieces, spoons, a table, chest, and two wooden pails. Furnishings might not be luxurious, or even comfortable, but household members had a place to sleep and the means to prepare and eat their meals.

As these colonists began to acquire consumer goods, some of their choices might seem unusual to a modern sensibility. Householders who were slightly better off, with money to spend on improving their homes, gave highest priority to greater comfort while sleeping by replacing the lumpy straw and flock bed ticks with feather mattresses. New bedding, usually including more elaborate linens and pillows, represented a major expenditure—at £2.5 to £3 almost as costly as all the possessions of the poorest households. Couples who owned just one bedstead (a wooden bed frame) often chose to improve its bedding before buying an additional bedstead to lessen crowding for large families or to provide a greater measure of privacy. Not even all wealthy households considered necessary purchases to include either warming pans, to take the chill off bedding during winter months, or chamber pots, to relieve oneself during the night; those goods appeared in fewer than one-half of the middling homes.

Once they had improved their sleeping quarters, poorer householders added variety to their diet by purchasing a pan for frying food as a change from one-meal stews prepared in iron pots. Housewives also acquired handmills, to relieve the tedium of grinding corn with a mortar and pestle, more often than they purchased a chair on which to sit. Candlesticks and candles, for lighting after sunset, took priority over tablecloths and napkins, although imported candles were used sparingly. Housewives began to buy smoothing irons, for pressing clothes after washing, before they began to acquire soap or washing tubs. Women valued the iron, which replaced heated stones, more than manufactured soap and more than a tub to replace a nearby stream or a cooking pot.

By the 1720s, Chesapeake households that had been settled for more than one generation enjoyed a gradual but definite improvement in material well-being. The changes were not dramatic, but rather resulted, for all but the wealthiest, from a slow process of small purchases made over time that gradually raised the quality and quantity of possessions. These acquisitions mark the first colonial evidence of participation in the consumer revolution, the burgeoning market for manufactured consumer goods that began to develop in England in the late seventeenth century. By the middle of the eighteenth century, the flood of imports had transformed the living standard at all levels of society.

Improvement in living conditions occurred earliest within elite households, as the two generations of the Addison family of southern Maryland vividly illustrate. John Addison arrived in the colony from England in 1674, eventually settling in what became Prince George's County. Addison was a merchant, planter, member of the council, and justice of both provincial and county courts. At his death, sometime in late 1705 or early 1706, he owned nearly 6,500 acres of land and fourteen slaves and left an estate appraised at nearly £3,000. Addison's household furnishings included bedsteads and their bedding, Russia leather chairs, and an oval dining table with napkins and tablecloths, all of which marked him as a member of the colony's elite. Nonetheless, Addison did not own any silver plate, and his tableware evidently was part of his forty pounds of pewter, valued at less than £2.

Addison's son Thomas, about twenty-six when his father died, followed in the elder Addison's footsteps as planter, merchant, councilor, and holder of numerous other offices. When he died in 1727, Thomas Addison owned about 15,000 acres of land, seventy-one slaves, and personal property appraised at nearly £5,800. The younger Addison, a wealthier man in a different time, spent his days in far more luxurious surroundings than his father had experienced. Furnishings of two rooms of Addison's house designated them as spaces for social gatherings: pictures and mirrors with gilded frames to reflect light from glass candelabra, a backgammon table where men could gamble on a game requiring both skill and luck, and tea tables spread with china tea sets and a copper coffee pot. Guests invited for dinner after Sunday services at the parish church sat down to tables graced with china plates and punch bowls, glass decanters, and silver-handled knives and forks. The younger Addison embellished each bed chamber with matching window curtains and bed hangings, all made of costly imported fabric. Addison's best bed, draped with yards of expensive silk, at nearly £50 constituted his most valuable, nonhuman property. For the region's poorest planters, all the property they possessed did not equal the value of Addison's best bed.

Just as the Chesapeake elite bought imported luxury goods to furnish their homes and adorn their persons with the latest British fashions, so the middling and lower sorts began to emulate their colonial betters—the local gentry—insofar as their means allowed. Improvements in manufacturing methods and more efficient trade networks helped bring a greater variety of British goods at lower cost. As the price of ceramics declined, for example, more and more middling housewives set their tables first with Delft earthenware, then with more fashionable creamware, purchasing an expanding array of plates, bowls, and serving pieces. By the 1730s, fine earthenware, bed and table linens, knives and forks, pictures, and silver tableware commonly appeared as furnishings of middling Chesapeake homes and occasionally could be found even in a poorer rural dwelling. The elite used genteel behavior and the props required for its performance to distance themselves from the lower sorts; middling and poorer planters sought similar goods as a way of bridging the distance between themselves and those above them on the social scale. Middling planters might acquire a mahogany table, a set of silver tablespoons, or a ceramic tea service. A poor planter could not hope to buy silver spoons or silk bed hangings, but he could furnish a table with individual tin knives and forks and drink cider or beer from a delft mug, without spending more than a few shillings of the family's hard-earned income.

By the second quarter of the century, members of the gentry also used the homes in which they lived and the social rituals that took place there to distinguish themselves from the rest of society. As they tightened their grasp on the region's political, economic, and social reins of power, and as rising tobacco prices provided additional profits and credit, elite planters began to transform their homes into ornate family seats that gave visible expression to their accomplishments. Between 1725 and 1735, for example, Lewis Burwell III built Kingsmill, a symmetrical, five-bay plantation house that measured 61 feet by 40 feet, with four rooms on each of two floors, a hip roof, and a tall chimney at each end. One-story service buildings flanked the formal garden in front of the house, and terraced gardens fell away behind to the bank of the James River. Farther up the bay, Charles Carroll of Annapolis during the same period built a brick home for himself adjoining the frame house inherited from his father. Although only one and one-half stories showed themselves to passersby on Duke of Gloucester Street, two and one-half stories commanded the view of terraced gardens and the creek beyond on the water side. In a town of mostly smaller, mostly wooden homes, no one could fail to notice Carroll's establishment or appreciate the importance of its occupant.

The interiors of gentry homes and the activities that took place in and around them changed as dramatically as did the exteriors. The entrance door, which in a one-story, two-room house led directly into living quarters, in the new homes built in Britain's prevailing Georgian style provided access only to a central passage. Closed doors flanking the passage separated public space from private quarters and opened only for family and friends. Elegantly furnished first-floor rooms supplied appropriate settings for social gatherings, as beds became relegated to second-floor sleeping chambers where only intimate friends were entertained.

Further differentiation took place through introduction of new social rituals. Tea drinking, for example, occurred in a ceremonial setting that featured silver and ceramic serving pieces and accessories. Guests also ate elaborate dinners at tables set with individual plates, glassware, and silverware. Terraced gardens with geometric arrangements of flower beds brought order and neatness to exterior surroundings while demonstrating the wealth and power of an owner who could afford the labor and expense of so controlling his landscape.

Elaborate houses and furniture, like Addison's best bed, thus had functions beyond providing shelter and a place to sleep. They positioned their owners at the top of a social hierarchy based on wealth, the only reliable measure of status in a society without inherited titles, long family lineages, or ancient country seats to serve that purpose, and in so doing affirmed those owners' right to serve as the region's political leadership. In the Chesapeake colonies, moreover, ownership of enslaved labor did more than provide workers to cultivate tobacco and other crops. Enslavement, a condition that defined the status of blacks, served to define the status of whites as well. Having enslaved workers to plant, harvest, and pack tobacco, butcher livestock, erect fencing, and dig ditches provided daily testimony to a master's wealth. To divert the efforts of some slaves from agriculture and other productive activities to domestic labor spoke of yet greater funds at the owner's disposal. To set the domestic staff to work cleaning, washing, and cooking in an imposing brick house newly built with the latest elements of Georgian style offered the most dramatic and visible proof of power and position.

By the end of the first quarter of the eighteenth century, Chesapeake settlers had established an economic and social framework that would prevail for the remainder of the colonial period and into the early national period. Agriculture dominated economic life, as most colonists earned their livelihood from products of land they owned or rented. By European standards, colonists enjoyed widespread ownership of land, but as population density increased in longer-settled areas, access to land for later generations often entailed movement to the frontier or to interior tracts on tidewater peninsulas. Many households struggled to acquire title to land, raising tenancy rates and extending the length of time individuals might spend laboring on another planter's land.

Changes in access to office and control of labor that resulted from the transition to a native-born population meant greater social and economic stratification and less social mobility within white society, but had the effect of making that society more orderly and more cohesive. As the ruling native-born elite developed a greater sense of legitimacy for its claims to leadership and status, the economic and political competition among immigrants that characterized much of the seventeenth century gradually gave way to jousting for position in cultural areas, such as horse racing, gambling, and political debate.

The developments of the early eighteenth century, including the wealth that supported improvements in living standards as well as consolidation of power by the ruling elite, ultimately derived from the ability of certain groups to exploit the labor of other groups. Indentured servants had initially provided most of the bound labor and continued to be part of the workforce through the eighteenth century, albeit as an ever-smaller percentage of the total. Tenants provided another source of labor, bartering their toil at tasks of farm building in exchange for access to land and other resources supplied by the land's owner. Small landowners might be another source of labor if they used land as collateral for borrowing and then defaulted on the mortgage. But by far the greatest contribution was made by enslaved workers, who in the eighteenth century became the largest component of the Chesapeake region's conscripted labor.

FIVE

A Society Enslaved

LEWIS BURWELL II, a wealthy Virginian with plantations on the Lower Peninsula between the James and York Rivers, added imported Africans to his workforce over a period of more than forty years before his death in 1710. He purchased new workers in small numbers, buying at most two or three at a time. Burwell acquired one man from a Royal African Company trader in 1691; another man, named Yambo, came as partial payment of a debt in 1693. Others, such as Yaddo, Cuffey, Colly, and Denbo, became Burwell's property through his two marriages. By the early eighteenth century, the workers toiling on Burwell lands included a number of family groups, some of whom likely were descended from Africans purchased as early as the 1660s. For example, by 1710, an enslaved couple, Jacob and his wife Frank, were the parents of five children: Sam, Lewis, Molly, Martha, and Frank. Another couple, Jack and Sue Parratt, had one daughter, Molly, and a son Billy, born in 1713, while Nann, bought by Burwell in 1691, was the mother of Abigail. Just a decade later, Jack, Amos, Molly, Billy, Sambo, Billy Parratt, Nat, Charles, a third Billy, Harry, Lewis, Jemmy, Frank, Sarah, and Ned were among the children who played together in woods and quarters when not engaged in the simple tasks that trained young slaves for a lifetime of work. As these children grew up and found partners, two and three generations became bound together as kin. By the mid-eighteenth century, enslaved workers held by Burwell's heirs inhabited five home plantations and more than a dozen quarters within a small geographic area, making possible broad multigenerational kin networks.

Charles Carroll (a distant cousin of Dr. Charles Carroll) arrived in St. Mary's City in 1688 owning neither land nor slaves. The ambitious Carroll soon used marital connections and an appointment as clerk of the land office to acquire property in and near Annapolis, Maryland's new capital, and began buying African and African American laborers. When he died in 1720, his estate included 112 enslaved workers on five plantations. During the ensuing decades, Carroll's eldest surviving son, known as Charles Carroll of Annapolis, reaped the benefit of natural increase among slaves his father had bought. Carroll's payment in the fall of 1733 for 133 shifts to clothe African American children at his home plantation, Doohoragen Manor, bears witness to the contribution childbearing by enslaved women made to his labor force. By midcentury, black residents of Carroll's Annapolis Quarter and at Doohoragen included at least two generations living amid grandparents, aunts and uncles, and cousins as well as parents and siblings. Fanny, born in 1705, worked at Riggs Quarter on Doohoragen and had been the property of the elder Carroll. An accounting of residents in 1773 noted that Fanny lived with two generations of descendants, including four children of her daughter Kate as well as at least four sons: Charles (a cook); Ned, who had seven children; Harry, who with his wife Moll had four children; and Bob, who lived at the sawmill with Frances Mitchell and their five children. At Annapolis Quarter, two children, eight grandchildren, and two great-grandchildren formed the nucleus of another family and work unit headed by Ironworks Lucy, whose name probably denotes an earlier connection with the Baltimore Ironworks. Only slaveholdings of the wealthiest planters encompassed enough people to create such dense, multigenerational kin networks living in close proximity. But similar networks developed across neighborhoods as lesser slaveholding families intermarried over several generations, dividing and regrouping their land and enslaved workers with each marriage. Extended family networks came to characterize African American communities just as they did those of British Americans.

By the early eighteenth century, elite Chesapeake planters had fully embraced the use of enslaved labor and had constructed a legal framework for slavery that protected their investment in bondspeople. The commitment of provincial and local officials to the policing of slaves and to the punishment of runaways drew upon the cooperation of men and women who themselves owned no slaves, as small and middling planters continued to rely primarily on family and servant labor. For the region overall, however, slavery developed as the primary system of economic production and its ideological justification influenced all forms of social interaction. Slaves continued to toil in fields, but they also staffed great houses, piloted boats, pursued a range of craft skills, worked in mills, iron furnaces, and forges—in short, enslaved labor proved adaptable to all economic areas. Over the course of the eighteenth century, slaveholdings grew in size and ownership spread more broadly among the free population, raising the proportion of blacks within each colony and drawing an expanding percentage of planters into slavery's web. As slavery became central to economic activity, and as legislation evolved to protect rights claimed by slaveowners, the region acquired the cultural features of a slave society, permeated by violence and laced with notions of inherent inequality.

For slaveowners, successful adoption of a system of racial slavery brought substantial benefits, but also carried potential risks. Elite planters worried most about slave revolts, but there were other causes for concern. White society threatened to divide along the fault line of slave ownership, as relatively inexpensive servant labor became scarcer and relatively abundant slave labor continued to be costly, beyond the means of many planters. Ownership of enslaved workers was a powerful status marker within the white population, bestowing significantly greater financial rewards, social prestige, and political power upon those with large holdings. Poorer whites who did not own slaves could have seen themselves as having more in common with blacks than with men whose wealth derived from slavery. But some white households that could not purchase African American workers still benefited from enslaved labor through rental or custodial arrangements, not only gathering profit from additional laboring hands but also keeping alive aspirations to ownership. At the same time, legislators in both colonies enacted laws severely circumscribing the lives of all black people, whether free or enslaved. These laws elevated the rights and privileges of all whites, no matter how poor, and created a shared racial identity that helped to keep white society from fracturing along lines of wealth and status.

The slaveowning elite, firmly in control of both colonial legislatures, wrote laws to protect its interests. As provincial law, slave codes placed everything within each colony's boundaries under the mantle of "slave society," but their relevance varied from area to area. Slavery was not the dominant labor system throughout the Eastern Shore or in western Maryland or along the Virginia frontier, where households used a mix of family labor, hired workers, and bound servants as well as slaves. Although laws regarding slavery applied to an entire colony, enforcement was not uniform, either in the judicial system or on individual plantations. In practice, daily life in a slave society was a matter of negotiation and adaptation, but always within a legal framework that protected ownership of bondspeople and a social hierarchy that rested on the foundation of enslavement.

Throughout eighteenth-century Virginia and Maryland, the relationship between masters and slaves held broad, abstract implications, but it was still the product of interactions between real people. Masters had power of life and death over their enslaved property, but rational men in practice had to balance sufficient discipline to compel labor and obedience with the need to avoid crippling injury or death of a valuable asset. Slaves had little incentive to work except fear of punishment or prospect of reward. Circumscribed as they were by Chesapeake society's laws and rules, however, Africans and African Americans found meaningful reasons to survive and ways to shape their lives: nurturing real and fictive kinship networks, adapting their masters' religion to serve their own hopes and cultural memories, controlling the work pace, and engaging in behaviors that rejected an identity as someone else's property.

Substantial numbers of native-born slaves, like those living on Burwell and Carroll plantations, became a marked regional feature by the century's second quarter, but natural increase was not the only source of growth for the enslaved population. Through the first half of the century, continued importation also played a significant role (although Africans did not arrive in numbers sufficient to reconstruct a community life sustained solely by African culture). From the late 1690s through the 1720s, slavers carried substantial numbers of Africans for sale to Chesapeake planters: forty-six hundred between 1698 and 1703; more than fourteen thousand from 1704 to 1718; another nineteen thousand between 1719 and 1729. In the next three decades, forced migration and natural increase together resulted in a dramatic upsurge in black population. From roughly thirteen thousand individuals in 1700, black population reached nearly one hundred and ninety thousand by 1760. This ever-growing source of labor drove geographic expansion and economic development even as dependence on coerced labor wove slavery's web around all aspects of colonial Chesapeake life, ensnaring both whites and blacks.

CREATING COMMUNITIES

Although slave ships transported cargoes to North America drawn from all levels of African society—rulers and slaves, traders and artisans, priests and farmers—the middle passage across the Atlantic washed away many of these distinctions. When ships passed between Capes Henry and Charles to enter the bay, the cargo was enslaved Africans whose worth, in the eyes of colonial planters, varied little from one individual to another. Yet within slavery, the experiences of Africans and their descendants were no more uniform than the status new arrivals had enjoyed in their native land. Ethnicity, age, gender, skill, time and place of arrival, and a master's position and temperament all interacted to shape the lives of individual slaves within the broad confines of a system that relegated them to the lowest place in colonial society.

From the late 1690s through the 1720s, when traders brought in large numbers of slaves, labor forces often included a number of single adult males, who might spend some portion of their lives living in a barracks with others like themselves and find a mate late in life, if at all. Over time, workforces on larger plantations became mixed in origin. Workers included native-born African Americans who enjoyed better health, spoke fluent English, and more readily understood how to maneuver through a world dominated by whites. Others were seasoned Africans who had lived in the Chesapeake region long enough to acclimate to a new disease environment and to develop familiarity with language, work routines, and survival skills. Still others were newly arrived Africans lacking both seasoning and acculturation. Periodic infusion of newcomers into social communities just taking shape on larger plantations likely created conflicts that strained, and sometimes broke, bonds being formed by shared work and residence.

As the native-born black population grew, the ratio of men to women became more balanced, making it easier to form families. Kinship networks developed not only within plantations but across the landscape as masters sold surplus slaves to neighbors and as slaves were given to or inherited by children living nearby. Roads and paths that connected plantations to stores, churches, courthouse, and other centers of white community life were used by blacks to move among neighboring plantations to visit relatives and friends. Population growth also expanded the number of large slaveholdings, where workers more often lived apart from their masters and experienced little direct supervision between sundown and sunup, thus creating additional opportunities to develop a communal life.

On the home plantation, slave cabins clustered together at a distance from the planter's own dwelling. Planters with more land also located work quarters near cultivated fields. With ten to fifteen adult hands considered the ideal number for a work gang, quarters typically provided homes for twenty-five to thirty people, consisting of working hands, children, and the elderly. Cabins were small and simple, constructed on posts placed directly in the ground, with earthen floors and wooden chimneys, and could vary considerably in size but were often 150 to 250 square feet. Thus housing of enslaved African Americans did not differ dramatically from spaces inhabited either by their African kin or by many free colonists. Houses in Africa were similarly small and constructed of natural materials that decayed within a few years and—like Chesapeake housing—could be repaired in place or rebuilt as settlements moved to fresh land. Most colonists also lived in small, simple wooden houses, with wooden chimneys and often earthen floors. Only in the last third of the century did substantial numbers of planters begin to live in larger and better-built homes, leaving enslaved blacks as the primary occupants of simple cabins.

Early cabins formed no particular pattern on the landscape, but over time their placement became more orderly, whether set out in rows or in circular or rectangular arrangements that enclosed a communal space similar to West African compounds.

Quarter at Carter's Grove. This artist's rendering of a reconstructed slave quarter at a plantation on Virginia's James River shows a variety of housing, from barracks for single men to individual or duplex houses for family groups. Fenced yards protected garden plots, chickens, and other fowl. Drawing by Jeffrey Bostetter. 1992-0191CN, The Colonial Williamsburg Foundation

Swept yards, bare of any vegetation, surrounded the cabins and reflected African practices. Blacks cultivated garden plots adjacent to their cabins or on the quarter's perimeter, growing a mix of vegetables that added variety to the diet, and raised the "dunghill fowl" (chickens) frequently described by travelers as ubiquitous on Chesapeake plantations. The central enclosed space provided the community's gathering place, where men, women, and children cooked, ate, drank, played, talked, sang, and smoked, as was true of villages in Africa. In living much of their life outdoors, a practice made necessary by the small size of their housing, blacks also shared experiences common to the region's free inhabitants.

Following English customs, indentured servants could expect

a certain amount of regular leisure time. When the workforce included a mix of servants and slaves, black and white workers probably experienced similar work routines, particularly on smaller plantations with too few laborers for separate work gangs. As slaves came to dominate the labor force, masters gradually established new, harsher work regimes. They minimized midday breaks in all but the hottest weather. Saturday became a full workday for both white servants and enslaved blacks, and Sunday work became much more common for slaves. Religious holidays now brought only about six days of rest per year, at Christmas, Easter, and Whitsuntide. Masters frequently demanded that enslaved workers strip tobacco, shuck and shell corn, or perform similar tasks in evening hours. More chores occupied slaves throughout winter months as well: draining swamps, clearing pastures, cutting and carting timber, and processing small grains.

Nearly all able-bodied enslaved men and women worked in the fields, cultivating tobacco and cereals—corn, wheat, or other grains. Women too old for field work cooked and looked after children too young to be pressed into service. Masters assigned elderly and disabled men to work as gamekeepers and cowherds responsible for plantation livestock. On large plantations, some black men practiced craft skills, generally as carpenters, coopers, shoemakers, or blacksmiths, positions often coveted by slaves and used as rewards by masters. On the largest plantations, with masters wealthy enough to divert a portion of their workers to conspicuous consumption, some slaves spent their days at domestic chores required by the planter's household. Women cooked, cleaned, washed clothes and linens, and looked after the master's children. Men tended gardens, groomed horses and drove carriages, waited on tables, and served as valets. Household slaves tended to be better clothed and fed, but because they were often on call around the clock and did not live in the quarters, they rarely experienced the respite from supervision that field hands enjoyed once the workday ended.

Masters generally provided slaves with little more than minimal clothing, a pot for cooking, a few basic tools, and simple bed ticks and blankets, although household slaves might receive better quality clothing. Regarded as property themselves, the enslaved had no legal right to property of their own, but in practice bondspeople acquired numerous personal possessions. Archaeologists have excavated spaces under slave cabins that held tools and more personal items, such as buttons, coins, and musical instruments. Most items were British or European manufactured goods associated with preparing and eating meals, including ceramics ranging from coarse earthenware to once-costly Chinese porcelain. In general, the objects were thirty to fifty years old when they ceased to be used, but some were newer, suggesting that their enslaved owners not only acquired goods handed down by masters when worn, broken, or out of fashion but also at times bought new items for themselves.

A variety of avenues gave enslaved workers entry into the market economy. Slaves who negotiated space and time to tend small gardens and raise chickens could purchase goods by selling produce, poultry, or eggs, as well as crafted objects to masters or local storekeepers. Domestic workers often received tips for services—grooming horses for a master's guests, for example, or doing laundry for a mistress's boarders. Men who made deliveries also received tips, such as Virginia slaves who carried special gifts of wild game and seafood from their masters to the governor in Williamsburg. Both plantation and store accounts record instances of enslaved workers making purchases and exchanges. One telling glimpse comes from the account book of William Johnston, a Yorktown storekeeper in the 1730s, whose customers included nine slaves who traded peas for consumer goods. Will, a slave of Colonel William Byrd II, traded four pecks of peas for a felt hat. "Billingley's Will" exchanged three bushels for a coverlet, and Thomas bought fabric, a handkerchief, and a knife and fork, using seven and one-half bushels as payment. George's peas added a length of fabric, a linen handkerchief, and a small quantity of lace to his possessions.

Archaeology also tells us much about the food eaten by the enslaved. Faunal remains indicate that animal protein came primarily from beef and pork, as was also true for most free settlers. Poultry was a less important source of meat. Slaves may have valued hens more for their eggs or their resale value than as protein for a one-pot meal. Bones from wild game—raccoon, deer, opossum, squirrel, duck, rabbit, and snapping turtle—and lead shot, gunflints, and gun parts among the artifacts indicate that enslaved men hunted to acquire additional meat for family meals. Slaves also gathered the bounty of the bay and rivers, leaving as evidence oyster shells, fish bones and scales, and lead fishing weights. The small fragments of recovered bones reveal that meat was generally used in stews that combined meat, vegetables, and broth to replicate traditional African fare. Stews also stretched available protein to feed many mouths, made poorer cuts of meat tastier and easier to eat, and saved labor because the mixture could be left to simmer while other chores were being done.

Because not all owners of slaves were planters with large, rural plantations, many housing arrangements differed from those described above. Other patterns persisted for urban slaves and for those owned by small and middling planters. Planters who owned only one or two slaves rarely provided separate housing for their bondspeople. The single slave of a small planter might sleep on a pallet by the kitchen hearth and have no private space. On middling plantations, a single building might house the owner's few enslaved workers. In town, slaves slept in kitchens, passages, stables, and other dependencies; no evidence exists for separate slave housing in either Annapolis or Williamsburg, even for the few households with as many as ten or a dozen black members. Because urban households often included skilled indentured or convict servants as well as a slave or two, slaves living in towns had more daily contact with bound white workers than did many plantation slaves.

Throughout much of the Chesapeake region during the eighteenth century, the expanding population of enslaved workers provided opportunities for some—though hardly all—to create families and kin networks. These clusters of related individuals formed the nuclei of black communities, not only within quarters of large holdings but also across plantations and neighborhoods. As Africans and African Americans worked to transform their forced living arrangements into meaningful relationships, the violence inherent in slavery and the constant threat of separation challenged their fragile communities with instability and insecurity.

DIVISIONS AND DISRUPTIONS

Living arrangements experienced by enslaved workers could vary considerably over an individual's lifespan. A young girl born on a large plantation, for example, might spend her childhood in a single family cabin with both parents; by midcentury, more than half the children on large plantations lived with both parents. By the time she was ten or eleven, she might be sold to a neighboring small planter and sleep on a pallet in the loft with the family's young children. Masters often separated black children between the ages of ten and fourteen from their kin when selling excess labor or shifting workers to keep quarters supplied with the preferred number of hands. In her late teens this young woman might find a mate on a neighboring plantation. If she were fortunate, her master would provide a cabin in which to raise her children, and where her partner could visit. Only one of every five women living on small plantations shared her home with a mate. As her children neared adulthood, this woman might experience another separation if her master sold or gifted one or more of her children.

Slave households dissolved and reformed because of circumstances over which the enslaved themselves had little control. Slave marriages had no legal status, and enslaved parents had no legal right to custody of their children. Although masters recognized marital and parental relationships in practice and understood that their laborers might toil more willingly as part of an intact family unit, slaves depended on owners' goodwill and good fortune for their family's security. A financial crisis or owner's death carried the potential for separation of slave families and kinship groups. Owners who found themselves in debt, for example, could sell their human property to extricate themselves from financial difficulties.

Slaves belonging to wealthy owners, while less likely to be sold to pay off debts, faced a different challenge: They belonged to the owners most likely to distribute slave property to family members through gifts or bequests. As early as 1695, for example, Lewis Burwell II may have transferred slaves to four married daughters, none of whom lived on the Lower Peninsula. At his death in 1710, Burwell left two young girls to each of two unmarried daughters, whose eventual marriages most likely removed the girls from their childhood kin network. Similar divisions occurred again and again, particularly if planters left slaves to daughters and divided land among sons. Marriages between men who owned land and women who owned slaves created productive plantation units for white owners, but frequently subjected black families to separation from kin and relocation to unfamiliar places. Removal to a new home, even in close proximity to the old, added another burden as the enslaved struggled to maintain family ties.

Although the legal system denied slaves an identity other than as property, Africans and African Americans recognized gradations of status and a perceptible hierarchy within their ranks. Some blacks specialized in craft work and rarely labored in the fields; others shouldered responsibility as leaders of work gangs or quarters; still others experienced more contact with whites, serving the master's family and guests as domestic staff for the "big house." These distinctions created social structures within the black community. Evolving kinship networks provided an additional framework of age and family position. An individual's place in that framework—as head of a lineage, for example—could convey status and authority within the network of a plantation's bondspeople or in a neighborhood, giving enslaved men and women an internal sense of worth independent of the external value assigned by a master.

Although colonial law denied enslaved blacks virtually every legal protection, bondspeople were not powerless as they negotiated and renegotiated their relationships with their masters. Africans, who came from societies that included slaves, brought their own cultural understandings about how slaves and masters should behave to these interactions. Communal memory and continued importation of workers from Africa reinforced this knowledge as slaves developed strategies to shape the master-slave relationship. Tactics ranged from routine delays and work slowdowns, through feigned stupidity and illness, to arson and sabotage. There were also, although infrequently, instances of murder and attempted rebellion.

Slaves belonging to large planters generally dealt on a daily basis not with their master but rather with overseers or drivers charged with extracting maximum labor from the workers they supervised and answerable to their employer for shortcomings and failures. Slaves became skilled at appealing directly to masters when overseers drove them too hard. They also became adept at using their control of tools, especially plows and carts, to establish the pace of work and at supplementing scanty food allotments through raids on stores of grain. Overseers and masters viewed the latter behavior as theft and pilferage; the enslaved saw the acts as legitimate enjoyment of the fruits of their labor.

On occasion, slaves simply ran off. Most runaways acted alone or in very small groups, but there were periodic reports of maroon communities forming on the edges of settled territory. (The term *maroon* derives from the Spanish word *cimmarón,* meaning wild in the sense of escaped or runaway.) In 1729, for example, fifteen slaves ran from a new plantation at the head of the James River. Runaways took tools, arms, clothing, and food and had time to begin clearing ground in the Shenandoah Valley before being recaptured. But maroon communities were more common and more successful in the Caribbean, where slaves greatly outnumbered whites. In Virginia and Maryland, by contrast, whites outnumbered blacks in most counties; white households were spread throughout the countryside, making detection of fugitives more likely; and slaves were clustered in relatively small groups where their movements were more easily observed by the whites among whom they lived.

A variety of motives inspired bondspeople who absented themselves from their master's control. Some, like those who sought out maroon communities, wished to escape completely from their status as someone else's property. For others, flight was one move in a series of actions designed to negotiate terms under which the slave would allow the master's continued use of his or her labor. Often absence was a temporary respite, time taken as a break from daily toil or used to visit family or friends on another plantation. Masters from southern Maryland who placed advertisements seeking information about runaways between 1730 and 1780, for example, believed that just over one-half of the slaves who had absconded left "to visit." These visits were more than mere social calls, however; their purpose was to reunite family members who had been separated by sale, inheritance, or relocation. Cuffee, whom his master "supposed to be gone to Piscataway, where he has a Wife; and formerly lived," was just one of hundreds of slaves who ran to a loved one as much as from a master.[1]

It is impossible to know how many slaves absented themselves long enough to be considered runaways, and equally difficult to estimate how many succeeded in avoiding recapture. Planta-

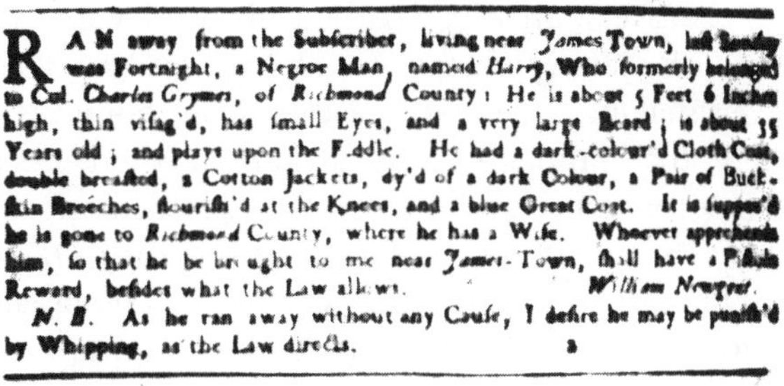

RAN away from the Subſcriber, living near *James Town*, last Sunday was Fortnight, a Negroe Man, named *Harry*, Who formerly belonged to Col. *Charles Grymes*, of *Richmond* County: He is about 5 Feet 6 Inches high, thin viſag'd, has ſmall Eyes, and a very large Beard; is about 35 Years old; and plays upon the Fiddle. He had a dark-colour'd Cloth Coat, double breaſted, a Cotton Jackets, dy'd of a dark Colour, a Pair of Buckſkin Breeches, flouriſh'd at the Knees, and a blue Great Coat. It is ſuppos'd he is gone to *Richmond* County, where he has a Wife. Whoever apprehends him, ſo that he be brought to me near *James-Town*, ſhall have a Piſtole Reward, beſides what the Law allows. *William Newgent.*

N. B. As he ran away without any Cauſe, I deſire he may be puniſh'd by Whipping, as the Law directs.

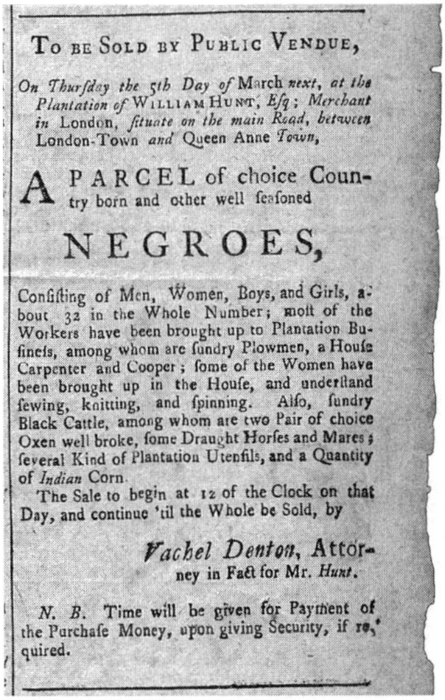

TO BE SOLD BY PUBLIC VENDUE,

On Thurſday the 5th Day of March *next, at the Plantation of* WILLIAM HUNT, *Eſq; Merchant in* London, *ſituate on the main Road, between* London-Town *and* Queen Anne *Town*,

A PARCEL of choice Country born and other well ſeaſoned

NEGROES,

Conſiſting of Men, Women, Boys, and Girls, about 32 in the Whole Number; moſt of the Workers have been brought up to Plantation Buſineſs, among whom are ſundry Plowmen, a Houſe Carpenter and Cooper; ſome of the Women have been brought up in the Houſe, and underſtand ſewing, knitting, and ſpinning. Alſo, ſundry Black Cattle, among whom are two Pair of choice Oxen well broke, ſome Draught Horſes and Mares; ſeveral Kind of Plantation Utenſils, and a Quantity of *Indian* Corn.

The Sale to begin at 12 of the Clock on that Day, and continue 'til the Whole be Sold, by

Vachel Denton, Attorney in Fact for Mr. *Hunt*.

N. B. Time will be given for Payment of the Purchaſe Money, upon giving Security, if required.

Runaway and Sale Advertisements. *Top,* a notice seeking recovery of a runaway slave, placed in the *Virginia Gazette* in 1746. *Left,* an advertisement that appeared in the *Maryland Gazette* in 1752 for the sale of a plantation's thirty-two slaves, livestock, and other goods. Collection of the Maryland State Archives, MSA SC 2731-1-8

tion record books occasionally contain names of slaves stricken from lists of property because they had escaped months ago and were unlikely to return. But the same books also contain payments of expenses for tracking and recapturing runaways. Some experiences may have been similar to that of Celia, who for at least three months was "entertained by Negroes, and [was] conveyed by them through most of the Counties on the Western Shore." There is no way to know if the blacks who helped her were free or enslaved, for runaways received aid from friends on other plantations as well as from free blacks. It is probable that more runaways suffered the fate of Jack, who was captured and put in jail; the sheriff "desired [his master] to take him away, and pay charges."[2] Native-born slaves, particularly those with greater fluency in English and experience of mobility, may have had the best chance of making a successful escape from bondage. It is telling, though, that although slaves far outnumbered servants, advertisements for runaway servants far exceeded those for slaves. Because slavery was legal in every British North American colony at this time—and because enslavement was a status largely defined by race—there was no settled area where a runaway slave might hope to be forever safe from discovery.

As effective as truancy and other methods of resistance might have been for slaves negotiating terms of work and organization of their communities, the brutality permeating slavery dictated that masters held the greater share of power. Successful employment of slave labor ultimately derived from the use of force. At little risk of legal sanctions except in cases of extreme barbarity, owners could whip, brand, or mutilate slaves who caused trouble, who destroyed property, who ran away, who failed to work, or who behaved in an insolent manner. Planters also employed psychological violence by selling or threatening to sell troublesome bondspeople. The use of physical force might make a single slave less fit for work, just as the sale of a loved one might further alienate a spouse or parent, but if such actions instilled enough fear in other slaves, masters found they were worth the price.

EXPANSION AND URBANIZATION

Masters could effectively use the threat of sale to coerce enslaved workers in part because geographic expansion during the eighteenth century created ever-greater distances between African Americans living in tidewater communities and plantations being established in the Piedmont. In this respect, however, the two Chesapeake colonies did not develop in tandem. Because Maryland's Piedmont area developed as a grain-producing region, its settlement proceeded largely without substantial investment in slavery. Wheat cultivation required numerous workers only at harvest, giving planters little incentive to purchase year-round laborers. In the Virginia Piedmont, however, tobacco provided the impetus for growth, and enslaved workers provided the necessary labor. Many newly arrived Africans were transported inland to plantations along the upper reaches of the colony's rivers and beyond the fall line into the Piedmont plateau. As natural increase among tidewater slaves provided owners with surplus workers, planters also moved native-born slaves west. By midcentury, only a minority of Virginia's Africans and African Americans resided in the tidewater area.

Several factors contributed to the westward shift of black labor. Elite planters used political connections to acquire new Piedmont land, cultivating some tracts with surplus workers moved from tidewater plantations and placed under the supervision of an overseer, while holding other land for future gifts to children. As land prices rose in tidewater counties, Piedmont tracts could be subdivided for lease or sale to landless colonists willing to migrate to frontier areas. Increased European demand encouraged expansion by raising tobacco prices, particularly for the oronoco variety, preferred by the French, that grew successfully in Piedmont soils. At the same time, elite planters and merchants used some of their profits from higher prices to offer credit to newcomers that enabled them to acquire enslaved workers. Within one generation after the first significant advance of slavery into the Piedmont area, about forty thousand blacks lived and labored there.

Unlike Piedmont plantations in Virginia that largely replicated earlier tidewater development, colonial settlements in western Maryland and beyond the Piedmont in Virginia grew out of different patterns of migration and economic activity. Maryland's western frontier, from the Pennsylvania border to the Potomac River, offered soil well-suited to the grain and cattle agriculture practiced by a growing population of German, Scottish, and Irish immigrants, who arrived at Philadelphia but quickly moved west and south through the backcountry. Waves of new settlers in search of land traveled along the Great Wagon Road that extended through the Appalachian valley from Pennsylvania to the Carolinas. Before midcentury, Native Americans who lived in Maryland's portion of the valley did not welcome settlers in their midst. Indians threatened reprisals if colonists "press too much upon Us for We have give no body Land," but in 1744 the Maryland assembly bought rights to land between the Potomac and Susquehanna Rivers from Native Americans of the Five Nations.[3] Members of the Maryland elite quickly patented the best land and disposed of it through outright sale, lease, or on credit, with the land as security.

In 1745, Daniel Dulany the Elder surveyed a site near the Monocacy River to provide a market town for western Maryland. He offered lots to artisans and tradesmen for purchase at modest prices or as leaseholds with an annual ground rent of one or two shillings. The proprietor granted the right to establish weekly markets and two annual fairs. German Lutheran and Reformed congregations built churches on lots Dulany donated. The area's rapid population growth led to creation of a new county just four years after Dulany began actively to promote settlement. By 1750, Frederick Town had become Maryland's most populous town, connected by wagon roads not only to Annapolis but also to the fall-line ports of Georgetown on the Potomac and Baltimore on the Patapsco. Herds of livestock made the journey to market on the hoof, while wagons carried grain to the port towns' mills.

By the 1750s, settlers began moving farther south into the Valley of Virginia, the area west of the Piedmont and the Blue Ridge Mountains, via the Great Wagon Road. As in Maryland, these German, Scottish, and Irish settlers concentrated on cultivating grains and raising herds of livestock, using family and hired labor. Their marketable produce traveled overland from northern portions of the valley to Virginia's river ports on the fall line: Alexandria on the Potomac and Fredericksburg on the Rappahannock. Secondary routes soon linked the valley's southern residents to Fredericksburg and to Richmond on the James River. Partly as a result of this westward expansion, after midcentury the Chesapeake region exported far more corn and perhaps half as much wheat as did the grain-producing middle Atlantic colonies of Pennsylvania and New York.

In 1748, migrants established Virginia's first small settlement farther west in the Allegheny Mountains. Known as Draper's Meadow, it was located near present-day Blacksburg. Two years later, a surveying party discovered a passage, now known as Cumberland Gap, through the mountains to the plateau beyond the Allegheny range. The surveyors were the first Virginians to reach the area where the modern states of Virginia, Kentucky, and Tennessee converge. But exploration was one thing, substantial occupation another. Even by the early 1770s, only about 6 percent of Virginia's population lived in the Shenandoah Valley or beyond. Competing interests of both the French and Native

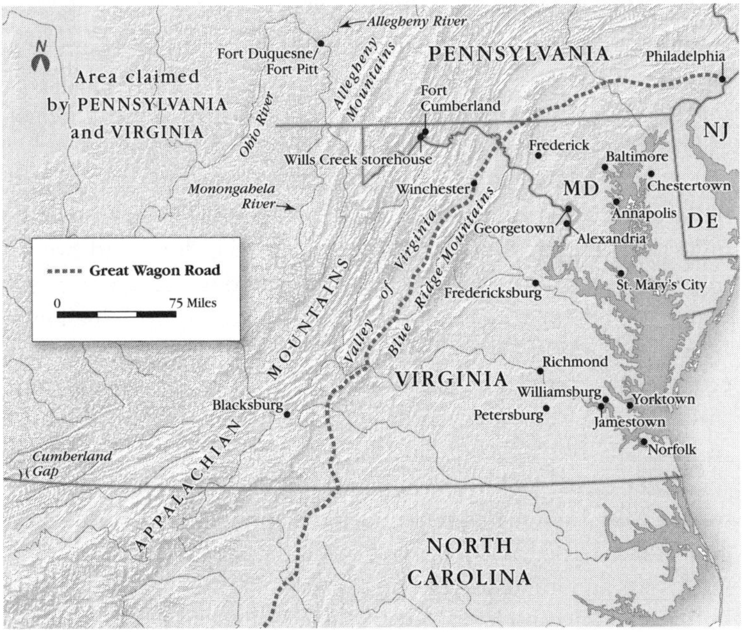

The Chesapeake region, c. 1765, with trans-Appalachian territory and principal colonial towns. Map by Robert Cronan, Lucidity Information Design, LLC

Americans delayed substantial movement into the mountains and territory to their west until after the Revolutionary War.

Agricultural and marketing changes that accompanied westward expansion gradually reworked the Chesapeake's urban landscape, particularly along the boundary between the coastal plain and the Piedmont plateau. Scottish factors and native-born merchants began to compete with English firms for business in the rapidly growing area. Scottish factors focused on the tobacco trade, leaving an opening for native-born merchants to build on tidewater connections with grain markets. These newcomers to the mercantile scene operated year-round stores that spurred growth in the few towns that already existed and stimulated the appearance of new villages in the backcountry and along the fall line. Because wheat generally went to market in the fall and surplus corn in the spring, teamsters and craftsmen who processed and moved the crops supplied tavern keepers and local stores with customers throughout the year. As crafts and services began to cluster together around headwaters and transfer points for cargoes, they drew in other artisans who could build houses, make shoes, and turn fabric into clothing, as well as professional men who could draw up legal documents or treat illnesses.

Grain production was the agricultural economy's most dynamic element at midcentury, and Chesapeake planters increasingly prospered from exports of corn, wheat, flour, and bread. Some areas, like the upper Eastern Shore and western Maryland, concentrated on wheat production in response to expanding overseas markets. Other planters in areas that produced good crops of tobacco diversified by marketing surplus corn and, less often, adding wheat to their crop mix. Still others, living in areas of poor soil not well-suited to either wheat or tobacco, such as the lower Eastern Shore, continued to produce corn for export to the West Indies. Planters also increased cultivation of lesser grains, like barley, oats, and rye; brewers purchased the barley, while oats and rye tended to be consumed on the plantations by humans and livestock.

As grain cultivation increased, the work experiences of enslaved men and women began to diverge significantly. Growing and processing grain created a larger market for craft workers, particularly woodworkers, blacksmiths, and coopers. Unlike the rough-hewn barns used to house tobacco, a mill required skilled carpenters for construction and maintenance, as well as trained millers to turn grains into marketable grades of flour. Wheelwrights produced carts and wagons that carried harvested grain to barns for threshing and to mills for grinding into flour, while coopers made barrels for shipping milled flour to overseas markets. The metalwork of cart wheels and traces, mill gears, and barrel hoops all called for blacksmithing skills. African Americans did not by any means monopolize these craft positions, but specialization in skilled craft work did become an alternative to repetitive field work for some enslaved men, even as women and older children continued the daily toil of tending hoe crops.

Customs records for the end of the colonial period demonstrate the greater diversification of the Chesapeake region's exports and overseas markets. Tobacco, shipped solely to Great Britain, in 1773 still accounted for 75 percent of the total value of commodity exports. The Navigation Acts similarly directed iron exports almost entirely to Great Britain. Although Chesapeake ironworks made a significant contribution to total British production, iron accounted for only 3 percent of exports from the two colonies. Grains and grain products (primarily flour) represented 19 percent of total commodity exports. Almost one-half went to southern Europe, and most of the rest was sent to the West Indies. Caribbean islands took nearly one-half the exported wood products, and Great Britain, needing colonial timber for the navy's masts and spars, accounted for most of the remainder. Comparing the 1773 figures with those recorded forty years earlier clarifies the changes that occurred. Tobacco exports nearly tripled in value, but the value of grains and grain products increased fifteenfold over the period, and the value of wood products grew by a factor of six. The Chesapeake economy had long since left behind the time when planters felt they had "no trade att home or abroad but that of tobacco."[4]

Economic diversification stimulated the growth of new towns and contributed substantially to the wealth that underwrote the flowering of Annapolis and Williamsburg. While smaller market towns functioned primarily as rural economic centers for tobacco and grain planters, Annapolis and Williamsburg expanded as social and cultural centers. Wealthy planters and legislators began to spend several months of the year in the colonial capitals, partly to do business in legislative sessions and provincial courts, but also to participate in a social season patterned after the dances, gaming clubs, card parties, and theaters enjoyed by fashionable Londoners. Income generated from shipbuilding and iron manufacture, land speculation, extensive law practices, and sale of agricultural products financed elegant town houses in each capital. A building boom in Annapolis, for example, produced roughly a dozen Georgian mansions in the 1750s and 1760s, introducing a new level of sophistication into the urban landscape.

The construction of these houses and similar homes in Williamsburg had a ripple effect in the local economy. Bustling work sites provided employment for a wide range of building craftsmen, from stonemasons who set massive foundations in place to carvers responsible for elaborate mantels and cornices that graced the interiors. Furnishing, clothing, and provisioning these wealthy households called on the services of cabinetmakers, tailors, barbers and wig makers, bakers and butchers, silversmiths and watchmakers. Dry-goods merchants imported mahogany furniture, fine silk and velvet fabrics, exotic foodstuffs, and other luxuries to enhance a genteel lifestyle.

The busier towns began to offer more employment opportunities for women. While the types of tasks performed by urban women did not differ greatly from those of rural women, urban women were more likely to use those skills to earn an income. Women often advertised their trades in a newspaper, took in orphan children to be instructed in their skills, appeared in court suits related to their work, and identified themselves by the craft work they performed. Thus in August 1745, a tailor's widow, Sarah Munro, offered "Quilting, of all Kinds, . . . such as Bed Quilts, Gowns, Petticoats, &c. performed . . . at her House in Annapolis, as well [done] as in England, and much cheaper." Mary Ann March and her daughter took in "Quilting, and any Needle Work, at very cheap Rates," but March also taught paying students "all Sorts of Embroidery."[5] Other women taught school and operated taverns. Tavern keeping, in particular, allowed a widowed woman to remain in her home making use of her domestic skills, as well as managerial talents, to support her family.

The colonial capitals offered their elite residents a much more varied social calendar than small towns and isolated plantations could provide on a regular basis. Traveling theater groups from England and other colonies visited both towns regularly, performing material ranging from Shakespeare to farces. In purpose-built theaters, the troupes entertained the gentry seated in reserved boxes; persons of lesser rank were packed onto benches in the pit and gallery. In Annapolis, balls at the Assembly Rooms, horse races on the course just outside the city gate, and social clubs like the Tuesday Club of the 1740s and 1750s brought elite gentlemen together in convivial settings. Gentry households represented no more than 10 percent of town residents, but they set the tone that caused the Reverend Jonathan Boucher to declare Annapolis, where he served as Anglican minister in the early 1770s, "the genteelest town in North America."[6]

BLURRING THE BOUNDARY

The majority of Africans and African Americans were enslaved, but from the earliest decades of settlement free inhabitants of the Chesapeake colonies included black men, women, and children, although always in small numbers. Some, like John Baptista in early Maryland, entered the region as servants and—like white servants—achieved freedom once their term of indenture ended. Some descendants of these early arrivals managed to protect their free-born status throughout the colonial period, albeit always with difficulty. Other Africans and African Americans acquired freedom through provisions in masters' wills. William Dixon, for example, a Quaker planter living on Maryland's Eastern Shore, freed two slaves in the will he wrote in 1708. In addition to bequeathing their freedom, Dixon left the couple fifty acres of land, instructed his executor to build dwelling and tobacco houses there, and gave them a mare, two head of cattle, and a sow to start their livestock herds. An owner could also free slaves by a manumission deed, a legal document declaring the individuals it named to be free persons. As an alternative route to freedom, some blacks succeeded in accumulating enough money to purchase themselves from their masters. The most common arrangement involved self-hire, whereby a master permitted an enslaved man or woman to work for someone else for wages. The terms usually required the slave to pay a set portion of the wages to the master, but the remainder could be used to buy goods or saved for self-purchase.

Most free African Americans, however, were not individuals who escaped the legal and physical net of slavery themselves, but rather descendants of mixed-race unions. Scattered court records and other documents reveal marriages between white and black partners in both colonies in the mid-seventeenth century, before the passage of laws that imposed severe penalties for such relationships. In Northampton County on Virginia's Eastern Shore, for example, at least five free black men and one enslaved man married white women in the 1650s and 1660s. As the black population grew and legislators took measures to secure their investment in enslaved labor, legal barriers made mixed-race marriages increasingly uncommon. The Maryland General Assembly first addressed the subject in 1664, declaring that any "freeborne English" woman who married any slave "shall Serve the master of such slave dureing the life of her husband."[7] Children born of unions that had already taken place became servants for thirty years. A revised statute of 1692 stipulated seven years of servitude for any free white woman who married an enslaved or free black man. Virginia legislation passed in 1691 imposed a penalty of banishment from the colony for any white person who married any person of color, whether black, mulatto, or Native American. A 1705 revision replaced banishment with six months imprisonment and a £10 fine. These laws succeeded in reducing —although not entirely eliminating—the incidence of interracial marriage in both colonies. Northampton County resident Tamer Smith, for example, spent six months in prison and paid the fine in order to marry Edmund Hitchens, a free mulatto, in 1738.

Laws limiting marriage, however, did little to prevent mixed-race sexual relationships and the likely result, mixed-race children. Many mulattoes were illegitimate children of free women, usually but not always servants, and black partners, who were almost always enslaved men. Prosecutions for interracial bastardy reflected the changing demography of the Chesapeake workforce across the colonial period. As plantation laborers began to include enslaved men, instances of white servant women accused of interracial bastardy—or, in the court's language, "bearing a mulatto child"—increased accordingly. Although the fathers were usually enslaved, the children were free because their mothers were free women. As illegitimate, mixed-race offspring of servant women, however, they occupied the very lowest tier in free society's hierarchy.

Legislatures and courts tried to keep up with the problem that free mixed-race women and children posed for their efforts to divide colonial population into two distinct groups defined by a combination of race and status: free whites and enslaved blacks. Laws mandated punishments intended to prevent mixed-race unions—or at least to ensure that the men and women who held bound labor would benefit from unions they could not prevent. Beginning in the 1690s, courts sold free women found guilty of interracial bastardy and their mulatto children for terms of servitude; in both colonies, the relevant laws initially applied only to white women, but were later revised to include free mulatto women. Virginia set the mother's punishment at five years of service or payment of a £15 fine (well beyond the means of most women), while Maryland set the term at seven years, with no escape through payment of a fine. Both colonies, moreover, mandated that mixed-race children of free mothers labor as servants until age thirty-one.

During the eighteenth century, free mixed-race children provided a significant source of labor for some Chesapeake planters. Most of the women punished for interracial bastardy were already servants laboring on plantations with both servant and enslaved workers, and their masters were the usual purchasers of their extended servitude. The women continued to live, therefore, on plantations with racially mixed labor forces as single, unmarried women through most of their childbearing years, increasing the likelihood that they would bear additional illegitimate children.

Selling mixed-race female children as servants raised the odds that these daughters would also bear illegitimate children, and it is not unusual to find examples of successive generations of women held as long-term servants as a consequence of interracial relationships. In 1730, for example, Talbot County justices sold the labor of Margaret Madden, an indentured servant, to Edward Needles, her master, for twenty-eight years, noting that "she by her own confession saith that she hath been convicted four times for fornication with a certain Negroe man."[8] The court also sold Grace Madden, Margaret's daughter, to Needles. In 1745, Grace gave birth to her first known illegitimate child, and faced prosecution for seven more children between that year and 1759. Because the father(s) of at least six were African or African American, Grace's multiple convictions added an additional forty-two years to her servitude. Grace retained the status of a free woman, with more legal rights than a slave could claim, but she experienced lifetime bondage. Grace's female children faced a high probability of following in the same path. The law succeeded in ensuring that planters ultimately benefited from the illicit sexual activity of their female servants, but punishment by servitude largely failed as a deterrent for interracial bastardy.

A second group of mixed-race children, those borne by enslaved women and fathered by free white men, rarely came to the attention of any court. Elizabeth Key's case was brought before the Virginia courts prior to the legal shift of the late seventeenth century that made a mother's status the determinant for children, and only because her father had explicitly provided for her freedom. Most mulatto children born by enslaved women became the property of planters, who were often their fathers, and their identity as enslaved mulattoes surfaces only occasionally in inventories or other contemporary documents. Only rarely did fathers acknowledge their children, free them, and provide for their support, in the manner of John Custis IV, a member of Virginia's council. Custis freed his son Jack, "born of the body of my Slave Alice," by a deed of manumission recorded in the York County Court. He gave Jack 250 acres of land in York County and ownership of Alice, her other children, and four additional enslaved boys of Jack's choosing. In his will, written in 1749, Custis stipulated that until he reached the age of twenty, Jack was to live with his white half brother Daniel. Custis directed his executor to build a "handsome strong convenient dwelling house" for Jack on the York County land and to furnish it with Russia leather chairs and couches, walnut tables, feather beds, and considerable other property, for Jack's use when he turned twenty.[9]

Religious beliefs, which likely motivated William Dixon to free his two slaves, became an increasingly important factor influencing attitudes toward slavery. Believing that each individual, whether white or black, contained the light of God, many members of the Society of Friends came to oppose the practice of one person holding in bondage another whom God considered his equal. The Virginia Yearly Meeting urged humane treatment and warned Quakers against participating in patrols searching for runaways but did not formally renounce slaveholding. Beginning in 1730, though, both the Philadelphia Yearly Meeting (which supervised Maryland's Eastern Shore meetings) and the Baltimore Yearly Meeting gradually moved toward firm opposition to buying, selling, and holding slaves. By the 1760s, these actions could be grounds for a local meeting to expel a member. Antipathy toward slave ownership on the part of Quaker meetings prompted some members to free their enslaved laborers, contributing to intermittent growth in the free black population.

The presence of free blacks and mulattoes, by blurring the sharp dividing line between free white on one side and enslaved black on the other, challenged slaveowners' control of blacks as property. Legislators continued to revise the laws that codified slavery in an effort to erect permanent, nonpermeable boundaries between black and white, enslaved and free. Slaves became subject to ever stricter controls and discipline, while the civil rights and civic responsibilities of free blacks—and Native Americans—narrowed considerably from those experienced by white men. In Virginia, for example, when the militia mustered according to rank, free men of color could not bring weapons and could only participate as "drummers, trumpeters, . . . or in such other servile labor as they shall be directed to perform."[10]

A wide-ranging Virginia statute passed in 1723 withheld the right to vote from all free people of color, regardless of their ability to meet property qualifications. Asked by British officials to explain the arbitrary denial, Governor William Gooch's reply clearly expressed the prevailing desire of legislators to treat all blacks very differently from all whites. Gooch wrote from Virginia that only by placing "a perpetual Brand upon Free-Negros & Mulattos by excluding them from that great Priviledge of a Freeman" [the right to vote] could white planters "make the free-Negros sensible that a distinction ought to be made between their offspring and the Descendants of an Englishman, with whom they never were to be Accounted Equal."[11] Other provisions forbid free blacks from purchasing white indentured servants or owning weapons. Laws also imposed more severe punishments for free blacks than for whites for certain crimes and mandated fines or imprisonment for striking a white person, regardless of the circumstances.

Over time, legislatures in both colonies also limited the ability of masters to free their slaves. A Virginia statute of 1691 required that any freed slave had to leave the colony, although the degree of enforcement is unknown. The 1723 statute cited above also prohibited manumission of any black, mulatto, or Indian slave except by approval of the governor and council and then only as a reward for public service. Noting that masters too often freed slaves who were "disabled and superannuated" (that is, unable to work because they were chronically ill, injured, or elderly) and who therefore "either perished through Want, or otherwise became a Burthen to others," Maryland legislators in 1752 ordered that masters could manumit such slaves only if they provided them with food and clothing for the remainder of their natural lives. Because "giving Freedom to Slaves, by any last Will and Testament, may be attended with many Evils," this legislation also banned manumission by will, a practice that was not reinstated until 1797.[12]

Few free black or mulatto inhabitants of the Chesapeake region shared the experience of Jack, the son of John Custis, who received land and other resources for his use as a free man. For most, slavery's legal framework and the demography of much of the settled area, where almost all people of African descent were enslaved, presented a constant challenge to their freedom. Despite these obstacles, small pockets of free families did persist on the margins of free society. By their very presence, free people of African descent challenged the foundation of the Chesapeake region's slave society, the profound separation in legal identity between a free white population, on one side, and an enslaved black population, on the other. To minimize the effect of their contradictory existence, both legislation and social practices evolved in ways that kept most free blacks confined to a narrow space between the lowest stratum of free white society and the ranks of the enslaved.

A HIERARCHICAL SOCIETY

In the middle of the eighteenth century, the non-Indian Chesapeake population totaled about two hundred and thirty thousand. Ninety-eight thousand people lived in Maryland and one hundred and thirty thousand in Virginia, with blacks accounting for 30 percent of Maryland's total and 44 percent of Virginia's. Using a Maryland census taken in 1755, we can reconstruct the broad outlines of Chesapeake society at midcentury, in which differences of gender, age, race, religion, wealth, and independence determined an individual's rights, privileges, and way of life.

Free white males made up just 15 percent of Maryland's population. Property requirements dictated that only an even smaller subset of men had the right to vote and to hold office, and these rights were further circumscribed by religion. Having lost officeholding privileges during the Protestant Revolution, Maryland Catholics were also barred from participating in elections after the Jacobite rebellion in Britain in 1715. Quakers could vote, but their objections to swearing the required oaths generally excluded them from holding office. Free black males who met Maryland's property qualifications could vote, but only a little more than four hundred free black and mulatto men lived in the colony (.003 percent of total population), and few met the property qualifications. Single and widowed free women could own property, execute contracts, and initiate suits, but could not vote or hold office. Married women and children derived their status from husbands and fathers and had no legal standing of their own. Free white women accounted for about 15 percent of the population, but it is not possible to isolate single or widowed women from the total. White children who were not servants constituted 30 percent of the colony's non-Indian residents.

Although indentured servants arrived in far fewer numbers than in the seventeenth century, workers were still entering Maryland under terms of servitude, particularly those with skills to offer. Wealthy planters, for example, often wrote to agents in Britain requesting gardeners or grooms or other men with specialized training. Transported British convicts, however, now accounted for about half of the servant population. The Transportation Act passed by Parliament in 1718 gave justices in Britain authority to sentence felons to terms of colonial servitude. Those guilty of noncapital crimes generally received a sentence of seven years; those convicted of capital offenses could be transported for a fourteen-year term or for life. Between 1718 and 1775, as many as fifty thousand transported convicts crossed the ocean, with the great majority sent to Chesapeake shores. The major markets for these workers were planters who did not have cash or credit to buy more costly slave labor, those who lived in areas where slavers rarely brought enough Africans to satisfy demand, craftsmen looking for inexpensive journeymen, and area ironworks. Indentured and convict servants, a group that included not only adults but also children, accounted for about 6 percent of the 1755 population.

The census tabulations divided Maryland's population of Africans and African Americans into several categories, distinguishing not only between free and enslaved but also between black and mulatto, although it is unlikely that every mixed-race individual was classified as mulatto. The figures yield a combined total of forty-six thousand blacks and mulattoes, of whom 92 percent were counted as black and 8 percent as mulatto. Only about seventeen hundred of these men, women, and children were not held in lifetime bondage. Those identified as black were almost always enslaved, with only 1 percent identified as free; by contrast, 41 percent of those classified as mulatto experienced the limited benefits of freedom extended to people of color in a slave society. Children under the age of sixteen accounted for 52 percent of the colony's black and mulatto population. These distributions underscore the fundamental symmetry between African ancestry and Chesapeake enslavement.

Looking more broadly at the two colonies, tenants and small landowners represented more than one-half of free householders. Although tenants had the extra expense of an annual rent for their land, living conditions for the two groups did not differ greatly. Shoemaker David Prichard was a typical member of this stratum of Chesapeake society. He had been an indentured servant in 1725, but by 1733 he headed his own household and had at least three children. He owned no land, but rented property in Island Hundred in Maryland's Talbot County, on which he kept horses, cows, and hogs, and grew tobacco and corn. The Prichards furnished their small dwelling with two beds, a pine table, a chest of drawers, one arm chair, and four side chairs. Mary Prichard prepared and served the family's meals in a kitchen space equipped with iron and tin utensils, pewter dishes, and a small amount of earthenware. She carried out her domestic chores aided by tubs for washing clothes, bedding, and table linens; a box iron for pressing cloth; and a wheel for spinning woolen yarn. In addition to his shoemaking equipment, Prichard owned two plows and some basic carpentry tools as well as a supply of leather and hides. But Prichard owned no labor, never served on a jury or in a minor office, was not eligible to vote, and accumulated only £55 of moveable property before his death in 1755.

Had Prichard's career been more prosperous, during his lifetime he might have moved up to the level of "middling" planter, in the process most likely acquiring land and slaves. The middling group comprised about one-quarter of the region's free householders. About 70 percent of middling planters owned land and on average held about two hundred acres. Roughly the same percentage owned slaves, usually having between one and five bondspeople in their household.

Noah Corner, for example, was a native-born carpenter and planter who lived on a 250-acre plantation on Maryland's Eastern Shore, where he grew tobacco, corn, wheat, and oats and raised cattle, horses, sheep, and pigs. Corner's riding horse, saddle, and bridle, valued together at £13, were worth nearly as much as all of Prichard's livestock; Corner's total investment in livestock, moreover, exceeded the value of Prichard's entire estate. Corner did not own a slave, but he bought one servant during his career and took in an orphan, whom he agreed to train as a house carpenter. The Corners furnished their home with four feather beds and bedsteads, a cot and cradle, three tables, three chests, eight rush-bottom chairs, and a walnut desk. An hour glass and a silver watch measured time, candlesticks held candles to provide light for reading, and a looking glass allowed Corner to adjust his brown wig. Rachel Corner's household duties included care of three children from her first marriage as well as at least three children of her second marriage. She prepared and served food for her family utilizing brass skillets and utensils, two dozen glass bottles, iron and tinware, pewter dishes and serving pieces, and a tea kettle. Her hackle, wool cards, and three spinning wheels allowed Rachel to process and spin flax and wool. Beeswax and tallow provided raw materials for the family's candles. As a freeholder, Corner could cast his vote for delegates to the legislature and he sat on several grand juries.

Although the upper echelon of the hierarchy that shaped colonial society encompassed only a very small percentage of the population, it embraced a wide range of wealth. Jeremiah Nicolls, for example, possessed far more property than Noah Corner, but was only a modestly wealthy member of the elite. Nicolls was the son of a minister whose fortuitous marriage allied him with a family of great wealth and position. Nicolls held the offices of justice of the peace and sheriff in Talbot County and acted as factor for a London tobacco firm. Twenty-five slaves, divided among his home plantation and two quarters, worked Nicoll's five hundred acres, cared for his livestock, and ran his ferry. Nicoll's mahogany tea table, violin, large library, extensive wine cellar, lavish wardrobe, gold rings and buttons, numerous pieces of silver plate, and small carriage all served notice of his position in the upper level of local society. Nicolls had ample land to divide among his four sons and could easily afford the £5 he left as a bequest to the county's free school. Noah Corner's home seems crowded with possessions when compared with David Prichard's, but the middling planter Corner had far more in common with Prichard than with a man such as Nicolls, who owned £1,500 in moveable property.

Gentry households accounted for no more than 10 percent of Chesapeake population, and the provincial elite, like the Burwells and Carrolls, encompassed even fewer of the region's inhabitants.

A scattering of artisans accumulated enough wealth to merit the title *gentleman* and enjoy the perquisites that went with it, but most gentry were planters, merchants, lawyers, and government officials. Protective of their position as society's leaders, Chesapeake gentry expected respect for their authority from all who ranked below them in the social hierarchy.

DEFERENCE AND DEFIANCE

In addition to visible differences in possessions and resources, the Chesapeake region's hierarchy also encompassed significant differences in access to political power and influence. Despite the substantial range of wealth within the gentry, elite men were united in their control of all levers of power within their society. Small planters might hold enough property to vote and middling planters routinely served on juries or acted as constables and road overseers, but elite men occupied virtually all of the positions of power in the public sphere. They held lucrative provincial offices as royal or proprietary appointees and served locally as justices of the peace and sheriffs. Small and middling planters and lesser gentry could express their preferences by voting for only two offices: vestrymen, who oversaw the affairs of Anglican parishes, and delegates to the lower houses of the colonial assemblies. Freeholders gave their votes to elite men seeking office with the expectation that those they elected would hold down the costs of government, enforce contracts and payment of debts, settle disputes over ownership of land, and manage parish affairs. Assemblymen enacted legislation that promoted the welfare and safety of independent, propertied white households; county justices and sheriffs enforced those laws for the same purposes.

Members of the elite courted support from middling and small planters in a variety of ways. Wealthy planters could use their control of county courts and vestries to award contracts for building projects, appoint tobacco inspectors, accept or reject petitions to operate ferries and taverns, grant relief from taxes or payments for medical care, and ratify agreements between parents and artisans that arranged training for children. For their own plantations and households, they hired free men to work as overseers of quarters and as stewards and clerks on the largest plantations; gave piecework employment for sewing and spinning to wives and daughters on neighboring plantations; rented property to men in need of land; and offered work to a wide variety of free craftsmen, sometimes on annual contracts but more often for specific jobs. In exchange for the patronage they extended through plantation management and the courts, elite planters expected deference and gratitude from those they favored—and support at the polls when they pursued public office.

Elite men also courted voters by displaying attention to their interests and views, most visibly by entertaining them generously at times of public gathering. These occasions involved giving "strong Liquors to the People . . . once at a Race, and the other Time at a Muster; and . . . on the Day of Election . . . strong Liquor . . . brought in a cart, near the Court-house Door, where many People drank thereof, whilst the Polls of the Election were taking."[13] The "strong Liquor" supplied by George Washington for an election in 1758 consisted of 150 gallons of rum punch, wine, brandy, beer, and hard cider liberally dispensed to some three hundred men. In such settings as militia musters, court and election days, races, and other community-wide gatherings, wealthy men mingled fraternally with their social inferiors in an outward semblance of equality. Providing hospitality to all voters was the mark of a gentleman worthy of respect and support.

As long as the gentlemen sent to Williamsburg and Annapolis remained mindful of their interests, ordinary planters were generally willing to accept the hospitality in exchange for their votes and deference to elite rule. When assemblymen enacted laws that ordinary planters viewed as harmful, however, they made their displeasure known at the polls. In 1722 and 1747, for example, Maryland voters turned out a large percentage of sitting delegates who supported tobacco legislation that small planters opposed. But the overall rarity of such events, coupled with willingness of voters to respond forcefully in specific instances, suggests a general acceptance of elite political rule.

In matters of religion, however, many Virginia and Maryland residents were less inclined to defer to gentry leadership. At mid-century the Chesapeake colonies witnessed the appearance of groups offering alternatives and challenges to the hegemony long enjoyed by the Anglican establishment. The confrontation was particularly acute in Virginia, where the Church of England had been the established religion from the colony's early days and dissenters had found little tolerance. Because Maryland's Catholic proprietors had welcomed diverse faiths in the seventeenth century, strong networks of families and institutions kept these religious communities active, despite the Church of England's position as the established religion after 1692. As a consequence, the introduction of new faiths in the eighteenth century was less disruptive north of the Potomac River.

Religious diversity increased in both colonies at midcentury with the influx into western areas of German settlers, who were members either of Lutheran and Reformed churches or of pietistic sects like the Mennonites. In addition, Scottish and some Irish settlers in the Virginia Piedmont raised the numbers of Presbyterians in that colony. Presbyterian ranks expanded throughout the tidewater area in the 1740s and 1750s as a result of the Great Awakening and the preaching of reform-minded New Light ministers, whose enthusiastic style won converts from the more sedate and intellectual Church of England. Itinerant preachers spoke of religious belief in emotional and personal terms, exhorting every individual to engage directly in the battle between good and evil. Revivals had the paradoxical effect of increasing religious fervor while disrupting the godly community. Throughout the region, congregations split in numerous ways: between new Presbyterian and older Anglican churches, between followers of reformist New Lights and those who favored conservative Old Side ministers, and between evangelicals and established political authority.

Revivals set in motion an even stronger challenge to the social order in Virginia in the 1760s. A group known as Separate Baptists confronted Anglicans in areas of religious practice, asserting that ministers required a divine call to preach more than formal training and basing church membership on an individual, emotional experience of conversion. These Baptists also insisted on a strict code of personal morality that rejected gambling, dancing, drinking, and diversions on the Sabbath, all pastimes enjoyed by Virginia's elite, and rejected the legal requirement that dissenting ministers be licensed to preach only at specific locations. Thus they challenged directly both the political authority and the behavioral model of gentry leadership, with its laxity in matters of piety but insistence upon symbols of hierarchy and preeminence. The Baptist appeal resonated most strongly in areas undergoing the greatest population growth, where political leaders asserted their authority but were too recently established to have earned the support of people whom they represented and governed.

Evangelical religious groups, whether Presbyterians, older Baptist sects, or newer Separate Baptists, met with an enthusiastic response from the region's black population. Baptists in particular welcomed black converts into their churches, even to the point of encouraging black preachers. Planters had earlier resisted the idea of converting enslaved workers to Christianity, fearing that conversion would promote resistance. But by the mid-eighteenth century, slaveowners felt more secure, and some came to believe that slaves who accepted Christian teachings might be more tractable and docile workers. Christianity as practiced by Africans and African Americans did not simply replicate white religious beliefs, however. Slaves incorporated African beliefs and practices into the religion of their white masters, shaping the evangelical message to suit their own heritage and circumstances. Rather than banish dancing, for example, congregations made it part of religious ritual and wove salvation after death into their spirituals as the promise of eventual freedom from bondage. Unlike evangelical whites, who stressed personal salvation of individuals, blacks placed greater emphasis on communal aspects of the new religious movements. Substantial conversion of African Americans, creation of black congregations, and a significant presence of black preachers did not begin until the last quarter of the century, but these developments stemmed from the activities of evangelicals who preached throughout the Chesapeake region in midcentury.

Although emotionally and spiritually powerful, the new spirit of religious belief within the black community did little to alter conditions of enslavement. The wealth and status of the colony's planters continued to rest on the backs of black workers held in bondage. None of the profit of their labor came back to the enslaved in the form of comfortable furniture, ample clothing, or lavish meals. Although the gulf that separated Chesapeake gentry from small planters, tenants, and the middling sort was far wider than that which separated poorer whites from blacks, colonial society divided along the axis of race rather than wealth. Slave codes established punishments for enslaved blacks that did not apply to white laborers, whether indentured, convict, or hired. Only slaves could be stripped naked for whippings, subjected to mutilation or dismemberment, forbidden to carry weapons, and required to carry a pass to travel away from their place of residence. Poor whites gained no tangible benefits from these laws, but such legislation clearly aligned them with more privileged whites rather than with the blacks whose material circumstances in too many ways mirrored their own.

Solidarity of race rather than of economic condition owed much as well to the fact that ownership of enslaved property became more widespread during the first half of the eighteenth century. At the beginning of the eighteenth century, only one Virginia household in five included any enslaved workers; by 1740, ownership had spread to one-half of the colony's households. Nonslaveholding whites had some basis for believing that in time they, too, might acquire slave property and the status of slaveowner. Moreover, white men who did not have outright ownership of enslaved workers often had use of their labor, through guardianships, marriage, sharing, and hiring. The employer of slaves could perhaps use accumulated profits from such workers to become the owner of slaves. The interests of various levels of white society thus converged to support a labor system based on black enslavement. Not all white households profited directly from the labor system's bounty, but those who truly suffered were the Africans and their descendants, most of whom remained in lifetime bondage. The full cost for the region as a whole, bound to a labor system that limited economic and personal freedom, would not be brought home until the nineteenth century.

Not every man and woman in the Chesapeake colonies who purchased bound labor profited from the investment, but any broad assessment must conclude that for white society as a whole enslaved labor was the route to substantial wealth. Over time and across the region, slavery generated assets—in the form of natural increase in the slave population, in the cleared fields, herds of livestock, and plantation houses and outbuildings that enslaved labor made possible, and in the increasingly abundant material possessions purchased with profits from workers' labor. For families like the Burwells and Carrolls, investment in African laborers proved the means to wealth, social standing, and political power. As the economy and culture of Virginia and Maryland matured, both rested squarely upon a foundation of coerced labor, enmeshing all inhabitants in the region's slave society.

By the third quarter of the eighteenth century, the Chesapeake region had experienced a century and a half of European settlement. The fragile roots planted in Jamestown in 1607 and St. Mary's City in 1634 had spread across the length and breadth of the Chesapeake Bay's coastal plain, crossed the Piedmont plateau, and begun to penetrate the mountains bordering the western edge of cultivated land and politically organized settlement. The fertile central core of plantations along the bay's western shore continued to emphasize tobacco production for export to Britain. Planters on the Eastern Shore, at the head of the bay, and along the western perimeter found profit in producing foodstuffs, livestock, and lumber for coastal, Caribbean, and southern European consumers. Tobacco exports remained steady, while wheat, corn, timber products, salted meat, iron, and ships provided the engine of robust economic growth. Planters at all levels of society benefited from the increasing complexity of economic activity, including opportunities for craft and professional employment afforded by the burgeoning population, greater density of settlement, and increasing urbanization.

Owners of large land- and slaveholdings benefited disproportionately, being the best positioned to take advantage of the widest array of new opportunities. Some of their profits were reinvested not only in land and labor but also in entrepreneurial activities. Much still remained for what might be termed social investment: acquisition of a well-furnished plantation house, surrounded by formal gardens, attended by liveried servants, inhabited by well-educated and well-read gentlemen and their families. Such investment provided gentry households with far more comforts than earlier generations had enjoyed, but also served the purpose of implicitly demonstrating their capacity and right to exercise power and leadership in all aspects of society. In the relatively stable and coherent society of the late colonial period, few beyond the unruly Baptists had reason to challenge those claims. Yet within a generation, the Chesapeake gentry would lead the region in joining colonists up and down the seaboard in a rebellion against King George III and Parliament—rejecting the hierarchy that had bound colony to mother country for nearly two centuries.

EPILOGUE

Grappling with an Empire

IT WAS A RAINY day in July 1754 when a company of nearly four hundred Virginia provincial troops and British regulars, led by a young lieutenant colonel named George Washington, confronted a force of French soldiers and their Native American allies in the Ohio country. Washington had been sent to assert Virginia's territorial claims, but found his men facing a large French contingent marching east from Fort Duquesne (present-day Pittsburgh). Washington retreated southeast to the aptly named Fort Necessity, a hastily built stockade situated in a marshy valley, vulnerable to musket fire from surrounding hills.

The French attacked the flimsy fort on 3 July and inflicted heavy losses. Washington, hoping to avert further British casualties and unaware that the French were low on ammunition, agreed to a cease-fire in order to discuss terms of his surrender. After signing the resulting surrender document on 4 July, Washington and his men abandoned the fort and moved eastward to a fortified storehouse at Wills Creek on the Virginia side of the Potomac River. The storehouse belonged to the Ohio Company, an enterprise organized by Virginians to settle territory west of the Appalachians. As Washington's men marched to this stronghold, the French destroyed Fort Necessity and other Ohio Company posts to obliterate—for the moment—all signs of the British in the Ohio country.

The confrontation at Fort Necessity ignited a new period of

military conflict between Britain and France, another episode in the long struggle between the two nations that had blazed off and on for several centuries. Known in the colonies as the French and Indian War, this round of fighting started in North America, but the two nations and their allies soon battled across three continents in a contest over territory, trade, naval supremacy, and religious beliefs. When peace returned for a time in 1763, the treaty ending this particular war represented a significant British victory. But victory carried with it the sources of the British Empire's next war, which began with North American protests against imperial policies. A shared sense of injustice and frustration with Parliament drew the Chesapeake colonies and their mainland siblings together, strengthening their connections with each other and ultimately, with a forceful declaration of independence, dissolving the ties that bound them to the mother country.

THE OHIO COMPANY AND WESTERN DEVELOPMENT

The Virginia and Pennsylvania colonies each had a charter that left its western boundary open-ended, and each had groups of land speculators who saw opportunity in that as-yet unsettled but potentially vast western territory. By the mid-1740s, Virginia had granted nearly one-third of a million acres on the Ohio River to wealthy speculators, who organized themselves as the Ohio Company and initiated plans to settle colonists on its land. In 1749, the company built a fortified storehouse at Wills Creek, a strategic position along the best route to the Ohio territory. For the moment the storehouse served as a trading post to nearby Native Americans. As colonists pushed westward looking for fresh land, the Ohio Company intended to sell its acreage and then supply the region's newly settled farmers with manufactured goods stockpiled in its storehouses.

The French, with their own claims to the fertile territory, did not sit idly by as the Ohio Company and similar groups from Pennsylvania and New York began to move pieces on the trans-Appalachian chessboard. They responded by constructing a series of forts to establish control of the land between the Great Lakes and the Ohio River. By the fall of 1753, three were under construction from Lake Erie southward along the Allegheny River. The French intended to build their fourth and final fort,

Fort Duquesne, at the forks of the Ohio River—precisely where Virginia traders had begun to erect a storehouse they planned to use as the Ohio Company's main fortified trading post.

Virginia's governor, Robert Dinwiddie, mindful of both his royal appointment to serve British interests and his personal investment in the Ohio Company, was eager to counter the French fort-building effort, but he had little room to maneuver. He had been arguing with the Virginia House of Burgesses since the summer of 1752 over his attempt to collect fees for putting his seal and signature on land patents without the sanction of a legislative act. To the burgesses, an important constitutional issue was at stake: if Dinwiddie collected fees without first securing their agreement, he would be collecting a tax without the consent of representatives of the colony's freeholders. In the midst of this dispute, the governor was in no position to ask the assembly to fund a campaign against the French.

Dinwiddie decided to try negotiations instead, and in the fall of 1753 he sent an emissary to ask the French to withdraw from the Ohio country. For this task Dinwiddie selected George Washington, then a twenty-one-year-old militia major with no knowledge of the French language but with connections to powerful men, experience in surveying in the Shenandoah Valley, sufficient physical stamina for the journey, and an enthusiasm for the task. Unimpressed by these assets, the French rejected his request for their withdrawal and continued building their forts. When Washington reported his mission's failure in January 1754, the Virginia council considered the situation and concluded that the colony had a duty to expel the French. With the council's approval, the governor promoted Washington to lieutenant colonel and authorized the expedition that eventually ended in surrender in July. Only after setting these events in motion, did Dinwiddie convene the burgesses to ask for an appropriation to fund the campaign. The legislature authorized £10,000, but, in an effort to maintain fiscal control, included provisions for strict oversight of expenditures.

When news of Washington's defeat at Fort Necessity reached Williamsburg, the burgesses refused to appropriate more money unless the governor conceded their exclusive right to levy internal fees and taxes. The quarrel between provincial assembly and royal governor thus being at a stalemate, Dinwiddie could not pay for a new expedition against the French. But the account of events that Dinwiddie sent to England reinforced existing British concern about the expanding French presence in North America. The king soon approved a proposal to send two army regiments under General Edward Braddock with orders to remove all French outposts deemed hostile to British interests. Britain would furnish the bulk of the troops, but colonial governors received instructions to provide supplies, provisions, and quarters for the troops as well as additional soldiers, either through volunteers or by calling up the militia.

The war with France began in their backyard and brought violence to settlements along the Chesapeake frontier, but neither Virginia nor Maryland made more than halfhearted attempts to support British policy. Although their two governors did what they could to supply assistance, internal priorities and political disputes in each Chesapeake colony kept the legislative assemblies from providing more than minimal aid to the war effort.

VIRGINIA AND MARYLAND DURING THE FRENCH AND INDIAN WAR

Braddock and his troops arrived in the Chesapeake region early in the spring of 1755. After joining provincial volunteers and militiamen in Maryland at Frederick Town, Braddock's forces numbered about two thousand men. The company prepared to march first to Maryland's Fort Cumberland (located across from the Wills Creek storehouse) and then on to the Ohio country. In the midst of these preparations, Benjamin Franklin, coordinator of communications and supplies from Pennsylvania, tried in vain to warn Braddock about the tactics of Native American warfare. In a reply swollen with condescension, Braddock assured Franklin that "These savages may indeed, be a formidable enemy to your raw American militia; but upon the king's regular and disciplined troops, sir, it is impossible they should make any impression."[1] His troops' discipline notwithstanding, Braddock lost more than half his men when the French and their "savage" allies met the British in July, ten miles southeast of Fort Duquesne.

In the wake of this defeat, frontier defenses collapsed throughout western Virginia, Maryland, and Pennsylvania. Braddock and his remaining troops fell back to Great Meadows, the site of Fort Necessity and Washington's earlier surrender, where the general died of his wounds. Remnants of the British forces then retreated all the way to Philadelphia. Their withdrawal left undefended the road that Braddock's men had constructed from Fort Cumberland through the backcountry. By autumn, more than one hundred Virginia settlers were reported dead or captured. Those who could fled eastward to more protected settlements. Writing to the governor, Washington described the difficulty of getting men and provisions delivered to Winchester, Virginia's westernmost supply depot, because the pass through the Blue Ridge Mountains was clogged with "Crowds of People who were flying [east], as if every moment was death."[2]

Maryland's governor, Horatio Sharpe, supported the military effort by calling up the militia, visiting soldiers in the field to bolster morale, and raising units by private subscription and personal encouragement of volunteers. But Sharpe had only limited success in persuading delegates to help pay for the war. The assembly passed supply bills in 1754 and 1756, but only with terms explicitly forbidden by Sharpe's proprietary instructions. The first bill assigned fees collected for licensing ordinaries to support of the military effort, despite orders to reserve that income for Lord Baltimore's private use. Taxes on landholding authorized in the second bill applied for the first time explicitly to land owned by the proprietor and leased to tenants. Crown pressure forced Lord Baltimore to accept the 1756 act, but he sent orders to the governor and council to stand firm in the future. As long as the proprietor refused to cede any of his private income for military expenses, delegates refused to pass supply bills, and Maryland provided no further public money or support.

For Virginia, a special ruling by England's Privy Council that resolved the fee controversy late in 1754 confirmed the governor's authority, giving Dinwiddie more room to maneuver. He called up militiamen from the northwestern counties, requisitioned muskets, and convened an assembly session in which burgesses voted to raise a provincial regiment of one thousand men, with Washington in command, and allocated money to supply equipment and pay soldiers. A significant shortfall between appropriations and the funds actually available required two substantial issues of paper money with no guaranteed backing to maintain its value. Moreover, the grandees who controlled the House of Burgesses worried more about a tidewater slave revolt

George Washington (1732–1799). Although Peale painted this portrait in 1772, Washington wore a colonel's uniform of the First Virginia Regiment, his rank eighteen years earlier at the beginning of the French and Indian War. By Charles Willson Peale, 1772. Courtesy of Washington and Lee University

than frontier danger from the French and Native Americans. Militias, patrolling tidewater and Piedmont counties to control slaves, received 55 percent of the war appropriation; only 45 percent funded the Virginia Regiment's defense of western settlements. Because meager pay drew few enlistments, the regiment never operated at more than half strength. In 1757, for example,

Washington could deploy at most only four hundred men to cover a frontier of 350 miles. He gave Dinwiddie a succinct assessment of the situation: unless an expedition was sent to destroy Fort Duquesne, "there will not . . . be one soul living on This side the Blue Ridge [next] autumn."[3]

Late in 1757, prospects for a successful campaign against the fort improved considerably. In London, William Pitt assumed control of British strategy and promoted new policies. To succeed in wresting away France's North American territory, Britain needed resources the colonies could supply, especially manpower, and Pitt revised Britain's approach to achieve that result. Colonies had men willing to serve, but only for short-term commitments; Pitt now allowed enlistment of provincial troops for a single season's campaign. Colonial economies lacked adequate supplies of cash and credit; Pitt pledged British subsidies and reimbursements to cover arms, ammunition, and provisions. Colonial legislatures objected to taxation; Pitt issued requisitions of materiel rather than requests for revenue. Colonial governors lacked patronage plums to entice reluctant legislators; Pitt's new policies included supply contracts and military commissions to exchange for votes of support.

The change of direction had little effect in Maryland, given the proprietor's adamant opposition to taxes on his land, but the new policies made a notable difference in Virginia. Once Britain agreed to repay military expenses, burgesses voted to raise a second regiment and offer a £10 bounty to volunteers. By the end of May, the First Virginia Regiment had nearly reached its full complement of one thousand and the Second Virginia Regiment had drawn nine hundred volunteers. Another of Pitt's policy changes gave provincial officers a rank superior to that of all British regular army officers of lesser rank, removing the distinction between colonial service and regular service that had discouraged elite Virginia men from enlisting. Thus, one volunteer for the Second Virginia was its leader, William Byrd III, a member of the council who far outranked George Washington in the colony's social hierarchy.

The crucial campaign, a march against Fort Duquesne by a combined British and colonial force numbering between six and eight thousand men, took place in the fall of 1758. As troops marched westward, the French commander, François-Marie Le

Marchande de Lignery, awaited their arrival with only three hundred regular troops and militia. Recognizing that he could not hold the fort when so badly outnumbered, on November 23 Lignery removed cannon and munitions, evacuated his men, set fire to the fort, and destroyed its buildings with gunpowder mines. British forces, close enough to hear the explosions, arrived the following day. Renaming the site Pittsburgh in honor of William Pitt, architect of their success, the soldiers once more established a British presence in Ohio country.

THE COMPLICATIONS OF VICTORY

With the western territory where the war began at last secured for Britain, the military focus moved away from the Chesapeake backcountry as British forces advanced north. The capture of Quebec in 1759 ended major North American engagements between Britain and France. When worldwide hostilities ceased in 1763, the Treaty of Paris ceded to the victorious British almost all the North American territory that France had claimed. Treaty terms more than doubled the size of the British Empire, but this great victory carried with it numerous burdens and new challenges. The war not only left Virginia with paper money that needed to be redeemed, but also left Britain with unprecedented debt and no easy solutions for its retirement. The British Empire gained nominal control over western lands that, although implicitly granted in early charters, had been occupied more effectively by the French than by British settlers. Now Parliament faced the complex problem of administering its new territory. The war had demonstrated the shortcomings of the existing governance system when several colonies conspicuously failed to support imperial policy. Britain's government now sought to strengthen control over its colonies. But every step forward to solve these problems resulted in two steps back, until the most influential segments of colonial society saw little benefit in remaining within the British Empire.

Parliament's first step dealt with control of the frontier. With fighting over, settlers began moving into the Ohio Valley, where Native Americans contested British claims. In the wake of an uprising that began near Detroit in May 1763 and spread east to the frontiers of Virginia and Pennsylvania, Parliament attempted to stabilize relations with Indians throughout the backcountry. A royal proclamation issued in October 1763 drew a line along the ridges of the Appalachian chain and barred Anglo-American settlers from the area, reserving it "for the present, and until our further pleasure be known" to the Indians who lived there.[4] Maryland had no claim to western territory, but Ohio Company members and similar speculative groups in southwestern Virginia saw their expectations of selling land and supplies to new migrants dashed. At the same time, men and women with little chance of advancement in settled Chesapeake areas had their hopes of better success across the mountains deferred indefinitely.

Other Parliamentary measures addressed the intertwined issues of defending the expanded empire, enforcing imperial law, and raising revenue. In these efforts, Parliament also acted to rein in colonial assemblies that had grown too independent. Regular British troops were stationed in the colonies, with colonists required to provision and house the soldiers. Parliament deployed naval vessels to patrol coastal waters and reorganized the customs service to prosecute smuggling, which had increased during the war and deprived Britain of significant revenue. Complaints by British merchants about depreciated paper money issued by Virginia and a few other colonies led to the Currency Act of 1764, prohibiting colonies from any future issues of paper money for payment of private debts.

The new parliamentary acts were law across the mainland colonies but did not equally affect every household or provoke the same degree of opposition everywhere. The burden imposed by the Stamp Act of 1765, however, was felt in every colony, and the tax weighed most heavily on the most influential segments of society. The act decreed that items widely used in places ranging from courtrooms to taverns required the purchase of stamped paper in addition to applicable duties. Merchants had to affix stamps to shipping documents; lawyers needed stamps for every legal paper passing through their hands; tavern owners and ordinary keepers required stamps not only for the license under which they operated but also for the cards and dice used by their patrons; and newspapers, books, pamphlets, and almanacs coming off the printers' presses all required proof of payment. Colonists had no choice but to purchase the stamps and thereby help defray the costs of a war that had eliminated the threat posed by the French.

Legislatures in Virginia and Maryland, as was true elsewhere, felt that Parliament's measures threatened powers they had become accustomed to exercising over their own affairs. Throughout the colonies, assemblies sent appeals to the king and Parliament explaining their objections. Virginia sent three: a petition to the king, an address to the House of Lords, and a remonstrance to the House of Commons. All stressed the difficult economic conditions colonists faced: provincial taxes at their highest level ever; more money needed to defend a frontier still vulnerable to Native American attacks; falling tobacco prices; no ability to ease the strain by issuing paper money; and alarming levels of personal debt. To levy a tax without their consent, the legislature told the House of Lords, made them "Slaves of *Britons*, from whom they are descended."[5]

The sparks lighted by this rhetoric first caught flame in Boston in the summer of 1765, when a mob destroyed the office of the colony's stamp distributor and then the furnishings of his home. Rhode Island and New York followed suit with equal success. At the end of August, it was Maryland's turn. Opponents gathered in Annapolis to hang an effigy of stamp agent Zachariah Hood, then tore down the warehouse rented to store the stamps while Hood fled to New York. In October, when a crowd of more than two thousand colonists met the ship carrying Virginia's agent, Colonel George Mercer, he too took the prudent course: he renounced his appointment.

Groups identifying themselves as the Sons of Liberty formed in the colonies in order to expand protests and set up committees of correspondence to coordinate with one another. Echoing a strategy used by New England merchants to protest the earlier Sugar Act, the Sons of Liberty urged colonists to boycott British imports. When the Stamp Act took effect in November 1765, colonists also boycotted activities that required a stamp: newspapers stopped printing, courts shut down, and ships could not clear customs. With colonial trade disrupted, London merchants lobbied for repeal. Parliament responded in January 1766 with two pieces of legislation, one declaring victory and the other capitulating. The Declaratory Act asserted Parliament's authority to levy taxes; a second act repealed the Stamp Act. The mainland colonies had their first experience of working together successfully in pursuit of a common goal. It would not be their last.

As Parliament wrestled with the legacy of Britain's victory over France, most free inhabitants of the Chesapeake colonies wished only to pursue happiness as they defined it: governing themselves through elected assemblies; making the most of economic opportunities unencumbered by burdensome taxes; expanding westward for a new start on fertile land; and enjoying all the rights and privileges of British subjects. Despite periodic contractions, their maturing economies successfully produced a range of goods for domestic and coastal markets. Several staple crops, lumber products, and provisions like barreled meat and corn supplied a diversified trade with overseas markets that ranged from the British Isles to southern Europe to the West Indies. A substantial portion of Chesapeake planters produced these goods using enslaved workers, who added wealth not only by their labor but also by natural increase in their numbers. As free Virginians and Marylanders confronted the challenges of new orders and restrictions that continued to arrive from Britain, they did so mindful of their traditional rights. Their protests against those orders and restrictions used arguments drawn from English precedents. But even as protests evolved into whispers of rebellion and war, most Chesapeake colonists expected to remain good and loyal subjects of the British Empire.

Continental Congress delegates on 2 July 1776 instead voted in favor of an independence declaration written by Virginia's Thomas Jefferson. The delegates pledged support to a document holding it to be "self-evident, that all men are created equal [and] endowed . . . with certain unalienable rights," among them "life, liberty and the pursuit of happiness." In 1776, the rhetorical phrase *all men* did not presume to embrace *all* men, let alone a broader reading of *men* as both male and female people. It required two centuries of struggle before the nation formed from Britain's American colonies truly began to encompass its African-American and female inhabitants within the rights promised by its founding document. Indian groups that still endeavor to remain self-governing on traditional homelands continue to struggle with issues of encroachment and dependence that have challenged Native Americans since Englishmen arrived in 1607. The union of "Independent States" that began at Jamestown but that dissolved all "allegiance to the British Crown" in the aftermath of the Seven Years' War has been, and continues to be, a work in progress.[6]

Notes

PROLOGUE. Leah and Rachel

1. John Smith, "A Map of Virginia . . ." (1612), in Karen Ordahl Kupperman, ed., *Captain John Smith: A Select Edition of His Writings* (Chapel Hill: University of North Carolina Press, 1988), 212.

2. Smith, "A Map of Virginia . . . ," in Kupperman, ed., *Captain John Smith*, 212.

3. Smith, "A Map of Virginia . . . ," in Kupperman, ed., *Captain John Smith*, 159, 160.

4. John Hammond, "Leah and Rachel, or, the Two Fruitfull Sisters Virginia and Mary-land" (1656), in Clayton Colman Hall, ed., *Narratives of Early Maryland, 1633–1684* (New York: Charles Scribner's Sons, 1910), 283, 284.

ONE. Great Expectations

1. *The Charter of Maryland, June 20, 1632* (Annapolis, MD: Hall of Records Commission, 1982), 10.

2. This terminology comes from J. Frederick Fausz, "Merging and Emerging Worlds: Anglo-Indian Interest Groups and the Development of the Seventeenth-Century Chesapeake," in Lois Green Carr et al., eds., *Colonial Chesapeake Society* (Chapel Hill: University of North Carolina Press, 1988), 47–98.

3. Richard Hakluyt, *Divers Voyages Touching the Discovery of America and the Islands Adjacent* (1582), John Winter Jones, ed. (London: Richards, Printer, 1850), 136.

4. "Arthur Barlowe's Narrative of the 1584 Voyage," in David B. Quinn and Alison M. Quinn, eds., *Virginia Voyages from Hakluyt* (London: Oxford University Press, 1973), 8, 7, 3.

5. "Ralph Lane's Narrative of the Settlement of Roanoke Island, 1585–1586," in Quinn and Quinn, eds., *Virginia Voyages*, 25.

6. Giovanni da Verrazano, "Narragansett Bay" (1524), in George Winship Parker, ed., *Sailors Narratives of Voyages along the New England Coast, 1524–1624* (Boston: Houghton, Mifflin, 1905), 5, 10.

7. Clifford M. Lewis, S.J. and Albert J. Loomie, S.J., eds., *The Spanish Jesuit Mission in Virginia, 1570–1572* (Chapel Hill: University of North Carolina Press, 1953), 89.

8. Lewis and Loomie, eds., *Spanish Jesuit Mission*, 90.

9. Lewis and Loomie, eds., *Spanish Jesuit Mission*, 134, 109.

10. "Observations by Master George Percy, 1607," in Lyon Gardiner Tyler, ed., *Narratives of Early Virginia, 1606–1625* (New York: Charles Scribner's Sons, 1907), 21.

11. Tyler, ed., *Narratives of Early Virginia*, 22.

12. John Smith, "The General Historie of Virginia" (1624), in Kupperman, ed., *Captain John Smith*, 60, 64.

13. "General Historie," in Kupperman, ed., *Captain John Smith*, 65.

14. "General Historie," in Kupperman, ed., *Captain John Smith*, 169.

15. William Strachey, "*For the Colony in Virginea Britannia. Lawes Divine, Morall and* Martiall, &c." (London: Walter Burre, 1612), 16.

16. Ralph Hamor, *A true discourse of the present estate of Virginia* (London: John Beale, 1615), 40.

17. "General Historie," in Kupperman, ed., *Captain John Smith*, 193.

18. Ferrar Papers, quoted in David R. Ransome, "Wives for Virginia, 1621," *William and Mary Quarterly*, 3rd series, 48, no. 1 (January 1991), 7, and Susan Myra Kingsbury, ed., *The Records of the Virginia Company of London* (Washington, DC: U.S. Government Printing Office, 1906–1935), 1:256.

19. "Letter of Sir Francis Wyatt, Governor of Virginia, 1621–1626," *William and Mary Quarterly*, 2nd series, 6, no. 2 (April 1926), 118.

20. *Charter of Maryland*, 15.

21. Jerome Hawley and John Lewger, "A Relation of Maryland" (1635), in Hall, ed., *Narratives of Early Maryland*, 72.

22. Hawley and Lewger, "Relation," 73.

23. Father Andrew White, "A Briefe Relation of the Voyage unto Maryland" (1634), in Hall, ed., *Narratives of Early Maryland*, 42.

TWO. Troubled Times

1. William Hand Browne et al., eds., *Archives of Maryland* (Baltimore: Maryland Historical Society, 1883–1972), 72 volumes, 4:314.

2. "Annual Letters of the Jesuits," in Hall, ed., *Narratives of Early Maryland*, 132, 135–36.

3. *Archives of Maryland*, 10:104.

4. George Alsop, "A Character of the Province of Maryland" (1666), in Hall, ed., *Narratives of Early Maryland*, 364.

5. Michael G. Kammen, ed., "Maryland in 1699: A Letter from the Reverend Hugh Jones," *Journal of Southern History* 29 (August 1963): 369, 371.

6. Alsop, "Character of the Province," 363.

7. Hammond, "Leah and Rachel," 290.

8. White, *A Brief Relation,* 40.

9. Contract of Richard Lowther, available online at http://jefferson.village.virginia.edu/etcbin/jamestown-browse?id=J1046.

10. *Archives of Maryland*, 53:431.

11. *Archives of Maryland,* 1:215.

12. *Archives of Maryland*, 41:499.

13. John Rolfe to Sir Edwin Sandys, January 1619/20, in Kingsbury, ed., *Records of the Virginia Company*, 3:245.

14. "No. 4. Secretary Kemp to Lord Baltimore," January 1638, Fund Publication, no. 28, *The Calvert Papers, Number One* (Baltimore: Maryland Historical Society, 1889), 149.

15. RB3/12/82–84, Recopied Deed Books, Barbados Archives, St. Michael, Barbados, quoted in John C. Coombs, "Building the Machine: The Development of Slavery and Slave Society in Early Colonial Virginia" (PhD diss., College of William and Mary, 2003), 64.

16. *Archives of Maryland*, 53:174.

17. Edmund Jennings to the Board of Trade, in Elizabeth Donnan, ed., *Documents Illustrative of the Slave Trade to America* (Washington, DC: Carnegie Institute of Washington, 1930), 4:89.

18. *Archives of Maryland*, 1:533.

19. *Archives of Maryland,* 4:234, 239.

20. "Extracts from Winthrop's *History of New England,* Relating to Virginia," *William and Mary College Quarterly Magazine* 12, no. 1 (July 1903), 58.

21. Treaty of 1646, Article 1, William Waller Hening, ed., *The Statutes at Large . . .* (New York: R. & W. & G. Bartow, 1823), 1:323.

22. Examination of Pascho Panton, Answer 1, 16 July 1645, in *Ingle* v. *The Looking Glass*, Examinations, Section I, High Court of Admiralty, HCA 13/60, PRO, quoted in Timothy B. Riordan, *The Plundering Time: Maryland and the English Civil War, 1645–1646* (Baltimore: Maryland Historical Society, 2004), 174.

23. *Archives of Maryland*, 1:270.

24. *Archives of Maryland*, 3:201.

25. *Archives of Maryland*, 1:246.

26. *Archives of Maryland*, 1:245.

27. Articles of surrender of the General Assembly, 12 March, 1651/52, Randolph MS, Virginia Historical Society, quoted in Warren M. Billings, *Sir William Berkeley and the Forging of Colonial Virginia* (Baton Rouge: Louisiana State University Press, 2004), 111.

28. Verlinda Stone to Lord Baltimore, included in John Langford,

"Refutation of Babylon's Fall" (1655), in Hall, ed., *Narratives of Early Maryland*, 266.

THREE. Transformations

1. Clayton Torrence, *Old Somerset on the Eastern Shore of Maryland: A Study in Foundations and Founders* (Baltimore, MD: Regional Publishing, 1979), 100.

2. Somerset County Court (Wills), MSA C1815–2:14, Maryland State Archives, Annapolis, MD.

3. Hening, ed., *Statutes at Large*, 2:346.

4. Robert Beverley, *The History and Present State of Virginia* (1705), Louis B. Wright, ed. (Charlottesville, VA: Dominion Books, 1968), 271.

5. Somerset County Court (Judicial Records), MSA C1774–6:55–71; quote at 63.

6. Somerset County Court (Judicial Records), MSA C1774–6:60, 59.

7. Middlesex Orders 3, 602–3, 1 January 1704/5, quoted in Darrett B. Rutman and Anita H. Rutman, *A Place in Time: Middlesex County, Virginia, 1650–1750* (New York: W. W. Norton, 1984), 221.

8. Somerset County Court (Judicial Records), MSA C1774–6:57.

9. "Answer of the Lord Baltimore to the Queryes about Maryland," *Archives of Maryland*, 5:266.

10. Beverley, *History and Present State of Virginia,* 57–58.

11. R[oger] G[reene], *Virginia's Cure: or an Advisive Narrative Concerning Virginia* . . . (London, 1662), 17, quoted in Edward Bond, *Spreading the Gospel in Colonial Virginia* (Lanham, MD: Lexington Books, 2004), 15.

12. Mary Taney, "Request for a Church," *Maryland Historical Magazine* 100, no. 1 (Spring 2005), 79.

13. *Archives of Maryland,* 3:362.

14. Matthew Hill to Richard Baxter, 1669, in Charles Augustus Briggs, *American Presbyterianism: Its Origin and Early History* . . . , Appendix 8 (New York: Charles Scribner's Sons, 1885), xlii.

15. Nathaniel Bacon to William Berkeley, 28 April 1676, quoted in Billings, *Sir William Berkeley*, 235.

16. "A Narrative of the Rise, Progresse, and Cessation of the late Rebellion in Virginia," in *Samuel Wiseman's "Book of Record": The Official Account of Bacon's Rebellion in Virginia, 1676–1677*, Michael Leroy Oberg, ed. (Lanham, MD: Lexington Books, 2005), 145.

17. Oberg, ed., *Wiseman's "Book of Record,"* 171.

18. "Nathaniel Bacon Esq'r his Manifesto Concerning the Present Troubles in Virginia," in *The Literatures of Colonial America,* Susan P. Castillo and Ivy Schweitzer, eds. (Hoboken, NJ: Wiley-Blackwell, 2001), 227.

19. Hening, ed., *Statutes at Large*, 2:337.

20. *Archives of Maryland*, 8:56.

21. *Archives of Maryland,* 8:105.

FOUR. Coming Together, Moving Apart

1. Kammen, ed., "Maryland in 1699," 371–72.

2. Jennifer Jones, "Middle Plantation in 1699," *Colonial Williamsburg Interpreter* 20 (Summer 1999): 3.

3. John Fontaine, "Journal of John Fontaine," in *Memoirs of a Huguenot Family*, Ann Maury, ed. (New York: George P. Putnam, 1853), 289.

4. "Extracts from the Account and Letter Books of Dr. Charles Carroll of Annapolis," *Maryland Historical Magazine* 24 (September 1929): 249.

5. William Byrd II to Charles Boyle, Earl of Orrery, 5 July 1726, quoted in T. H. Breen, *Tobacco Culture: The Mentality of the Great Tidewater Planters on the Eve of Revolution* (Princeton, NJ: Princeton University Press, 1985), 85.

6. *Archives of Maryland*, 33:467.

7. *Maryland Gazette*, 2 May 1754, M1279, *Maryland Gazette* Collection, MSA SC 2731:487.

FIVE. A Society Enslaved

1. *Maryland Gazette*, 7 June 1749, MSA SC M1278:955.

2. *Maryland Gazette*, 28 August 1751, MSA SC M1278:1458 and 1 December 1763, M1280, MSA SC 2731:1094.

3. *Archives of Maryland*, 28:11.

4. Kammen, ed., "Maryland in 1699," 371.

5. *Maryland Gazette*, 2 August 1745, MSA SC M1278:86 and 27 March 1751, MSA SC M1278:1360.

6. Rev. Jonathan Boucher, *Reminiscences of an American Loyalist, 1738–1789* (Boston: Houghton Mifflin, 1925), 65.

7. *Archives of Maryland*, 1:533–34.

8. Talbot County Court (Judgments), MSA C1875–34:312.

9. John Custis IV will, 14 November 1749, Custis Family Papers, MSS lc 9698a, 52–53, VHS, quoted in Emory G. Evans, *A Topping People: The Rise and Decline of Virginia's Old Political Elite, 1680–1790* (Charlottesville: University of Virginia Press, 2009), 143.

10. Hening, ed., *Statutes at Large*, 7:95.

11. William Gooch to Board of Trade, 1736, CO 5/1322, f. 153, quoted in Ira Berlin, *Many Thousands Gone: The First Two Centuries of Slavery in North America* (Cambridge, MA: Belknap Press of Harvard University Press, 1998), 123.

12. Session Laws, 1752, Early State Records, MSA SC M3179:847.

13. *Journals of Burgesses, 1727–34, 1736–40*, 370, entry for 9 December 1738, quoted in Rhys Isaacs, *The Transformation of Virginia, 1740–1790* (Chapel Hill: University of North Carolina Press, 1982), 112.

EPLIOGUE. Grappling with an Empire

1. *Autobiography of Benjamin Franklin,* quoted in Land, *Colonial Maryland: A History* (Millwood, NY: KTO Press, 1981), 216.

2. George Washington to Robert Dinwiddie, 11 October 1755; available at http://rotunda.upress.virginia.edu/founders/GEWN.html.

3. George Washington to Robert Dinwiddie, 24 October 1757; available at http://rotunda.upress.virginia.edu/founders/GEWN.html.

4. Royal Proclamation, 7 October 1763; available at http://avalon.law.yale.edu/18th_century/proc1763.asp.

5. Memorial to the House of Lords, 18 December 1764, quoted in Fred Anderson, *Crucible of War: The Seven Years' War and the Fate of Empire in British North America, 1754–1766* (New York: Vintage Books, 2001), 613.

6. "The Declaration of Independence," in Richard D. Heffner, *A Documentary History of the United States*, 3rd ed. (New York: Mentor, 1976), 15, 18.

Essay on Sources

General Works

Despite the universal identification of Virginia and Maryland as Britain's Chesapeake colonies, an appellation that recognizes the regional connection shared by these two entities, very few scholarly monographs approach the colonial history of the two sisters as a whole. The Chesapeake colonies are given equal weight, however, in two key collections of essays: David W. Ammerman and Thad W. Tate, *The Chesapeake in the Seventeenth Century: Essays on Anglo-American Society* (Chapel Hill: University of North Carolina Press, 1978) and Lois Green Carr, Philip D. Morgan, and Jean B. Russo, eds., *Colonial Chesapeake Society* (Chapel Hill: University of North Carolina Press, 1988). For colony-specific narratives that encompass the full colonial period, see Warren M. Billings, John E. Selby, and Thad W. Tate, *Colonial Virginia: A History* (White Plains, NY: KTO Press, 1990) and Aubrey C. Land, *Colonial Maryland: A History* (Millwood, NY: KTO Press, 1981). For collections of primary source material for the early years of settlement in each colony, see Clayton Colman Hall, ed., *Narratives of Early Maryland, 1633–1684* (New York: Charles Scribner's Sons, 1910) and Lyon Gardiner Tyler, ed., *Narratives of Early Virginia, 1606–1625* (New York: Charles Scribner's Sons, 1907).

A number of works analyze the development of the Chesapeake colonies within the larger context of North American and Atlantic history. For examples, each of which includes useful bibliographic material, see John J. McCusker and Kenneth Morgan, *The Early Modern Atlantic Economy* (Cambridge: Cambridge University Press, 2000); Jack P. Greene, *Pursuits of Happiness: The Social Development of Early Modern British Colonies and the Formation of American Culture* (Chapel Hill: University of North Carolina Press, 1988);

and John J. McCusker and Russell R. Menard, *The Economy of British America, 1607–1789* (Chapel Hill: University of North Carolina Press, 1985).

Two books signal new efforts to approach the history of the Chesapeake colonies from a regional perspective that moves freely across provincial boundaries: Lorena S. Walsh, *Motives of Honor, Pleasure, and Profit: Plantation Management in the Colonial Chesapeake, 1607–1763* (Chapel Hill: University of North Carolina Press, 2010) and James D. Rice, *Nature and History in the Potomac Country: From Hunters-Gatherers to the Age of Jefferson* (Baltimore: Johns Hopkins University Press, 2009). Although neither author endeavors to describe the colonial history of the region per se, each presents an astonishing breadth of information with deft command of recent scholarship in multiple fields, including not only history but also demography, archaeology, anthropology, and economics.

Early Exploration and Settlement

Numerous works discuss Europe's age of exploration and overseas settlement. Among those that focus upon England and North America, see Peter C. Mancall, ed., *Envisioning America: English Plans for the Colonization of North America, 1580–1640* (Boston, MA: Bedford Books, 1995); Kenneth R. Andrews, *Trade, Plunder, and Settlement: Maritime Enterprise and the Genesis of the British Empire, 1480–1630* (Cambridge: Cambridge University Press, 1984); K. R. Andrews, N. P. Canny, and P. E. H. Hair, eds., *The Westward Enterprise: English Activities in Ireland, the Atlantic, and America, 1480–1650* (Liverpool: Liverpool University Press, 1978); and David B. Quinn, ed., *North America from Earliest Discovery to First Settlements: The Norse Voyages to 1612* (New York: Harper & Row, 1977).

For early interactions between Europeans and Indians in North America generally, see Daniel K. Richter, *Facing East from Indian Country: A Narrative History of Early America* (Cambridge, MA: Harvard University Press, 2001); Karen Ordahl Kupperman, *Indians and English: Facing Off in Early America* (Ithaca, NY: Cornell University Press, 2000); Peter C. Mancall and James H. Merrill, eds., *American Encounters: Natives and Newcomers from European Contact to Indian Removal, 1500–1850* (New York: Routledge, 2000); and Colin G. Calloway, *New Worlds for All: Indians, Europeans, and the Remaking of Early America* (New York: Oxford University Press, 1994).

For histories of Chesapeake Indian populations prior to and during the establishment of England's Chesapeake colonies, see Karenne Wood, ed., *The Virginia Indian Heritage Trail* (Charlottesville: Virginia Foundation for the Humanities, 2007); Martin D. Gallivan, *James River Chieftains: The Rise of Social Inequality in the Chesapeake* (Lincoln: University of Nebraska Press, 2003); Helen C. Rountree and E. Randolph Turner, *Before and After Jamestown: Virginia's Powhatans and Their Predecessors* (Gainesville: University Press of Florida, 2002); Helen C. Rountree and Thomas E. Davidson, *Eastern Shore Indians of Virginia and Maryland* (Charlottesville: University Press of

Virginia, 1997); Helen C. Rountree, *Pocahontas's People: The Powhatan Indians of Virginia through Four Centuries* (Norman: University of Oklahoma Press, 1990); and James H. Merrell, "Cultural Continuity among the Piscataway Indians of Colonial Maryland," *William and Mary Quarterly* 36 (1979): 548–570.

The 2007 quadricentennial of Jamestown's founding kindled numerous new works about Virginia's earliest years, including Karen Ordahl Kupperman, *The Jamestown Project* (Cambridge, MA: Belknap Press of Harvard University Press, 2009); Peter C. Mancall, ed., *The Atlantic World and Virginia, 1550–1624* (Chapel Hill: University of North Carolina Press, 2007); Helen C. Rountree, Wayne E. Clark, and Kent Mountford, *John Smith's Chesapeake Voyages, 1607–1609* (Charlottesville: University of Virginia Press, 2007); James P. P. Horn, *A Land as God Made It: Jamestown and the Birth of America* (New York: Basic Books, 2006); William M. Kelso, *Jamestown: The Buried Truth* (Charlottesville: University of Virginia Press, 2006); and Danielle Moretti-Langholtz, *A Study of Virginia Indians and Jamestown: The First Century* (Williamsburg, VA: Prepared for the Colonial National Historical Park, National Park Service, U.S. Dept. of the Interior, 2005).

Additional works that focus upon early Virginia include April Lee Hatfield, *Atlantic Virginia: Intercolonial Relations in the Seventeenth Century* (Philadelphia: University of Pennsylvania Press, 2004); Frederic W. Gleach, *Powhatan's World and Colonial Virginia: A Conflict of Cultures* (Lincoln: University of Nebraska Press, 1997); Karen Ordahl Kupperman, *Captain John Smith: A Select Edition of His Writings* (Chapel Hill: University of North Carolina Press, 1988); and Edmund S. Morgan's highly influential *American Slavery, American Freedom: The Ordeal of Colonial Virginia* (New York: Norton, 1975). For recent scholarship offering new perspectives on significant aspects of Virginia's early history, see Douglas Bradburn and John C. Coombs, eds., *Early Modern Virginia: New Essays on the Old Dominion* (Charlottesville: University of Virginia Press, 2011).

Lacking the distinction of being the first enduring English colony in North America, Maryland also lacks extensive scholarship about the colony's foundation and early period of settlement. For a brief narrative of Maryland's early years, see Lois Green Carr, Russell R. Menard, and Louis Peddicord, *Maryland at the Beginning* (Annapolis: Maryland State Archives, 1991). The essays in David C. Quinn, ed., *Early Maryland in a Wider World* (Detroit, MI: Wayne State University Press, 1982) place the colony's beginnings in a broad historical context.

Servitude and Slavery

The extensive literature about bound labor in colonial North America is weighted heavily toward studies of slavery. Useful exceptions include Kenneth Morgan's synthesis of recent scholarship for both slavery and servitude, *Slavery and Servitude in Colonial North America: A Short History* (New

York: New York University Press, 2001) and two studies that consider the overlapping boundaries of servitude and slavery in early Virginia: J. Douglas Deal, *Race and Class in Colonial Virginia: Indians, Englishmen, and Africans on the Eastern Shore during the Seventeenth Century* (New York: Garland Publishing, 1993) and T. H. Breen and Stephen Innes, *"Myne Owne Ground": Race and Freedom on Virginia's Eastern Shore, 1640–1676* (New York: Oxford University Press, 1980). David Galenson's study of indentured servants, *White Servitude: An Economic Analysis* (Cambridge: Cambridge University Press, 1981) considers indentured servitude across colonies. For information about convict servitude, see A. Roger Ekirch, *Bound for America: The Transportation of British Convicts to the Colonies, 1718–1775* (Oxford: Oxford University Press, 1987). Christine Daniels discusses the interplay between servitude and the legal system in colonial Maryland in "'Liberty to Complaine': Servant Petitions in Maryland, 1652–1797" in Christopher L. Tomlins and Bruce H. Mann, eds., *The Many Legalities of Early America* (Chapel Hill: University of North Carolina Press, 2001).

Kenneth Morgan, *Slavery in America: A Reader and Guide* (Athens: University of Georgia Press, 2005) and Peter J. Parish, *Slavery: History and Historians* (New York: Harper & Row, 1989) provide succinct summaries of interpretive arguments about slavery as well as extensive bibliographic information for the broader slavery literature. Provocative recent works on slavery in the British colonies include Jennifer L. Morgan, *Laboring Women: Reproduction and Gender in New World Slavery* (Philadelphia: University of Pennsylvania Press, 2004); Ira Berlin, *Many Thousands Gone: The First Two Centuries of Slavery in North America* (Cambridge, MA: Belknap Press of Harvard University Press, 1998); and Ira Berlin and Philip D. Morgan, eds., *Cultivation and Culture: Labor and the Shaping of Slave Life in the Americas* (Charlottesville: University Press of Virginia, 1993). Most discussion of colonial slavery centers on African workers and their descendants, with the notable exception of Alan Gallay, *The Indian Slave Trade: The Rise of the English Empire in the American South, 1670–1717* (New Haven, CT: Yale University Press, 2003). For current perspectives on the transatlantic trade in African slaves, see the January 2001 issue of the *William and Mary Quarterly*, especially Lorena S. Walsh's essay "The Chesapeake Slave Trade: Regional Patterns, African Origins, and Some Implications." For more about slavery's archaeological record, see Leland Ferguson, *Uncommon Ground: Archaeology and Early African America* (Washington, DC: Smithsonian Institution Press, 1992).

A number of significant works focus upon slavery in one or both of the Chesapeake colonies. These include John C. Coombs, *The Rise of Virginia Slavery, 1630–1730* (Charlottesville: University of Virginia Press, forthcoming); Anthony S. Parent Jr., *Foul Means: The Formation of a Slave Society in Virginia, 1660–1740* (Chapel Hill: University of North Carolina Press, 2003); Philip D. Morgan, *Slave Counterpoint: Black Culture in the Eighteenth-Century*

Chesapeake and Lowcountry (Chapel Hill: University of North Carolina Press, 1998); Lorena S. Walsh, *From Calabar to Carter's Grove: The History of a Virginia Slave Community* (Charlottesville: University Press of Virginia, 1997); Kathleen M. Brown, *Good Wives, Nasty Wenches, and Anxious Patriarchs: Gender, Race, and Power in Colonial Virginia* (Chapel Hill: University of North Carolina Press, 1996); Mechal Sobel, *The World They Made Together: Black and White Values in Eighteenth-Century Virginia* (Princeton, NJ: Princeton University Press, 1987); and Morgan, *American Slavery, American Freedom*. Thad W. Tate, *The Negro in Eighteenth-Century Williamsburg* (Williamsburg, VA: Colonial Williamsburg Foundation, 1965) provides a notable published study of Chesapeake slavery in an urban environment.

Demography, Settlement Patterns, and Standards of Living

The broad foundation of current interpretations about the development of the Chesapeake colonies stems from groundbreaking scholarship of the 1970s that used nonliterary sources and quantitative methods. Much of this research appears in articles rather than monographs. For a sample of the most influential work, see essays by Russell R. Menard, Lorena S. Walsh, and Allan Kulikoff, in Aubrey C. Land, Lois Green Carr, and Edward C. Papenfuse, eds., *Law, Society, and Politics in Early Maryland* (Baltimore: Johns Hopkins University Press, 1977); Lois Green Carr and Lorena S. Walsh, "The Planter's Wife: The Experience of White Women in Seventeenth-Century Maryland," *William and Mary Quarterly* 34 (1977), 542–71; Russell R. Menard, "The Maryland Slave Population, 1658 to 1730: A Demographic Profile of Blacks in Four Counties," *William and Mary Quarterly* 32 (1975), 29–54; and the essays collected in Tate and Ammerman, eds., *The Chesapeake in the Seventeenth Century*, and Carr, Morgan, and Russo, eds., *Colonial Chesapeake Society*.

Works that interweave demographic history with information about settlement patterns and standards of living include James P. P. Horn, *Adapting to a New World: English Society in the Seventeenth-Century Chesapeake* (Chapel Hill: University of North Carolina Press, 1994); James R. Perry, *The Formation of a Society on Virginia's Eastern Shore, 1615–1655* (Chapel Hill: University of North Carolina Press, 1990); Allan Kulikoff, *Tobacco and Slaves: The Development of Southern Cultures in the Chesapeake, 1680–1800* (Chapel Hill: University of North Carolina Press, 1986); Gloria L. Main, *Tobacco Colony: Life in Early Maryland, 1650–1720* (Princeton, NJ: Princeton University Press, 1982); and Darrett B. Rutman and Anita H. Rutman, *A Place in Time: Middlesex County, Virginia, 1650–1750* (New York: Norton, 1986).

For information about ethnic groups that migrated from the British Isles and northern Europe to the Chesapeake colonies, see Patrick Griffin, *The People with No Name: Ireland's Ulster Scots, America's Scots Irish, and the Creation of a British Atlantic World, 1689–1764* (Princeton, NJ: Princeton University Press, 2001); Marianne Wokeck, *Trade in Strangers: The Beginnings of*

Mass Migration to North America (University Park: Pennsylvania State University Press, 1999); and Alan L. Karras, *Sojourners in the Sun: Scottish Migrants in Jamaica and the Chesapeake* (Ithaca, NY: Cornell University Press, 1992).

Economic Development

The research of the 1970s not only sparked new interest in Chesapeake demography but also stimulated related analyses of economic development. For examples of "local studies" that explore economic as well as social issues, see Perry, *Formation of a Society*; Kevin Kelly, *Economic and Social Development of Seventeenth-Century Surry County, Virginia* (New York: Garland Publishing, 1989); Jean B. Russo, *Free Workers in a Plantation Economy: Talbot County, Maryland, 1690–1759* (New York: Garland Publishing, 1989); Rutman and Rutman, *A Place in Time*; and Richard R. Beeman, *The Evolution of the Southern Backcountry: A Case Study of Lunenberg County, Virginia, 1746–1832* (Philadelphia: University of Pennsylvania Press, 1984). Douglas Bradburn and John C. Coombs offer a provocative reevaluation of 1970s scholarship in "Smoke and Mirrors: Reinterpreting the Society and Economy of the Seventeenth-Century Chesapeake," *Atlantic Studies* 3 (2006), 131–57.

For the centrality of maritime activity and mercantile pursuits in Virginia and Maryland, see Arthur Pierce Middleton, *Tobacco Coast: A Maritime History of Chesapeake Bay in the Colonial Era* (Newport News, VA: Mariners' Museum, 1953). Lois Green Carr, Russell R. Menard, and Lorena S. Walsh analyze the processes of farm building and property accumulation during the early stages of English settlement in *Robert Cole's World: Agriculture and Society in Early Maryland* (Chapel Hill: University of North Carolina Press, 1991). The conflict between English farming practices and Native American economies is a central theme in Rice, *Nature and History in the Potomac Country* and in Virginia DeJohn Anderson, *Creatures of Empire: How Domestic Animals Transformed Early America* (New York: Oxford University Press, 2006).

For a useful discussion of unsuccessful efforts to diversify the Chesapeake economy during the seventeenth century, see chapters 5 and 9 of Warren M. Billings, *Sir William Berkeley and the Forging of Colonial Virginia* (Baton Rouge: Louisiana State University Press, 2004). Robert Beverley, *The History and Present State of Virginia* [1705], ed. Louis B. Wright (Chapel Hill: University of North Carolina Press, 1947) provides a contemporary perspective on Virginia's economic development midway through the colonial period. The expansion of wheat cultivation in the northern Chesapeake is discussed in Paul G. E. Clemens, *The Atlantic Economy and Colonial Maryland's Eastern Shore: From Tobacco to Grain* (Ithaca, NY: Cornell University Press, 1980).

Additional works that describe aspects of colonial Chesapeake economy include Laura Croghan Kamoie, *Irons in the Fire: The Business History of the Tayloe Family and Virginia's Gentry, 1700–1860* (Charlottesville: University of Virginia Press, 2007); Ann Smart Martin, *Buying into the World of Goods: Early Consumers in Backcountry Virginia* (Baltimore: Johns Hopkins University Press, 1993); Gregory A. Stiverson, *Poverty in a Land of Plenty: Tenancy in Eighteenth-Century Maryland* (Baltimore: Johns Hopkins University Press, 1977); and Edward C. Papenfuse, *In Pursuit of Profit: The Annapolis Merchants in the Era of the American Revolution, 1763–1805* (Baltimore: Johns Hopkins University Press, 1975). The latter work also summarizes the early development of Maryland's major colonial port; Thomas C. Parramore et al., *Norfolk: The First Four Centuries* (Charlottesville: University Press of Virginia, 1994) describes the early development and growth of Virginia's equivalent maritime center.

Religion and Culture

For discussion of religious practices and the diversity of faiths in the Chesapeake colonies, see the introduction to Edward L. Bond, *Spreading the Gospel in Colonial Virginia: Sermons and Devotional Writings* (Lanham, MD: Lexington Books, 2004); John D. Krugler, *English and Catholic: The Lords Baltimore in the Seventeenth Century* (Baltimore: Johns Hopkins University Press, 2004); Edward L. Bond, *Damned Souls in a Tobacco Colony: Religion in Seventeenth-Century Virginia* (Macon, GA: Mercer University Press, 2000); Arthur Pierce Middleton, *Anglican Maryland, 1692–1792* (Virginia Beach, VA: Donning, 1992); Sobel, *The World They Made Together*; Rhys Isaac, *The Transformation of Virginia, 1740–1790* (Chapel Hill: University of North Carolina Press, 1982); Clayton Torrence, *Old Somerset on the Eastern Shore of Maryland: A Study in Foundations and Founders* (Baltimore: Regional Publishing, 1979); and Kenneth Carroll, *Quakerism on the Eastern Shore* (Baltimore: Maryland Historical Society, 1970).

For works that explore the cultural life of elite planters, see Emory G. Evans, *A "Topping People": The Rise and Decline of Virginia's Old Political Elite, 1690–1780* (Charlottesville: University of Virginia Press, 2009); Trevor G. Burnard, *Creole Gentlemen: The Maryland Elite, 1691–1776* (New York: Routledge, 2002); Kenneth A. Lockridge, *The Diary and Life of William Byrd II of Virginia, 1674–1744* (Chapel Hill: University of North Carolina Press, 1987); T. H. Breen, *Tobacco Culture: The Mentality of the Great Tidewater Planters on the Eve of Revolution* (Princeton, NJ: Princeton University Press, 1981); and Hunter D. Farish, ed., *Journal and Letters of Philip Vickers Fithian: A Plantation Tutor of the Old Dominion, 1773–1774* (Charlottesville: University Press of Virginia, 1968). Studies that discuss the culture and consumer behavior of nonelites as well as the elite include essays in Cary Carson, Ronald Hoffman, and Peter J. Albert, eds., *Of Consuming Interests: The Style of Life in the Eighteenth Century* (Charlottesville: University Press of Virginia, 1994); Richard L. Bushman, *The Refinement of America: Persons, Houses, Cities* (New

York: Knopf, 1992); Daniel Blake Smith, *Inside the Great House: Planter Family Life in Eighteenth-Century Chesapeake Society* (Ithaca, NY: Cornell University Press, 1986); and Isaac, *The Transformation of Virginia*.

Works of historical archaeology that uncover the material culture of Chesapeake residents include William M. Kelso, *Jamestown: The Buried Truth*; Mark P. Leone, *The Archaeology of Liberty in an American Capital: Excavations in Annapolis* (Berkeley: University of California Press, 2005); Danielle Moretti-Langholtz, *A Study of Virginia Indians and Jamestown*; Anne Elizabeth Yentsch, *A Chesapeake Family and Their Slaves: A Study in Historical Archaeology* (Cambridge: Cambridge University Press, 1994); Ferguson, *Uncommon Ground*; and Ivor Noël Hume, *Martin's Hundred* (Charlottesville: University Press of Virginia, 1991).

Local Government, Provincial Politics, and Imperial Crises

Works that discuss the establishment of local government and legal systems in the two Chesapeake colonies include Alan F. Day, *A Social Study of Lawyers in Maryland, 1660–1775* (New York: Garland Publishing, 1989); David W. Jordan, *Foundations of Representative Government in Maryland, 1632–1715* (New York: Cambridge University Press, 1987); the introduction and first three essays in Bruce C. Daniels, *Town and Country: Essays on the Structure of Local Government in the American Colonies* (Middletown, CT: Wesleyan University Press, 1978); and essays by Lois Green Carr and David Jordan, in Land, Carr, and Papenfuse, eds., *Law, Society, and Politics*. For a recent biography of William Berkeley that encompasses many of the issues of local governance and provincial politics in Virginia during the seventeenth century, see Billings, *Sir William Berkeley and the Forging of Colonial Virginia*. Ronald Hoffman, *Princes of Ireland, Planters of Maryland: A Carroll Saga, 1500–1782* (Chapel Hill: University of North Carolina Press, 2002) offers a similar blend of biography and political history for Maryland during the eighteenth century.

A handful of monographs provide more detail about specific events in the political histories of Maryland and Virginia. For Maryland's crisis during the mid-seventeenth century, see Timothy B. Riordan, *The Plundering Time: Maryland and the English Civil War, 1645–1646* (Baltimore: Maryland Historical Society, 2004). Lois Green Carr and David William Jordan analyze the Protestant Revolution's causes, course, and consequences in *Maryland's Revolution of Government, 1689–1692* (Ithaca, NY: Cornell University Press, 1974). For a documentary history of Bacon's Rebellion in Virginia, see Charles M. Andrews, ed., *Narratives of the Insurrection, 1675–1690* (New York: Scribner's, 1915); for narrative accounts, see Billings, *Sir William Berkeley*; Morgan, *American Slavery, American Freedom*; and Wilcomb E. Washburn, *The Governor and the Rebel: A History of Bacon's Rebellion in Virginia* (Chapel Hill: University of North Carolina Press, 1957).

For more information about the Seven Years' War, see Fred Anderson,

Crucible of War: The Seven Years' War and the Fate of Empire in British North America, 1754–1766 (New York: Knopf, 2000); Eric Hindraker, *Elusive Empires: Constructing Colonialism in the Ohio Valley, 1673–1800* (New York: Cambridge University Press, 1997); and Francis Jennings, *Empire of Fortune: Crowns, Colonies, and Tribes in the Seven Years' War in America* (New York: Norton, 1988).

An array of works describes, analyzes, and interprets the events leading to the American Revolution. Useful introductions to the subject include Theodore Draper, *A Struggle for Power: The American Revolution* (New York: Times Books, 1996) and Edmund S. Morgan, *The Birth of the Republic: 1763–89* (Chicago: Chicago University Press, 1992). For discussions that focus on the Chesapeake colonies, see Rhys Isaac, *Landon Carter's Uneasy Kingdom: Revolution and Rebellion on a Virginia Plantation* (Oxford: Oxford University Press, 2004); Woody Holton, *Forced Founders: Indians, Debtors, Slaves, and the Making of the American Revolution in Virginia* (Chapel Hill: University of North Carolina Press, 1999); and Ronald Hoffman, *A Spirit of Dissension: Economics, Politics, and the Revolution in Maryland* (Baltimore: Johns Hopkins University Press, 1973).

Index